A Glossary of Literary Terms

A Glossary of Literary Terms

Third Edition

M. H. Abrams, *Cornell University*

Holt, Rinehart and Winston, Inc.
New York Chicago San Francisco Atlanta
Dallas Montreal Toronto London Sydney

Foreword to the Third Edition

This new edition of *A Glossary of Literary Terms* has provided the opportunity to make changes that I have long had in mind. I have shortened a few articles, expanded many others, and tried to clarify and sharpen all of them. The number of terms has been increased by about one-third. Some of the added items are traditional ones, such as *aestheticism and decadence; Bildungsroman; courtly love; deism; Menippean satire; periods of English literature; rhetoric and rhetorical criticism; surrealism*. Other terms indicate the directions taken by literature and literary criticism in recent years; for example, the *anatomy; black humor; distance and involvement; epiphany; literature of the absurd; persona, tone, and voice*. In addition, the examples used to illustrate a term have been extended to include more American writers, as well as recent works that a student is likely to have read.

The bibliographical references in the various articles have been brought up-to-date, and considerably enlarged, in the belief that an important function of the *Glossary* is to encourage the student to investigate a topic further. Books currently available in paperback are indicated by an asterisk before the title.

The most conspicuous change in the format is one that was recommended by many users: the provision of an Index of Terms at the end of the volume. This feature has made it possible to eliminate the many blank entries in the text whose only function was to serve as cross-references. All the articles of the text proper are still entered in alphabetic sequence; the terms defined and discussed within that article are printed in **boldface,** while important terms that occur in the article, but are defined elsewhere, are printed in *italics*. The most convenient way to use the *Glossary* is to refer first to the Index. There the reader will find, in **boldface,** the page number of the main discussion of a term; he will also find the page numbers of those occurrences of the term in other articles that clarify its significance and exemplify its uses. A number of entries in the Index are also supplemented by references to closely associated terms. These secondary references expedite the fuller exploration of a subject, as well as the finding of items that serve the needs of a particular course in literature. They identify, for example, the entries most relevant to the analysis of *style*, the articles that define the types of *figurative language* or literary *genres*, and the diverse articles that treat the species, component elements, history, and criticism of the *drama, lyric,* or *novel.*

To make the volume self-sufficient, simplified guides to pronunciation have been entered, in the Index of Terms, for terms that are most likely to be mispronounced by a student. The key to these guides will be found on the first page of the Index.

I have retained, although with some simplification, my original procedure of organizing the *Glossary* as a series of brief essays, in which minor terms are for the most part discussed under the major or generic terms to which they are related, and in which words that are often employed either in conjunction or as contraries (*distance and involvement, empathy and sympathy, objective and subjective, primitivism and progress*) are discussed together. The advantages of this procedure are many. A list of isolated dictionary definitions is not only forbidding but misleading, since the use and range of many terms only become clear in a context of the items to which they are related. Such a presentation also makes it possible to supplement the preferred definition of a word with enough indications of its semantic changes and of its diversity in present usage, to provide a chart by which to steer through the shifting referents and submerged ambiguities of standard literary discussion. Above all, the essay form provides an opportunity to write discussions that are readable as well as utilitarian, while the Index, and the use of **boldface** and *italic* type, make it easy to find any term that is incorporated within an essay.

My first acknowledgment must be to the late scholars Dan S. Norton and Peters Rushton, whose *Glossary of Literary Terms* (1941) provided the original impetus for the present book. This new edition has profited greatly from the learning of various colleagues at Cornell, especially Professor Edgar Rosenberg, and from the generous advice of teachers at many universities, who suggested changes and additions that would make the book more useful to their students. I am especially grateful to: Thomas R. Arp, Southern Methodist University; G. N. Bergquist, Creighton University; Jack L. Capps, United States Military Academy; Ralph Flood, Temple University; Lloyd J. Kubenka, Creighton University; Robert E. Kuehn, Yale University; Daniel F. Littlefield, Oklahoma State University; Jerome J. McGann, University of Chicago; Alan H. Nelson, University of Chicago; and Leo Rockas, Briarcliff College, New York. Miss Margaret Ferguson has been a helpful and unfailingly cheerful research assistant, and Miss Marie Lonning and Miss Johnna Barto, of Holt, Rinehart and Winston, have been wise and patient editors. These advisers have helped me to come closer to my original goal: to write the kind of handbook that I wish had been available to me when I was a college student of literature.

M. H. Abrams

Ithaca, New York
August 1970

A Glossary of Literary Terms

ACT. A major division in the action of a play. Such a division was introduced into England by Elizabethan dramatists, who imitated the Roman playwright Seneca by structuring the action so that it fell into five acts. Late in the nineteenth century, a number of writers followed the example of Chekhov and Ibsen by constructing plays in four acts. In the present century the most common form for nonmusical dramas has been three acts.

Acts are often subdivided into **scenes,** which in modern plays usually consist of units of action in which there is no change of place or break in the continuity of time. (Some recent plays dispense with the division into acts, and are structured as a sequence of scenes, or episodes.) In the conventional theater with a proscenium arch and curtain, the end of a scene is usually indicated by a dropped curtain, and the end of an act by a dropped curtain and an intermission.

AESTHETICISM and DECADENCE. Aestheticism, or "the Aesthetic Movement," was a European phenomenon during the latter nineteenth century that had its chief philosophical headquarters in France. Its roots lie in the German theory, proposed by Kant (1790), that aesthetic contemplation is "disinterested," indifferent both to the reality and to the utility of the beautiful object; it was also influenced by the view of Edgar Allan Poe (in "The Poetic Principle," 1850) that the supreme work is a "poem *per se*," a "poem written solely for the poem's sake." In defiance against the indifference or hostility of their society to any art that did not inculcate current utilitarian and social values, French writers developed the doctrine that art is the supreme value among the works of man because it is self-sufficient and has no aim beyond its own perfection: the end of a work of art is simply to exist, and to be beautiful.

French Aestheticism, as a self-conscious movement, is often said to date from Théophile Gautier's witty defense of his claim that art lacks all utility (Preface to *Mademoiselle de Maupin*, 1835), and it was developed by Baudelaire, Flaubert, Mallarmé, and many other writers. A rallying cry of Aestheticism became the phrase "l'art pour l'art"— **art for art's sake.** This claim usually involved also the view of life for art's sake, with the artist envisioned as a priest who renounces the practical and self-seeking concerns of ordinary existence in the service of what Flaubert and others called "the religion of beauty."

Some proponents of Aestheticism also espoused views and values which developed into a movement called the **Decadence.** The term was based on the literature and art of the latter Roman Empire, and

1

of Greece in the Byzantine era, which were said to possess the subtle savor and beauties of a culture and art which have passed their vigorous prime and fallen into decay. Such was also held to be the state of European civilization in the later nineteenth century. The precepts of the Decadence were summarized by Gautier, in the "Notice" he prefixed to an edition of Baudelaire's poems, *Les Fleurs du Mal*, in 1868. Central to this movement was the view that art is totally opposed to "nature," both in the sense of biological nature and of the standard, or "natural," norms of morality and sexual behavior. The thoroughgoing Decadent writer cultivates high artifice, and often the bizarre, in his subject matter and style, recoils from the fecundity and exuberance of instinctual and organic life, prefers elaborate dress over the living form and cosmetics over the natural hue, and often sets out to violate what is "natural" in human experience by resorting to drugs, depravity, or sexual deviation in the attempt to achieve (in a phrase often echoed from the poet Rimbaud) "the systematic derangement of all the senses." The movement reached its height in the last two decades of the century; an extreme product was the novel, *À Rebours* (*Against the Grain*), written by J. K. Huysmans in 1884. This period is also known as the **fin de siècle** (end of the century); the phrase connotes the lassitude, satiety, and ennui expressed by many writers of the Decadence.

The doctrines of French Aestheticism were introduced into England by Walter Pater, with his emphasis on painstaking artifice and stylistic subtlety, his recommendation to crowd one's life with the maximum of exquisite sensations, and his concept of the supreme value of beauty and of "the love of art for its own sake." (See his Conclusion to *The Renaissance*,[1] 1873.) Both the Aesthetic and Decadent Movements are represented by such writers of the 1890s as Oscar Wilde, Arthur Symons, Ernest Dowson, and Lionel Johnson, and the artist Aubrey Beardsley. In the search for strange sensations, a number of English Decadents in this period experimented with drugs and with illicit or perverse amours; several of them died young. Representative literary products are Wilde's novel *The Picture of Dorian Gray* (1891) and his play *Salomé* (1893); also the poems of Ernest Dowson.

The influence of certain aesthetic and decadent tendencies—such as the view of the "autonomy" (self-sufficiency) of art, the concept of the poem or novel as a constructed object, the distrust of spontaneous "nature" as against art and artifice—have been important in the writings of such prominent recent authors as W. B. Yeats, T. E. Hulme, and T. S.

[1] An asterisk before a title indicates that a paperback edition of the book is available (as listed in *Paperbound Books in Print*, 1969).

Eliot, as well as in the theory of the *New Critics*. And the decadent emphasis in literature on drugged perception, sterile or deviant sexuality, and the deliberate inversion of conventional moral and social values, has recently reappeared, with modern variations, in the Beat poets and novelists and in the work of the French writer Jean Genêt.

See A. C. Bradley, "Poetry for Poetry's Sake," in *Oxford Lectures on Poetry* (1909); Holbrook Jackson, *The Eighteen Nineties* (1913); William Gaunt, *The Aesthetic Adventure* (1945); A. E. Carter, *The Idea of Decadence in French Literature, 1830–1900* (1958); Frank Kermode, *Romantic Image* (1957); Enid Starkie, *From Gautier to Eliot* (1960).

AFFECTIVE FALLACY.   In an essay published in 1946 W. K. Wimsatt, Jr., and Monroe C. Beardsley defined the affective fallacy as the error of evaluating a poem by its effects—especially its emotional effects—upon the reader. As a result of this fallacy "the poem itself, as an object of specifically critical judgment, tends to disappear," so that criticism "ends in impressionism and relativism." This attempt to separate the appreciation and evaluation of a poem from its emotional and other effects on the reader has been severely criticized, on the grounds that a work of literature which leaves the reader unresponsive and impassive is not experienced as literature at all. M. C. Beardsley has since modified the earlier claim by the admission that "it does not appear that critical evaluation can be done at all except in relation to certain types of effect that aesthetic objects have upon their perceivers." So modified, the doctrine becomes a claim for *objective criticism*, in which the critic does not describe the effects of a work upon himself, but concentrates upon the analysis of the specific attributes and devices of the work by which such effects are achieved.

See Wimsatt and Beardsley, "The Affective Fallacy," reprinted in W. K. Wimsatt, Jr., *The Verbal Icon* (1954); Monroe C. Beardsley, *Aesthetics: Problems in the Philosophy of Criticism* (1958), p. 491 and Chap. 11.

AGE OF SENSIBILITY.   The period between the death of Alexander Pope (1744) and the publication of Wordsworth and Coleridge's *Lyrical Ballads* (1798). The older and alternative name for this half-century, the **Age of Johnson,** stresses the dominant position of Dr. Johnson (1709–1784) and his circle of fellow men of letters, including Oliver Goldsmith, Edmund Burke, James Boswell, and Edward Gibbon. These men on the whole represented a culmination of the literary and critical modes of *neoclassicism* and the world view of the *Enlightenment*. The more recent name, **Age of Sensibility,** instead places its stress on the emergence, in the 1740s and later, of new cultural attitudes, theories of literature, and types of poetry—a growing sympathy for the Middle Ages, *cultural primitivism*, an intense interest in ballads and other folk literature, and a turn from neoclassic "correctness" and emphasis on judgment and restraint to an emphasis on instinct and feeling, the development of a *literature of sensibility*, and the exaltation of "original genius" and the "bardic" poetry of the sublime and visionary imagination. Thomas Gray expressed the new sensibility and values in his "Stanzas to Mr. Bentley":

> But not to one in this benighted age
> Is that diviner inspiration given,
> That burns in Shakespeare's or in Milton's page,
> The pomp and prodigality of Heaven.

Other poets manifesting similar shifts in thought and taste were William Collins and Joseph and Thomas Warton (poets who, together with Gray, began in the 1740s the vogue for what Johnson slightingly referred to as "ode, and elegy, and sonnet"), Christopher Smart, William Cowper, and Robert Burns. Thomas Percy published his influential *Reliques of Ancient English Poetry* (1765), which included many folk ballads and a few medieval metrical romances, and James Macpherson in the same decade published his greatly doctored versions of the poems of the Gaelic bard, Ossian (Oisin), which had an immense vogue throughout Europe. In the last decade of the period William Blake signaled the arrival of a new era in his *Songs of Innocence and of Experience, The Marriage of Heaven and Hell*, and his early books of visionary prophecy, written in what he called "the voice of the Bard," including *The Book of Urizen* and *The Book of Los.*

See W. J. Bate, *From Classic to Romantic* (1946); Northrop Frye, "Towards Defining an Age of Sensibility," in *Fables of Identity* (1963), and ed., *Romanticism Reconsidered* (1965); F. W. Hilles and Harold Bloom, eds., *From Sensibility to Romanticism* (1965).

ALLEGORY. An allegory is a narrative in which the agents and action, and sometimes the setting as well, are contrived not only to make sense in themselves, but also to signify a second, correlated order of persons, things, concepts, or events. There are two main types:

(1) Historical and political allegory, in which the characters and the action represent, or "allegorize," historical personages and events. So in Dryden's *Absalom and Achitophel* (1681) King David represents Charles II, Absalom represents his natural son the Duke of Monmouth, and the biblical plot allegorizes a political crisis in contemporary England. (2) The allegory of ideas, in which the characters represent abstract concepts and the plot serves to communicate a doctrine or

thesis. Both types of allegory may either be sustained throughout a work, as in *Absalom and Achitophel* and Bunyan's *The Pilgrim's Progress* (1678), or exist merely as an episode in a nonallegorical work. One example of episodic allegory is the encounter of Satan with his daughter Sin, as well as with Death—the son born of their incestuous relationship—in *Paradise Lost* (Book II). Another example, so brief that it is a tableau rather than a developed narrative, is the passage in Gray's "Elegy Written in a Country Churchyard":

> Can Honour's voice provoke the silent dust,
> Or Flatt'ry sooth the dull cold ear of Death?

The central device in the typical allegory of ideas is the personification of abstract entities such as virtues, vices, states of mind, and types of character; in the more explicit allegories, such reference is specified by the character's name. Thus Bunyan's *The Pilgrim's Progress* allegorizes the doctrines of Christian salvation by telling how Christian, warned by Evangelist, flees the City of Destruction and makes his way laboriously to the Celestial City; en route he encounters such characters as Faithful, Hopeful, and the Giant Despair, and passes through places like the Slough of Despond, the Valley of the Shadow of Death, and Vanity Fair. A passage from this work will indicate the nature of a clear-cut allegorical process:

> Now as Christian was walking solitary by himself, he espied one afar off come crossing over the field to meet him; and their hap was to meet just as they were crossing the way of each other. The Gentleman's name was Mr. Worldly-Wiseman; he dwelt in the Town of Carnal-Policy, a very great Town, and also hard by from whence Christian came.

Allegory is a strategy which may be employed in any literary form or genre. *The Pilgrim's Progress* is a moral and religious allegory in a prose narrative; Spenser's *Faerie Queene* fuses moral, religious, historical, and political allegory in a verse romance; the third book of Swift's *Gulliver's Travels* (the voyage to Laputa and Lagado) is an allegorical satire directed primarily against philosophical and scientific pedantry; and William Collins' "Ode on the Poetical Character" is a formal lyric poem which allegorizes a topic in literary criticism—the nature, dignity, and power of the poet's creative imagination.

Various literary forms may be regarded as special types of allegory, in that they narrate one coherent set of circumstances which signify a second order of correlated meanings. A **fable** is a short story that exemplifies a moral thesis or a principle of human behavior; usually in its conclusion either the narrator or one of the characters states the moral in the form of an *epigram*. Most common is the **beast fable,** in which animals talk and act like the human types they represent. In the familiar fable of the fox and the grapes, the fox—after vainly exerting all his wiles to get the grapes hanging beyond his reach—concludes that they are probably sour anyway: the express moral is that men belittle what they cannot get. An early set of beast fables was attributed to Aesop, a Greek slave of the sixth century B.C.; in the seventeenth century a Frenchman, Jean de la Fontaine, wrote a set of witty fables in verse which are the classics of this literary kind. Chaucer's *The Nun's Priest's Tale*, the story of the cock and the fox, is a beast fable; John Gay wrote a collection of fables in the eighteenth century; James Thurber's *Fables for Our Time* (1940) is a recent set of short fables; and in *Animal Farm* (1945) George Orwell expanded the beast fable into a sustained satire on the political and social conditions of our age.

A **parable** is a short narrative presented so as to stress the implicit but detailed analogy between its component parts and a thesis or lesson that the narrator is trying to bring home to us. The parable was one of Christ's favorite devices as a teacher; examples are His parables of the good Samaritan and of the prodigal son. Here is Christ's parable of the fig tree, Luke 13:6–9:

> He spake also this parable: A certain man had a fig tree planted in his vineyard; and he came and sought fruit thereon, and found none. Then said he unto the dresser of his vineyard, "Behold, these three years I come seeking fruit on this fig tree, and find none: cut it down; why cumbereth it the ground?" And he answering said unto him, "Lord, let it alone this year also, till I shall dig about it, and dung it. And if it bear fruit, well: and if not, then after that thou shalt cut it down."

An **exemplum** is a story told as a particular instance of the general text of a sermon. The device was extremely popular in the Middle Ages, when extensive collections of exempla were prepared for use by preachers. In Chaucer's *The Pardoner's Tale* the Pardoner, preaching on the thesis "Greed is the root of all evil," incorporates as exemplum the tale of the three revelers who set out to find Death, but find a heap of gold instead, then kill one another in the attempt to gain sole possession of the treasure. By extension the term "exemplum" is also applied to tales used in a formal, though nonreligious, exhortation. Thus Chaucer's Chanticleer borrows the preacher's technique in the ten exempla he tells in a vain effort to persuade his skeptical wife, Dame Pertelote the hen, that bad dreams forebode disaster.

See *Didactic* and *Symbol*; and consult C. S. Lewis, **The Allegory of Love* (1936), Chap. 2; Edwin Honig, **Dark Conceit: The Making of Allegory* (1959); Angus Fletcher, *Allegory: The Theory of a Symbolic Mode* (1964). On the exemplum, see G. R. Owst, *Literature and Pulpit in Medieval England* (2d ed., 1961), Chap. 4.

ALLITERATION   is the repetition of speech sounds in a sequence of nearby words; the term is usually applied only to consonants, and only when the recurrent sound occurs in a conspicuous position at the beginning of a word or of a stressed syllable within a word. In Old English **alliterative meter,** alliteration is the organizing device of the verse line: each line is divided into two half-lines of two stresses by a decisive pause, or *caesura*, and at least one, and usually both, of the two stressed words in the first half-line alliterates with the first stressed word of the second half-line. (In this versification a vowel was considered to alliterate with any other vowel.) A number of Middle English poems, such as "Piers Plowman" and *Gawain and the Green Knight*, continued to use and play variations upon the old alliterative meter. (See *strong-stress meters*.) In the opening line of "Piers Plowman," for example, all four of the stressed words alliterate:

> In a *s*omer *s*eson, whan *s*oft was the *s*onne . . .

In later English versification, however, alliteration is used only for special stylistic effects, such as to reinforce the meaning, to link related words, or to provide tone color. An example is the repetition of the *s*, *th*, and *w* sounds in Shakespeare's Sonnet XXX:

> When to the *s*essions of *s*weet *s*ilent *th*ought
> I *s*ummon up remembrance of *th*ings past,
> I *s*igh the lack of many a *th*ing I *s*ought
> And *w*ith old *w*oes new *w*ail my dear time's *w*aste.

Various other repetitions of speech sounds are identified by technical terms. **Consonance** is the repetition of a sequence of consonants, but with a change in the intervening stressed vowel: live–love, lean–alone, pitter–patter. W. H. Auden's " 'O where are you going?' said reader to rider," makes prominent use of this device; the last stanza reads:

> "Out of this house"—said *rider* to *reader*,
> "Yours never will"—said *farer* to *fearer*,
> "They're looking for you"—said *hearer* to *horror*,
> As he left them there, as he left them there.[1]

Assonance is the repetition of identical or similar vowel sounds—especially in stressed syllables—in a sequence of nearby words. Note the recurrent long *i* in the opening lines of Keats's "Ode on a Grecian Urn":

> Thou still unrav*i*shed br*i*de of qu*i*etness,
> Thou foster ch*i*ld of *s*ilence and slow t*i*me.

[1] From "O where are you going?" Copyright 1934 and renewed 1962 by W. H. Auden. Reprinted from *Collected Shorter Poems, 1927–1957*, by W. H. Auden, by permission of Random House, Inc., and Faber and Faber Ltd.

The assonantal effect at the beginning of William Collins' "Ode to Evening" depends on a sequence both of similar and of identical vowels:

> If aught of oaten stop or pastoral song,
> May hope, chaste Eve, to soothe thy pensive ear.

For a special case of the repetition of vowels and consonants in combination, see *Rhyme*.

ALLUSION   in a work of literature is a brief reference, explicit or indirect, to a person, place, or event, or to another literary work or passage. In Thomas Nashe's "Litany in Time of Plague,"

> Brightness falls from the air,
> Queens have died young and fair,
> Dust hath closed Helen's eye,

there is an explicit allusion to Helen of Troy. Most allusions serve to enlarge upon or enhance a subject, but some are used in order ironically to undercut it by the discrepancy between the subject and the allusion. In the lines from T. S. Eliot's *The Waste Land*, describing a modern woman at her dressing table,

> The Chair she sat in, like a burnished throne,
> Glowed on the marble,[1]

the ironic allusion, by the indirect mode of echoing Shakespeare's words, is to *Antony and Cleopatra* (II. ii. 196 ff.):

> The barge she sat in, like a burnish'd throne,
> Burn'd on the water.

For discussion of a poet who makes persistent and complex use of this device, see Reuben A. Brower, *Alexander Pope: The Poetry of Allusion* (1959).

In older literature the author assumed that his allusions would be recognized by the educated readers of the day. But a number of modern authors (including Joyce, Pound, and Eliot) often employ allusions that are highly specialized, or else are based on the author's private reading and experience, in the knowledge that very few readers will recognize them without the help of scholarly annotation.

AMBIGUITY.   In ordinary usage "ambiguity" is commonly applied to a fault in style: the use of a vague or equivocal expression when what is wanted is precision and singleness of reference. Since William Empson published *Seven Types of Ambiguity* (1930), however, the

---

[1] From *The Waste Land* by T. S. Eliot (1922). Reprinted by permission of Harcourt, Brace & World, Inc., and Faber and Faber Ltd.

term has been widely used in criticism to identify a special poetic device: the use of a word or expression such that two or more distinct references, or else two or more diverse kinds of connotation, are equally relevant. **Multiple meaning** and **plurisignation** are alternate terms for this use of language; they have the advantage of avoiding the pejorative aspect of the word "ambiguity."

When Shakespeare's Cleopatra, exciting the asp to a frenzy, says (V. ii. 306 ff.),

> Come, thou mortal wretch,
> With thy sharp teeth this knot intrinsicate
> Of life at once untie. Poor venomous fool,
> Be angry, and dispatch,

her speech is richly multiple in significance. For example, "mortal" means "fatal" or "death-dealing," and at the same time signifies that the asp is itself mortal, or subject to death. "Wretch" in this context serves to express both contempt and pity (Cleopatra goes on to refer to the asp as "my baby at my breast, / That sucks the nurse asleep"). And the two meanings of "dispatch"—"make haste" and "kill"—are both relevant.

"Intrinsicate" in the same passage exemplifies a special type of multiple meaning, the **portmanteau word.** The term was introduced into literary criticism by Humpty Dumpty, the expert on semantics in Lewis Carroll's *Through the Looking Glass*. He is explicating to Alice the meaning of the opening lines of "Jabberwocky":

> 'Twas brillig, and the slithy toves
> Did gyre and gimble in the wabe.

"Slithy," Humpty Dumpty explained, "means 'lithe and slimy'. . . . You see it's like a portmanteau—there are two meanings packed up into one word." A portmanteau word thus is coined by fusing together two or more words. Shakespeare's "intrinsicate," for example, is a fusion of "intrinsic" and "intricate." James Joyce exploited this device to the full in order to sustain the multiple levels of meaning in his dream narrative *Finnegans Wake*; an example is his comment on girls who are "yung and easily freudened."

William Empson (who named and enlarged upon a literary phenomenon that had been noted by earlier writers) helped set current a mode of explication which has greatly expanded our sense of the complexity and richness of poetic language. The risk, exemplified both by Empson and other recent critics, is that the intensive search for ambiguities easily leads to **over-reading:** ingenious, overdrawn, and sometimes self-contradictory explications that violate the norms of the English language and ignore the controls upon reference exerted by the context of a literary passage.

For related terms see *Connotation and Denotation* and *Pun*. Refer to Empson, and to Philip Wheelwright, *The Burning Fountain* (1954), especially Chap. 4. For critiques of Empson's theory and application of the concept of ambiguity, see John Crowe Ransom, "Mr. Empson's Muddles," *The Southern Review*, IV (1938), and Elder Olson, "William Empson, Contemporary Criticism and Poetic Diction," in *Critics and Criticism*, ed. R. S. Crane (1952).

ANGRY YOUNG MEN   designates a group of British novelists and playwrights of the 1950s and later who—in an era of greatly increased upward mobility of the social classes—manifest hostility toward the traditions, standards, and manners of what has come to be called "the Establishment." A number of their works depict in comic or satiric fashion the oppressiveness, hypocrisy, and stultifying values in the English school or university, or in the social, commercial, or industrial world. Examples are novels such as Kingsley Amis' *Lucky Jim* (1954), John Braine's *Room at the Top* (1957), Alan Sillitoe's *Loneliness of the Long Distance Runner* (1960), and plays such as John Osborne's *Look Back in Anger* (1957). The mode survives in the late 1960s, in the cinema *If . . .* , directed by Lindsay Anderson, and has influenced the English *literature of the absurd*. See John Russell Taylor, *Anger and After* (1962).

ANTITHESIS   is a contrast or opposition in meaning, emphasized by a parallel in grammatical structure. An example is Alexander Pope's description of Atticus in his *Epistle to Dr. Arbuthnot*, "Willing to wound, and yet afraid to strike." In the second line of Pope's description of the Baron's designs against Belinda, in *The Rape of the Lock*, the grammatical parallelism is strengthened by alliteration in the nouns:

> Resolved to win, he meditates the way,
> By *f*orce to ravish, or by *f*raud betray.

An example of antithesis in prose is this sentence from Samuel Johnson's *Rasselas*, Chap. 26: "Marriage has many pains, but celibacy has no pleasures."

ARCHAISM.   The use in literature of words and expressions that have become obsolete in common speech. Spenser in *The Faerie Queene* deliberately employed archaisms (many of them derived from Chaucer's English) in the attempt to achieve a specialized poetic style, and one that is particularly appropriate to his revival of the medieval *chivalric romance*. The translators of the King James Version of the Bible (1611) gave weight, dignity, and sonority to their prose by archaic revivals. Both Spenser and the King James Bible have in their turn been major sources of archaisms in Milton and many later poets. When Keats, for example, described the Grecian Urn as "with *brede /* Of marble men and maidens *overwrought*," he used archaic words for "braid" and "worked [that is, ornamented] all over." Until recent times many poets have continued to say "I ween," "methought," "steed," "taper" (for candle), and "morn," but only in verse.

ARCHETYPE. On the one side the literary theory of the archetype derives from the school of comparative anthropology at Cambridge University, of which the basic work is J. G. Frazer's *The Golden Bough* (1890–1915); this book traced elemental patterns of myth and ritual which, it claimed, recur in the legends and ceremonials of the most diverse cultures. On the other side the theory derives from the depth psychology of C. G. Jung, who applied the term "archetype" to "primordial images," the "psychic residue" of repeated types of experience in the lives of our very ancient ancestors which, Jung said, are inherited in the "collective unconscious" of the human race and are expressed in myths, religion, dreams, and private fantasies, as well as in works of literature.

The term has been much employed in literary criticism, especially since the appearance of Maud Bodkin's *Archetypal Patterns in Poetry* (1934). In criticism "archetype" is applied to narrative designs, character types, or images which are said to be identifiable in a wide variety of works of literature, as well as in myths, dreams, and even ritualized modes of social behavior. Similarities within these diverse phenomena are held to reflect a set of universal, primitive, and elemental patterns, whose effective embodiment in a literary work evokes a profound response from the reader. Some archetypal critics have dropped Jung's theory of the collective unconscious; in the words of Northrop Frye, this theory is "an unnecessary hypothesis," and the recurrent archetypal patterns are simply there, "however they got there."

Among the prominent practitioners of various forms of archetypal criticism, in addition to Maud Bodkin, are G. Wilson Knight, Robert Graves, Philip Wheelwright, Richard Chase, and Joseph Campbell. In a remarkable and widely influential book, *The Anatomy of Criticism* (1957), Northrop Frye developed the archetypal approach into a radical and inclusive revision of the traditional grounds both of the theory of literature and the practice of literary criticism. Since all these critics tend to emphasize the underlying mythical patterns in literature, on the assumption that myths are closer to the elemental archetype than are the artful products of sophisticated writers of literary works, archetypal criticism is usually associated with *myth criticism*. The death–rebirth theme is often said to be the archetype of archetypes, and is held to be grounded in the cycle of the seasons and the organic cycle of human life; this archetype, it has been claimed, informs primitive rituals of the sacrificial king, myths of the god who dies to be reborn, and a multitude of diverse literary works, including the Bible, Dante's *Divine Comedy*, and Coleridge's *Rime of the Ancient Mariner*. Among other, more limited, archetypal themes, images, and characters which have been frequently traced in literature are the journey underground, the heavenly ascent, and the search for the father; the paradise–Hades image; the Promethean rebel–hero, the earth goddess, and the fatal woman.

Consult, in addition to the works mentioned above, C. G. Jung, "On the Relation of Analytical Psychology to Poetic Art" (1922), in *Contributions to Analytical Psychology* (1928), and "Psychology and Literature," in *Modern Man in Search of a Soul* (1933); G. Wilson Knight, *The Starlit Dome* (1941); Robert Graves, *The White Goddess* (1948); Richard Chase, *Quest for Myth* (1949); Joseph Campbell, *The Hero with a Thousand Faces* (1949); Philip Wheelwright, *The Burning Fountain* (1954), and *Metaphor and Reality* (1962); Northrop Frye, "The Archetypes of Literature," in *Fables of Identity* (1963). For critiques of archetypal theory and practice see H. M. Block, "Cultural Anthropology and Contemporary Literary Criticism," *Journal of Aesthetics and Art Criticism*, XI (1952); Murray Krieger, ed., *Northrop Frye in Modern Criticism* (1966).

ATMOSPHERE   (alternative terms are **mood** and **ambience**) is the tonality pervading a literary work, which sets up in the reader expectations as to the course of events, whether happy or (more commonly) disastrous. Shakespeare establishes the tense and fearful atmosphere of *Hamlet* at the beginning, by the terse and nervous dialogue of the sentinels as they anticipate a reappearance of the ghost; Coleridge engenders a compound of religious and superstitious terror by his manner of describing the initial scene of *Christabel*; and Hardy in *The Return of the Native* makes Egdon Heath an immense and brooding presence which reduces to pettiness and futility the human struggle for happiness for which it is the setting.

AUGUSTAN AGE.   The original Augustan Age was the brilliant literary period of Vergil, Horace, and Ovid under the Roman emperor Augustus (27 B.C.–A.D. 14). Since the eighteenth century, however, the term has also been applied to the period in England from approximately 1700 to 1745, on the ground that the leading writers of the period (such as Pope, Swift, Addison, and Steele) greatly admired the Roman Augustans, themselves drew the parallel between the two ages, and deliberately imitated their literary forms and subjects, their emphasis on social concerns, and their ideals of moderation, decorum, and urbanity.

BALLAD.   Of the **popular ballad** (known also as the **folk ballad** or **traditional ballad**) a convenient short definition is that it is a song, transmitted orally, which tells a story. In all probability the original version was composed by a single author, but he is unknown; and since each singer who learns the ballad by word of mouth is apt to introduce changes in both the text and the tune, a popular ballad exists in many variant forms. Typically, the popular ballad is dramatic and impersonal: the narrator begins with the climactic episode, tells the story tersely by means of action and dialogue (sometimes, by means of dialogue alone), and tells it without expressing his personal attitudes or feelings.

The most common stanza form—called the **ballad stanza**—is a *quatrain* in alternate four- and three-stress iambic lines, in which only the second and fourth lines rhyme. This is the form of "Sir Patrick Spens"; the first stanza of this ballad also exemplifies the conventionally abrupt opening and the typical manner of proceeding by briefly sketched setting and action, sharp transition, and curt dialogue:

> The king sits in Dumferling towne,
>   Drinking the blude-red wine:
> "O whar will I get a guid sailor,
>   To sail this schip of mine?"

Many ballads employ set formulas, such as (1) stock descriptive phrases like "milk-white steed" and "blood-red wine," (2) the *refrain* ("Edward," "Lord Randal"), and (3) **incremental repetition,** in which a line or stanza is repeated, but with an addition that advances the story ("Lord Randal," "Child Waters").

British ballads have been gathered by a variety of collectors since the eighteenth century, but the standard collection is Francis J. Child's *English and Scottish Popular Ballads* (1882–1898), which includes 305 ballads, together with many variant versions. Bertrand H. Bronson has edited *The Traditional Tunes of the Child Ballads* (3 vols.; 1959–1966). Popular ballads are still being sung—and collected, usually with a tape recorder—in the British Isles and the remote rural areas of America. To the songs it inherited from Great Britain America has added native forms of the ballad, such as those sung by lumberjacks and cowboys. A number of recent folk singers, from Woody Guthrie to Bob Dylan, themselves compose ballads; most of these, however, such as "Bonnie and Clyde," are closer to the journalistic "broadside ballad" than to the primitive and heroic mode of the popular ballads in the Child collection.

A **broadside ballad** is a ballad printed on one side of a single sheet (called "a broadside"), dealing with a current event or issue, and sung to a well-known tune. Beginning with the sixteenth century, these broadsides were hawked in the streets or at country fairs in Great Britain.

A **literary ballad** is a narrative poem written by a learned poet in deliberate imitation of the form and spirit of the popular ballad. Some of the greatest of these were composed in the Romantic period: Coleridge's *Rime of the Ancient Mariner* (which, however, is much longer and more elaborately developed than the folk ballad), Scott's "Proud Maisie," and Keats's "La Belle Dame sans Merci."

See Gordon H. Gerould, *The Ballad of Tradition* (1932), and M. J. C. Hodgart, *The Ballads* (2d ed., 1962). For the broadside ballad see *The Common Muse*, eds. V. de Sola Pinto and Allan E. Rodway (1957).

BATHOS and ANTICLIMAX.   Bathos is Greek for "depth," and it has been an indispensable term to critics since Alexander Pope, parodying Longinus' famous essay *On the Sublime* (that is, "loftiness"), wrote in 1727 an essay *On Bathos, or Of the Art of Sinking in Poetry.* Pope solemnly assures his readers that he undertakes "to lead them as it were by the hand . . . the gentle down-hill way to Bathos; the bottom, the end, the central point, the *non plus ultra*, of true Modern Poesy!" The word ever since has been used for an unintentional descent in literature when, straining to be pathetic or passionate or elevated, the writer overshoots the mark and drops into the trivial or the ridiculous. Among his examples Pope records "the modest request of two absent lovers" in a contemporary poem:

> Ye Gods! annihilate but Space and Time,
> And make two lovers happy.

The slogan "For God, for Country, and for Yale!" is bathetic because it moves to intentional climax in rhetorical order and to unintentional descent in significance—at least for someone who is not a Yale man. The greatest of poets sometimes fall unwittingly into the same rhetorical figure. In the early version of *The Prelude* (1805; Book IX) Wordsworth, after recounting at length the tale of the star-crossed lovers, Vaudracour and Julia, tells how Julia died, leaving Vaudracour to raise their infant son:

> It consoled him here
> To attend upon the Orphan and perform
> The office of a Nurse to his young Child
> Which after a short time by some mistake
> Or indiscretion of the Father, died.

The Stuffed Owl: An Anthology of Bad Verse, eds. D. B. Wyndham
Lewis and Charles Lee (rev. ed., 1948), is a rich mine of bathos.

Anticlimax is sometimes used as an equivalent of bathos. In a second
usage, however, "anticlimax" is nonpejorative, and denotes a writer's
intentional drop from the serious and elevated to the trivial and lowly,
in order to achieve a comic or satiric effect. Thus Thomas Gray, in
his mock-heroic "Ode on the Death of a Favorite Cat," drowned when
she tried to catch a goldfish, gravely inserts the observation:

> What female heart can gold despise?
> What cat's averse to fish?

And in *Don Juan* (I. ix.) Byron thus epitomizes the gallant quality
of Juan's father:

> A better cavalier ne'er mounted horse,
> Or, being mounted, e'er got down again.

BIOGRAPHY.   Late in the seventeenth century Dryden neatly defined
biography as "the history of particular men's lives." The name now
connotes a relatively full account of the facts of a man's life, involving
the attempt to set forth his character, temperament, and milieu, as well
as his experiences and activities. English biography proper—as distinguished from the generalized chronicles of the deeds of a king, or
the stylized and pious lives of the Christian saints—appeared in the
seventeenth century; an example is Izaak Walton's *Lives* (of John
Donne, George Herbert, Richard Hooker, and others), written between
1640 and 1678. In the eighteenth century both the theory and the
practice of biography as a special literary art were greatly advanced;
it was the age of Dr. Johnson's monumental *Lives of the English Poets*
(1779–1781) and James Boswell's *Life of Samuel Johnson* (1791),
which many readers hold to be the greatest of all biographies. In our
own time biography has become one of the most popular of literary
forms, and a biographical title usually stands high on the best-seller list.

Autobiography is a biography written by the subject about himself.
It is to be distinguished from the **memoir**—in which the emphasis is
not on the author's developing self, but on the people he has known
and the events he has witnessed—and from the private **diary** or
journal, which is a day-to-day record of the events in a man's life which
he writes for his own use and pleasure, with little or no thought of
publication. Examples of the latter form are the seventeenth-century
Diaries of Samuel Pepys and John Evelyn, and the *Journals* of James
Boswell. The first fully developed autobiography is also one of the
greatest: the *Confessions* of St. Augustine, written in the fourth century A.D. The design of this profound and subtle spiritual history

centers on the author's mental crisis and a recovery in which he discovers his Christian identity and vocation in life. This design has been repeated in many later autobiographies, whether these, like Augustine's, are religious confessions of crisis and conversion, such as John Bunyan's *Grace Abounding to the Chief of Sinners* (1666), or secular works in which the crisis is resolved by the author's discovery of his identity and vocation as a poet or artist, such as Wordsworth's great autobiography in verse, *The Prelude* (completed 1805, published 1850). Among the notable British and American autobiographies in prose are those by Benjamin Franklin, John Stuart Mill, Anthony Trollope, Henry Adams, and Sean O'Casey.

On biography: Harold Nicolson, *The Development of English Biography* (1928); Donald A. Stauffer, *English Biography before 1700* (1930), and *The Art of Biography in Eighteenth-Century England* (1941); Leon Edel, *Literary Biography* (1957). On autobiography: Wayne Shumaker, *English Autobiography* (1954); Roy Pascal, *Design and Truth in Autobiography* (1960); John N. Morris, *Versions of the Self: Studies in English Autobiography from John Bunyan to John Stuart Mill* (1966).

BLANK VERSE   consists of lines of *iambic pentameter* which are unrhymed—hence the term "blank." Of all verse forms it is closest to the natural rhythms of English speech, yet the most flexible and adaptive to diverse levels of discourse; as a result, it has been more frequently and variously used than any other type. Soon after blank verse was introduced by Surrey in his translations from *The Aeneid* (about 1540), it became the standard meter for Elizabethan and later poetic drama; a free form of blank verse is still the medium in such recent plays as those of Maxwell Anderson and T. S. Eliot. Milton used blank verse for his epic poems, James Thomson for his descriptive and philosophical *Seasons* (1726–1730), Wordsworth for his autobiographical *Prelude*, Tennyson for the narrative *Idylls of the King*, Browning for *The Ring and the Book* and many dramatic monologues, and T. S. Eliot for much of *The Waste Land*. Many meditative lyrics have also been written in blank verse, including Coleridge's "Frost at Midnight," Wordsworth's "Tintern Abbey," Tennyson's "Tears, Idle Tears," and Wallace Stevens' "Sunday Morning."

The formal divisions in blank verse poems, setting off each sustained unit of meaning, are called **verse paragraphs.**

See *Meter*; and refer to Moody Prior's critical study of blank verse in **The Language of Tragedy* (1964).

BOMBAST   originally meant "cotton stuffing"; the word was adopted to signify verbose and inflated diction that is disproportionate to the

matter it expresses. The high style of even so fine a poet as Christopher
Marlowe is at times inappropriate to its occasion, as when Faustus
declares (*Dr. Faustus* III. i. 47 ff.):

> Now by the kingdoms of infernal rule,
> Of Styx, Acheron, and the fiery lake
> Of ever-burning Phlegethon I swear
> That I do long to see the monuments
> And situation of bright-splendent Rome;

which is to say: "By Hades, I'd like to see Rome!" Bombast is a frequent component in the *heroic drama* of the late seventeenth and early
eighteenth centuries. The pompous language of that drama is amus-
ingly parodied in Henry Fielding's *Tom Thumb the Great* (1731), as
in the famous opening of Act II. v, in which the lover cries:

> Oh! Huncamunca, Huncamunca, oh!
> Thy pouting breasts, like kettle-drums of brass,
> Beat everlasting loud alarms of joy;
> As bright as brass they are, and oh! as hard;
> Oh! Huncamunca, Huncamunca, oh!

Fielding points out in a note the inspiration for this parody in James
Thomson's lines in *The Tragedy of Sophonisba* (1730):

> Oh! Sophonisba, Sophonisba, oh!
> Oh! Narva, Narva, oh!

BOWDLERIZE. To expurgate from a work passages considered inde-
cent or indelicate. The word derives from the Reverend Thomas
Bowdler, who tidied up his *Family Shakespeare* in 1815 by omitting
"whatever is unfit to be read by a gentleman in a company of ladies."
Gulliver's Travels and Shakespeare are often bowdlerized in editions
intended for children, and until quite recently, even some compilers
of anthologies for college students have availed themselves of Bowdler's
prerogative in editing Chaucer.

BURLESQUE is often defined as "an incongruous imitation"; that is, it
imitates the matter or manner of a serious literary work, or literary
genre, but makes the imitation amusing by a ridiculous disparity
between its form and style and its subject matter. The burlesque may
be written for the sheer fun of it; usually, however, it is a form of *satire*.
The butt of the satiric ridicule may be the literary work or type that
is being imitated, or the subject matter to which the imitation is incongruously applied, or (often) both of these together.

"Burlesque," "parody," and "travesty" are sometimes applied interchangeably; simply to equate these terms, however, is to surrender
useful critical distinctions. It is better to follow the critics who use

"burlesque" as the generic name and use the other terms to discriminate various species of burlesque. The application of these terms will be clearer if we make two preliminary distinctions: (1) In a burlesque imitation, the form and style may be either lower or higher in status and dignity than the subject to which it is incongruously applied. If the form and style is elevated and the subject is low or trivial, we have "high burlesque"; if the subject is serious and dignified and the style and manner of treatment is low and undignified, we have "low burlesque." (2) A burlesque may also be distinguished according to whether it imitates a particular work or author, or a general type or genre. Applying these two distinctions, we get the following species of burlesque.

(I) Varieties of high burlesque:

(1) A **mock epic** or a **mock-heroic** poem imitates the elaborate form and ceremonious style of the *epic* genre, and applies it to a commonplace or trivial subject matter. In a masterpiece of this form, *The Rape of the Lock*, Pope views through the grandiose epic perspective a quarrel between the belles and elegants of his day over the theft of a lady's curl. The story includes such elements of epic protocol as supernatural *machinery*, a voyage on board ship, a visit to the underworld, and a heroically scaled battle between the sexes— although with metaphors, hatpins, and snuff for weapons. The term "mock-heroic" is often applied to other dignified poetic forms which are purposely mismatched to a lowly subject; for example, to Thomas Gray's comic "Ode on the Death of a Favorite Cat."

(2) A **parody** imitates the serious materials and manner of a particular work, or the characteristic style of a particular author, and applies it to a lowly or grossly discordant subject. John Phillips' "The Splendid Shilling" (1705) parodied the style of Milton's *Paradise Lost* by exaggerating its high formality and applying it to the description of a tattered poet composing in a drafty attic. Henry Fielding parodied Richardson's novel *Pamela* in *Joseph Andrews* by putting a hearty male hero in place of Richardson's sexually beleaguered heroine. Here is Hartley Coleridge's parody of the first stanza of Wordsworth's "She Dwelt among the Untrodden Ways":

> He lived amidst th' untrodden ways
>   To Rydal Lake that lead,
> A bard whom there were none to praise,
>   And very few to read.

From the early nineteenth century to the present, parody has been the favorite form of burlesque. Among the gifted parodists of this century have been Max Beerbohm in England (see his *A Christmas

Garland, 1912), and such writers for *The New Yorker* as James Thurber, Robert Benchley, and E. B. White.

(II) Varieties of low burlesque:

(1) The **Hudibrastic poem** is named from Samuel Butler's *Hudibras* (1663), which satirizes rigid Puritanism by describing the adventures of a Puritan knight, Sir Hudibras; instead of the doughty deeds and dignified style of the traditional genre of the *chivalric romance,* however, we find the knightly hero experiencing humiliating misadventures which are described in *doggerel* verses and a ludicrously colloquial idiom.

(2) The **travesty,** like the parody, mocks a particular work; but it does so by treating its lofty subject in a jocular and undignified manner and style. As Boileau put it, in a travesty of Vergil's *Aeneid* "Dido and Aeneas are made to speak like fishwives and ruffians."

The modern sense of "burlesque" as a theater form derives, historically, from plays which mocked serious types of drama by an incongruous imitation. John Gay's *Beggar's Opera* (1728), for example, was a high burlesque of Italian opera, as were a number of musical plays by Gilbert and Sullivan in the Victorian era. What American theatergoers now call "burlesque," however, is a variety show in which there is little mockery of serious drama but a great deal of slapstick and bawdry for its own sake; the climactic episode is commonly the striptease.

See George Kitchin, *A Survey of Burlesque and Parody in English* (1931); Richmond P. Bond, *English Burlesque Poetry, 1700–1750* (1932); and these anthologies: Walter Jerrold and R. M. Leonard, eds., *A Century of Parody and Imitation* (1913); Robert P. Falk, ed., *The Antic Muse: American Writers in Parody* (1955); Dwight MacDonald, ed., *Parodies: An Anthology* (1960).

CAROLINE AGE.   The reign of Charles I, 1625–1649; the name is derived from "Carolus," the Latin version of "Charles." This was the time of the English Civil War, fought between the supporters of the King (known as "Cavaliers") and the supporters of Parliament (known as "Roundheads" from their custom of wearing their hair cut short). Milton began his writing during this period; and it was the age of the religious poet George Herbert and of the prose writers Robert Burton and Sir Thomas Browne.

Associated with the court were the **Cavalier poets,** composers of witty and polished lyrics of gallantry. The group includes Richard Lovelace, Sir John Suckling, and Thomas Carew. Robert Herrick, although a country parson, is often classified with the Cavalier poets because, like them, he was a **Son of Ben**—that is, an admirer and follower of Ben Jonson—in many of his lyrics of love and gallant compliment.

For suggested readings, see *Jacobean Age*.

CARPE DIEM,   meaning "seize the day," is a Latin phrase from Horace's *Odes* (I. xi) which has become the name for a very common literary *motif*, especially in lyric poetry. The speaker in a carpe diem poem emphasizes that life is short and time is fleeting in order to enjoin the auditor—who is often a reluctant virgin—to make the most of present pleasures. A frequent emblem of the brevity of physical beauty and the finality of death is the rose, as in Spenser's *Faerie Queene* (II. xii. 74–75: "Gather therefore the Rose, whilst yet is prime"), Herrick's "To the Virgins, to Make Much of Time" ("Gather ye rose-buds, while ye may"), and Waller's "Go, lovely rose." The greatest poems of this kind communicate the poignant sadness—or desperation—of the pursuit of pleasures under the sentence of death; see Andrew Marvell's "To His Coy Mistress," and the set of variations on the carpe diem motif, "The Rubáiyát of Omar Khayyám" by the Victorian poet Edward Fitzgerald.

CELTIC RENAISSANCE,   also known as the **Irish Literary Revival,** identifies the creative period in Irish literature from about 1885 to the death of William Butler Yeats in 1939. Some of this literature was written in the native Irish tongue, which is a Celtic dialect, but the major authors wrote in English. The movement was stimulated by the works of Yeats; other important poets were AE (G. W. Russell), James Stephens, and Oliver St. John Gogarty. The dramatists included, in addition to Yeats himself, Lady Gregory (who was also an important patron and publicist for the movement), John Millington Synge and Sean O'Casey.

See E. A. Boyd, *Ireland's Literary Renaissance* (1916, rev. ed., 1922).

CHARACTER and CHARACTERIZATION.   (1) **The character** is a literary genre: a short, and usually witty, sketch in prose of a distinctive type of person. The genre was inaugurated by Theophrastus, a Greek author of the second century B.C., who wrote a lively book called *Characters*. The form had a great vogue in the earlier seventeenth century; the books of characters then written by Joseph Hall, Sir Thomas Overbury, and John Earle influenced later writings in the essay, history, and fiction. The title of some of Overbury's sketches will indicate the nature of the form: "A Courtier," "A Wise Man," "A Fair and Happy Milkmaid." See Richard Aldington's anthology, *A Book of "Characters"* (1924).

(2) **Characters** are the persons, in a dramatic or narrative work, endowed with moral and dispositional qualities that are expressed in what they say—the **dialogue**—and what they do—the **action.** The grounds in a character's temperament and moral nature for his speech and actions constitute his **motivation.** A character may remain essentially "stable," or unchanged in his outlook and dispositions, from beginning to end of a work (Prospero in *The Tempest,* Micawber in Dickens' *David Copperfield*), or he may undergo a radical change, either through a gradual development or as the result of an extreme crisis (Shakespeare's King Lear, Pip in Dickens' *Great Expectations*). Whether he remains stable or changes, we require "consistency" in a character—he should not suddenly break off and act in a way not plausibly grounded in his temperament as we already have come to know it.

E. M. Forster, in *°Aspects of the Novel* (1927), introduced popular new terms for an old distinction in discriminating between flat and round characters. A **flat character** (also called a "type," or "two-dimensional"), Forster says, is built around "a single idea or quality" and is presented in outline and without much individualizing detail, and so can be fairly adequately described in a single phrase or sentence. A **round character** is complex in temperament and motivation and is represented with subtle particularity; thus he is as difficult to describe with any adequacy as a person in real life, and, like most people, he is capable of surprising us. Almost all dramas and narratives, properly enough, have some characters who serve as mere functionaries and are not characterized at all, as well as other characters who are quite flat: there is no need, in Shakespeare's *Henry IV, Part 1,* for Mistress Quickly to be as globular as Falstaff. The degree to which a character needs to be three-dimensional depends on his function in the plot, and in many types of plot, such as in the detective novel or adventure novel or farce comedy, even the protagonist usually possesses only two dimensions. Sherlock Holmes and Long John Silver do not require, for their own excellent literary roles, the roundness of a Hamlet, a Becky Sharp, or a Jay Gatsby.

A broad distinction is frequently made between alternative methods available to an author in "characterizing" the persons in a narrative, showing and telling. In **showing** (also called "the dramatic method"), the author merely presents his characters talking and acting and leaves the reader to infer what motives and dispositions lie behind what they say and do. In **telling,** the author himself intervenes authoritatively in order to describe, and often to evaluate, the motives and dispositional qualities of his characters. For example, in the fine opening chapter of *Pride and Prejudice* Jane Austen first shows us Mr. and Mrs. Bennet as they talk to one another about the young man who has just rented Netherfield Park, then tells us about them, and so confirms and expands the inferences and judgments that the reader has begun to make from what he has already been shown:

> Mr. Bennet was so odd a mixture of quick parts, sarcastic humour, reserve, and caprice, that the experience of three-and-twenty years had been insufficient to make his wife understand his character. *Her* mind was less difficult to develop. She was a woman of mean understanding, little information, and uncertain temper.

Especially since the theory and practice of Flaubert and Henry James, it has been common to consider "telling" a violation of artistry and to recommend only the technique of "showing" characters: the author, it is often said, should efface himself in order to write "objectively," "impersonally," or "dramatically." Such judgments, however, glorify a modern kind of artistic limitation which is suited to particular kinds of novelistic effects, and decry a supplementary method of characterization which all the greatest novelists, until recently, have employed to produce masterpieces. (See *Point of view.*)

On the problems and methods of characterization, including discussions of showing and telling, see in addition to E. M. Forster (above), Percy Lubbock, *The Craft of Fiction* (1926); W. C. Booth, *The Rhetoric of Fiction* (1961), especially Chaps. 1–4; W. J. Harvey, *Character and the Novel* (1966); Robert Scholes and Robert Kellog, *The Nature of Narrative* (1966).

CHIVALRIC ROMANCE or MEDIEVAL ROMANCE.   A form of narrative which developed in twelfth-century France, spread to the vernacular literatures of other countries, and displaced in popularity the various *epic* and heroic types of narrative. ("Romance" originally signified a work written in the French language, which evolved from a dialect of the Roman language, Latin.) Romances were at first written in verse, but later in prose as well. The **romance** is distinguished from the epic in that it represents, not a heroic age of tribal wars, but a courtly and chivalric age, often one of highly developed manners and civility; its standard plot is one of quest and adventure, undertaken by a single knight; it introduces a heroine, and frequently its central interest is *courtly love*, together with tournaments fought and dragons and monsters slain for a damsel's sake; it stresses the chivalric ideals of courage, honor, mercifulness to an opponent, and exquisite and elaborate manners; and it delights in wonders and marvels. Supernatural events in the epic had their causes in the will and actions of the gods; romance shifts the supernatural to fairyland, and makes much of the mysterious effect of magic, spells, and enchantments.

The materials of medieval romances are divided by scholars into three types of subjects: (a) "The Matter of Britain" (especially stories centering on the court of King Arthur); (b) "The Matter of Rome" (stories based on classical antiquity); and (c) "The Matter of France" (Charlemagne and his knights). The cycle of tales which developed around the pseudo-historical British King Arthur produced many of the finest romances, some of them (stories of Sir Perceval and the quest for the Holy Grail) with a religious instead of a purely secular interest. Chrétien de Troyes, the great twelfth-century French poet, wrote Arthurian romances; *Gawain and the Green Knight* is a superb verse, or "metrical," romance about an Arthurian knight, written in fourteenth-century England; and Malory's *Morte d'Arthur* (fifteenth century) is an English prose version of the cycle of romances about Arthur and his Knights of the Round Table.

See W. P. Ker, *Epic and Romance* (1897); L. A. Hibbard, *Medieval Romance in England* (rev. ed., 1961); R. S. Loomis, *The Development of Arthurian Romance* (1963) and *The Grail* (1963). For modern adaptations and extensions of the concept of the romance genre, see *myth critics*, and Eleanor T. Lincoln, *Pastoral and Romance: Modern Essays in Criticism* (1969).

CHORUS. Among the ancient Greeks the chorus was a group, wearing masks, who sang or chanted verse while performing dancelike maneuvers at religious festivals. A similar chorus played a part in Greek tragedies, where (in the plays of Aeschylus and Sophocles) they served mainly as commentators on the action who represented traditional moral, religious, and social attitudes; beginning with Euripides, however, the chorus assumed primarily a lyrical function. The Greek *ode*, as developed by Pindar, was also chanted by a chorus.

Roman playwrights, such as Seneca, took over the chorus from the Greeks, and in the mid-sixteenth century some English dramatists (for example, Norton and Sackville in *Gorboduc*) imitated the Senecan chorus. The classical type of chorus was never widely used by English writers. There is one tragic masterpiece, however, which includes this feature—John Milton's *Samson Agonistes*—and in recent times, T. S. Eliot made effective use of the classical chorus in his religious tragedy, *Murder in the Cathedral*.

During the Elizabethan Age the term "chorus" was applied also to a single character who spoke the prologue and epilogue to a play, and sometimes introduced each act as well. This character served as the author's vehicle for commenting on the play and for communicating to the audience exposition about its subject, offstage events, and setting; see Marlowe's *Dr. Faustus* and Shakespeare's *Henry V*. In Shakespeare's *Winter's Tale*, the fifth act begins with "Time, the

Chorus," who asks the audience that they "impute it not a crime / To me or my swift passage that I slide / O'er sixteen years," then summarizes what has happened during those years and announces that the setting for this act is Bohemia. A recent and extended use of a chorus in this sense is the Stage Manager in Thornton Wilder's *Our Town*.

Modern scholars use the term **choral character** to identify a character within the play itself who stands largely apart from the action and by his comments provides the audience with a special perspective (often an ironic perspective) through which to view characters and events. Examples in Shakespeare are the Fool in *King Lear*, Enobarbus in *Antony and Cleopatra*, and Thersites in *Troilus and Cressida*; a modern instance is Seth Beckwith in O'Neill's *Mourning Becomes Electra*. "Choral character" is sometimes applied also to persons in a novel who represent a communal point of view, or the perspective of a cultural group; instances are Thomas Hardy's peasants, and the old Negro women in William Faulkner.

CHRONICLE.   Chronicles, the predecessors of modern "histories," were accounts, in prose or verse, of national or worldwide events over a considerable period of time. If the chronicles deal with events year by year, they are often called **annals.** Unlike the modern historian, most chroniclers tended to take their information as they found it, and made little attempt to separate fact from legend. The most important English chronicles are the *Anglo-Saxon Chronicle*, started by King Alfred in the ninth century and continued until the twelfth century, and the *Chronicles of England, Scotland, and Ireland* (1577–1587) by Raphael Holinshed and other writers; the latter documents were an important source of materials for Elizabethan drama.

CHRONICLE PLAYS   were dramatic renderings of the historical materials in the English *Chronicles* by Raphael Holinshed and others. They leaped into high popularity late in the sixteenth century, when the patriotic fervor following the defeat of the Spanish Armada in 1588 brought a demand for plays dealing with events of English history. The early chronicle plays presented a loosely knit series of events during the reign of an English king and depended for effect mainly on a bustle of stage battles, pageantry, and spectacle. Marlowe, however, in his *Edward II* (1592) selected and rearranged materials from Holinshed's *Chronicles* to compose a unified drama of character, and Shakespeare's series of chronicle plays, encompassing the succession of English kings from Richard II to Henry VIII, includes such major achievements as *Richard II*, *Henry IV, Parts 1 and 2*, and *Henry V*.

The Elizabethan chronicle plays are often called **history plays.** This latter term is also applied more broadly to any drama based mainly on historical materials, including such recent examples as Arthur Miller's *The Crucible* (1953), which treats the Salem witch trials of 1692, and Robert Bolt, *A Man for All Seasons* (1962), on Sir Thomas More.

On chronicle plays see E. M. W. Tillyard, *Shakespeare's History Plays* (1946); Lily B. Campbell, *Shakespeare's "Histories"* (1947); Irving Ribner, *The English History Play in the Age of Shakespeare* (rev. ed., 1965).

CLICHÉ,   which is French for the stereotype used in printing, signifies an expression which deviates enough from ordinary usage to call attention to itself and has been used so often that it is felt to be hackneyed or cloying. "I beg your pardon" or "Sincerely yours" are standard usages which do not call attention to themselves; but "point with pride," "my better half," "the eternal verities," "lock, stock, and barrel" are considered clichés. Some clichés are foreign phrases which are used as an arch or elegant equivalent for the English term (*aqua pura, terra firma*). Others are hackneyed literary echoes. "The cup that cheers" is an inaccurate quotation from Cowper's *The Task*, referring to tea— "the cups / That cheer but not inebriate."

> Come, and trip it as you go
> On the light fantastic toe,

was charming in Milton's "L'Allegro," but "to trip the light fantastic" has become an annoying substitute for "to dance." In his *Essay on Criticism* (II, 11. 350 ff.) Alexander Pope comments satirically on some clichés which eighteenth-century **poetasters** (untalented pretenders to the poetic art) used to eke out their rhymes:

> Where'er you find "the cooling western breeze,"
> In the next line it "whispers through the trees";
> If crystal streams "with pleasing murmurs creep,"
> The reader's threatened (not in vain) with "sleep."

See Eric Partridge, *A Dictionary of Clichés* (4th ed., 1950).

COMEDY.   A comedy is a work in which the materials are selected and managed primarily in order to interest and amuse us: the characters and their discomfitures engage our delighted attention rather than our profound concern, we feel confident that no great disaster will occur, and usually the action turns out happily for the chief characters. The term "comedy" is customarily applied only to dramas; it should be noted, however, that the comic form, so defined, also occurs in prose fiction and narrative poetry.

Within the broad spectrum of dramatic comedy, the following types are frequently distinguished:

(1) **Romantic comedy,** as developed by Shakespeare and some of his Elizabethan contemporaries, is concerned with a love affair that involves a beautiful and idealized heroine (sometimes disguised as a man); the course of this love does not run smooth, but overcomes all difficulties to end in a happy union. Many of the boy-meets-girl plots of later writers are instances of romantic comedy. In *The Anatomy of Criticism* (pp. 182–183), Northrop Frye points out that some of Shakespeare's romantic comedies involve a movement from the normal world of conflict and trouble into "the green world"—the Forest of Arden in *As You Like It*, or the fairy-haunted wood of *A Midsummer Night's Dream*—in which the problems and injustices of the ordinary world are magically dissolved, enemies reconciled, and true lovers united. Frye regards this phenomenon (together with other aspects of these comedies, such as their festive conclusion in the social ritual of a wedding, a feast, a dance) as evidence that comic plots reflect primitive myths and rituals celebrating the victory of spring over winter.

(2) **Satiric comedy** attacks the disorders of society by making ridiculous the violators of its standards of morals or manners. In *Volpone* and *The Alchemist*, by Shakespeare's contemporary Ben Jonson, the greed and ingenuity of one or more highly intelligent but rascally swindlers, and the equal greed but stupid gullibility of their victims, are made grotesquely ludicrous rather than lightly amusing. Both of these satiric comedies end unhappily for the rogues who are their protagonists; the comic effect is sustained, however, because these personages have been rendered in such a way as to repel rather than engage our sympathies.

(3) The **comedy of manners** was early exemplified by Shakespeare's *Love's Labour's Lost* and *Much Ado about Nothing*, and was brought to a high polish in **Restoration comedy.** This form deals with the relations and intrigues of gentlemen and ladies living in a polished and sophisticated society, and relies for comic effect in great part on the wit and sparkle of the dialogue—often in the form of *repartee*, a witty conversational give-and-take which constitutes a kind of verbal fencing match—and to a lesser degree, on the ridiculous violations of social conventions and decorum by stupid characters such as would-be wits, jealous husbands, and foppish dandies. Excellent examples are Congreve's *The Way of the World* and Wycherley's *The Country Wife*. A middle-class reaction against the immorality of situation and the frequent indecency of dialogue in the courtly Restoration comedy resulted in the *sentimental comedy* of the eighteenth century. Oliver Goldsmith (*She Stoops to Conquer*) and his contemporary Richard

Sheridan (*The Rivals* and *A School for Scandal*) revived the wit and gaiety, but deleted the indecency, of Restoration comedy. The comedy of manners lapsed in the early nineteenth century, but was revived by many skillful practitioners, from A. W. Pinero and Oscar Wilde (*The Importance of Being Earnest*, 1895) to George Bernard Shaw, Somerset Maugham, Noel Coward, and other writers of our own era.

(4) **Farce** is a type of comedy designed to provoke the audience to simple, hearty laughter—"belly laughs," in the parlance of the theater. To do so it commonly employs highly exaggerated or caricatured character types, puts them into improbable and ludicrous situations, and makes free use of broad verbal humor and physical horseplay. Farce was a component in the comic episodes in medieval *miracle plays*, such as the Wakefield plays "Noah" and the "Second Shepherd's Play." In the enduring English drama, farce is usually an episode in a more complex form of comedy—for example, the knockabout scenes in Shakespeare's *The Taming of the Shrew* and *The Merry Wives of Windsor*. Brandon Thomas' *Charley's Aunt*, however, an American play of 1892 which has often been revived, is a true farce throughout. The one-reelers, as well as some of the full-length cinemas, by such comedians as Charlie Chaplin, Buster Keaton, and W. C. Fields, were excellent farce. Currently farce is employed mainly in single scenes of musical revues and as standard fare in television comedy.

(5) A distinction is frequently made between high and low comedy. **High comedy,** as described by George Meredith in a classic essay on *The Idea of Comedy* (1877), evokes "intellectual laughter"—thoughtful laughter from spectators who remain emotionally detached from the action—at the spectacle of folly, pretentiousness, and incongruity in human behavior. Meredith finds its highest form within the comedy of manners, in the wit combats (sometimes identified now as the "love duels") between such intelligent, sophisticated, highly verbal, and well-matched lovers as Benedick and Beatrice in Shakespeare's *Much Ado about Nothing* and Mirabell and Millamant in Congreve's *The Way of the World*. **Low comedy,** at the other extreme, makes little or no intellectual appeal, but undertakes to arouse laughter by jokes, or "gags," and by slapstick humor or boisterous or clownish physical activity; it is, therefore, one of the common components of farce.

See also *Comedy of humours. Tragicomedy, Sentimental comedy,* and *Wit, Humor, and the Comic.* On comedy and its varieties refer to A. H. Thorndike, *English Comedy* (1929); H. T. E. Perry, *Masters of Dramatic Comedy* (1939); Louis Kronenberger, *The Thread of Laughter* (1952); W. K. Wimsatt, Jr., ed., *English Stage Comedy* (1954); Leo Hughes, *A Century of English Farce* (1956); Elder Olson, *The Theory of Comedy* (1968). For works emphasizing the relation of comedy to forms of myth and ritual, see Northrop Frye, *Anatomy of Criticism* (1957), pp. 163–186; and C. L. Barber, *Shakespeare's Festive Comedy* (1959).

COMEDY OF HUMOURS. A type of comedy which Ben Jonson, the Elizabethan playwright, based on the ancient but still current physiological theory of the **four humours.** The "humours" were held to be the four primary fluids—blood, phlegm, choler (or yellow bile), and melancholy (or black bile)—whose "temperament," or mixture, determined both a man's physical state and his character type. An imbalance of one or another humour in a temperament was said to produce four kinds of disposition, whose names have survived the underlying theory: sanguine (from the Latin *sanguis*, blood), phlegmatic, choleric, and melancholic. In Jonson's **comedy of humours** each of the major characters, instead of being a well-balanced individual, has a preponderant humour that gives him a characteristic distortion or eccentricity of disposition. Jonson expounds his theory in the "Induction" to his play *Every Man in His Humour* (1598) and exemplifies the mode in his later comedies as well.

COMIC RELIEF   is the use of humorous characters, speeches, or scenes in a serious or tragic work, especially a dramatic work. Such elements were almost universal in Elizabethan tragedy. Sometimes they occur merely as intrusive episodes of dialogue or horseplay for purposes of alleviating tension and adding variety; in the best plays, however, they are made integral to the plot, in a way that counterpoints and enhances the tragic significance. Examples of such complex uses of comic elements are the gravediggers in *Hamlet* (V. i); the scene of the drunken porter after the murder of the king in *Macbeth* (II. iii); the speeches of the Fool in *Lear*; and the roles of Mercutio and the old Nurse in *Romeo and Juliet*.

See Thomas De Quincey's classic essay "On the Knocking at the Gate in *Macbeth*" (1823).

COMMEDIA DELL'ARTE   was a form of comic drama developed about the mid-sixteenth century by guilds of professional Italian actors. The actors, playing stock characters, largely improvised the dialogue around a given **scenario**—a brief outline of a drama, indicating the entrances of the main characters and the sequence of the action. In a typical play, a pair of young lovers outwit a rich old father ("Pantaloon"), aided by a clever and intriguing servant ("Harlequin"), in a plot enlivened by the buffoonery of "Punch" and other clowns. Wandering Italian troupes played in all the large cities of Renaissance

Europe, and influenced various writers of comedies in Elizabethan England and, later, Molière in France. The modern Punch and Judy show is a descendant of this old Italian comedy.

See Kathleen M. Lea, *Italian Popular Comedy, 1560–1620* (2 vols.; 1934).

COMMONWEALTH PERIOD, also known as the **Puritan Interregnum,** extends from the end of the Civil War and the execution of Charles I in 1649 to the restoration of the Stuart monarchy under Charles II in 1660. In this period England was ruled by Parliament under the Puritan leader Oliver Cromwell; his death in 1658 signaled the dissolution of the Commonwealth. Drama almost disappeared for the eighteen years after the Puritans, on moral and religious grounds, closed the public theaters in September 1642. It was the age of Milton's political pamphlets, of Hobbes's *Leviathan* (1651), of the prose writers Sir Thomas Browne, Thomas Fuller, Jeremy Taylor, and Izaak Walton, and of the poets Vaughan, Waller, Cowley, Davenant, and Marvell.

CONCEIT.   Originally meaning a concept or image, "conceit" came to be the name for figures of speech which establish a striking parallel—usually an elaborate parallel—between two apparently dissimilar things or situations. The term, once derogatory, is now best employed as a neutral identification of a poetic device. Two types of conceit are often distinguished:

(1) The **Petrarchan conceit** is a type of figure used in love poems which had been novel and effective in the Italian poet Petrarch, but often became hackneyed in his imitators, the Elizabethan sonneteers. The figure consists of detailed and exaggerated comparisons applied to the disdainful mistress, as cold and cruel as she is beautiful, and to the distresses and despair of the worshipful lover. (See *Courtly love.*) Sir Thomas Wyatt, for example, in his sonnet "My Galley Chargèd with Forgetfulness," circumstantially parallels the lover's state to a ship laboring in a storm; and in another sonnet, "Like to These Unmeasurable Mountains," he compares it to an Alpine landscape. A third sonnet by Wyatt begins with a familiar Petrarchan conceit, an *oxymoron* describing the simultaneous fever and chills experienced by a sufferer from the disease of love:

> I find no peace; and all my war is done;
> I fear and hope; I burn and freeze in ice.

Shakespeare (who at times employed this type of conceit himself) satirized some standard objects pressed into service for similes by Petrarchan sonneteers, in his sonnet beginning

> My mistress' eyes are nothing like the sun;
> Coral is far more red than her lips' red:
> If snow be white, why then her breasts are dun;
> If hairs be wires, black wires grow on her head.

(2) The **metaphysical conceit** is a characteristic figure in John Donne and other *metaphysical poets* of the seventeenth century. It was described by Dr. Johnson, in a famed passage in his "Life of Cowley," as wit which is

> a kind of *discordia concors*; a combination of dissimilar images, or discovery of occult resemblances in things apparently unlike. . . . The most heterogeneous ideas are yoked by violence together.

The metaphysical poets exploited all knowledge—commonplace or esoteric, practical, theological, or philosophical, true or fabulous—for the vehicles of these figures; and their comparisons, whether succinct or expanded, were novel, witty, and at their best startlingly effective. In sharp contrast to both the concepts and figures of conventional Petrarchism is Donne's "The Flea," a poem that uses a flea who has bitten both lovers as the basic reference for its argument against the lady's coyness. In Donne's "The Canonization," as the poetic argument develops, the comparisons for the relationship between lovers move from the area of commerce and business, through various actual and mythical birds and diverse forms of historical memorials, to a climax which equates the sexual acts and the moral status of worldly lovers with the ascetic life and heavenly destination of unworldly saints. The most famous sustained conceit is Donne's parallel (in "A Valediction: Forbidding Mourning") between the continuing relationship of his and his lady's soul, despite their physical parting, to the coordinated movements of the two feet of a draughtsman's compass. A well-known instance of the chilly and hyperbolical ingenuity of the overdriven metaphysical conceit is Richard Crashaw's description, in "Saint Mary Magdalene," of the tearful eyes of the repentant Magdalene as

> two faithful fountains
> Two walking baths, two weeping motions,
> Portable and compendious oceans.

Following the great revival of the metaphysical poets in the 1920s, a number of modern poets exploited this type of conceit. Examples are T. S. Eliot's comparison of the evening to "a patient etherized upon a table" in "The Love Song of J. Alfred Prufrock," and the series of startling figurative vehicles in Dylan Thomas' "In Memory of Ann Jones." The vogue for such conceits extended even to popular love songs, in the 1920s and later, by well-educated composers such as Cole Porter: "You're the Cream in My Coffee" and "You're the Tops."

See K. K. Ruthven, *The Conceit (1969).

CONCRETE and ABSTRACT. In traditional philosophy a "concrete term" is defined as a word which denotes a particular person or thing, and an "abstract term" is defined as a word (such as "brightness," "beauty," "evil," "despair") which denotes qualities that do not exist except as attributes of particular persons or things. A sentence is said to be concrete if it makes an assertion about a particular subject (T. S. Eliot's "Grishkin is nice . . ."), and abstract if it makes an assertion about an abstract subject (Pope's "Hope springs eternal in the human breast"). With reference to literature, however, these terms are often used in an extended way: a passage is called abstract if it represents its subject matter in general or non-sensuous words or with only a thin realization of its experiential qualities, but is called concrete if it represents its subject matter with striking particularity and sensuous detail. In his "Ode to Psyche" Keats's

> 'Mid hush'd, cool-rooted flowers, fragrant-eyed,
> Blue, silver-white, and budded Tyrian,

is a concrete description which involves all five senses. And in the opening of his "Ode to a Nightingale," Keats communicates concretely, by a combination of literal and figurative language, exactly how it felt to experience the full-throated song of the nightingale:

> My heart aches, and a drowsy numbness pains
> My sense, as though of hemlock I had drunk,
> Or emptied some dull opiate to the drains. . . .

It is frequently asserted that "poetry is concrete," or, as John Crowe Ransom put it in *The World's Body* (1938), that its proper subject is "the rich, contingent materiality of things." Most poetry is certainly more concrete than other modes of language. It should be kept in mind, however, that poets do not hesitate to use abstract language when the poetic situation or purpose calls for it. Keats, though he was one of the most concrete of poets, began *Endymion* with a sentence containing only abstract terms:

> A thing of beauty is a joy forever:
> Its loveliness increases; it will never
> Pass into nothingness; . . .

And some of the most moving and memorable passages in poetry are not concrete; for example, the statement about God in Dante's *Paradiso,* "In His will is our peace," or the bleak comment by Edgar in the last act of *King Lear,*

> Men must endure
> Their going hence, even as their coming hither;
> Ripeness is all.

See J. C. Ransom, *The World's Body* (1938); R. H. Fogle, *The Imagery of Keats and Shelley* (1949), Chap. 5.

CONFIDANT (the feminine form is "confidante") is a character in a drama or novel who plays only a minor role in the action, but serves the protagonist as a trusted friend to whom he can confess his intimate thoughts. The confidant thus provides the playwright with a plausible device for communicating to the audience the mind and intentions of his principal character without the use of such stage devices as the *soliloquy* or the *aside*; an example is Horatio in Shakespeare's *Hamlet,* and Cleopatra's maid Charmion in his *Antony and Cleopatra.*

A famous confidant in prose fiction is Dr. Watson in A. Conan Doyle's stories about Sherlock Holmes. The device is particularly useful to modern writers who, like Henry James, have largely renounced the novelist's earlier privilege of intruding in order to address himself directly to the reader. To the confidant James also applied the term **ficelle**, French for the strings by which the puppeteer manages his puppets. Discussing Maria Gostrey, Strether's confidante in *The Ambassadors*, James remarks that she is a "ficelle" who is not, "in essence, Strether's friend. She is the reader's friend much rather." (James, *The Art of the Novel*, ed. R. P. Blackmur, 1934, pp. 321–322.)

On the nonintrusive author, see *Point of view*. On the confidant, refer to W. J. Harvey, *Character and the Novel* (1966).

CONNOTATION and DENOTATION.   In literary usage (logicians use these words in a different way) the **denotation** of a word is its primary meaning, such as the dictionary ordinarily specifies; its **connotation** is the range of secondary or accompanying meanings which it commonly suggests or implies. Thus "home" denotes the place where one lives, but connotes privacy, intimacy, and coziness; that is the reason real estate agents like to use "home" instead of "house" in their advertisements. "Horse" and "steed" denote the same quadruped, but "steed" has a different connotation, deriving from the romantic narratives in which this word ordinarily occurs.

The connotation of a word is only a potential range of secondary meanings; which, if any, of these connotations are evoked depends on the particular context in which it is used. Poets typically establish contexts which bring into play some part of the connotative as well as the denotative meaning of words. In his poem "Virtue" George Herbert wrote,

> Sweet day, so cool, so calm, so bright,
> The *bridal* of the earth and sky. . . .

The denotation of "bridal"—a union between human beings—serves as part of the ground for applying the word as a metaphor to the union of earth and sky; but the metrical and verbal context in which the word occurs also evokes such connotations of "bridal" as sacred, joyous, and ceremonial. (Note that "marriage," although metrically and denotatively equivalent to "bridal," would have been less effective in this context, because more commonplace and modern in its connotation.) Even the way a word is spelled may alter its connotation. Keats, in the passage of his "Ode to a Nightingale,"

> Charmed magic casements, opening on the foam
> Of perilous seas, in *faery* lands forlorn,

altered his original spelling of "fairy" in order to make available the connotations of antiquity and of the magic world of Spenser's *Faerie Queene* in the older form, "faery."

A related distinction frequently made since the 1920s is that between **emotive language** and **referential** (or **cognitive**) **language.** Referential language—the language of pure description and exposition, of which the language of science is an instance—makes neutral assertions about matters of fact. Emotive language—including the language of poetry— may make reference to facts, or represent an object or state of affairs, but it also expresses and evokes feelings and attitudes toward the matters referred to. The difference is that between a weather report —"the day is fair and cool, with no wind"—and the lines from Herbert cited above. The distinction was popularized in criticism by I. A. Richards, *Principles of Literary Criticism* (1924).

On connotation and denotation see Isabel C. Hungerland, *Poetic Discourse* (1958), Chap. 1, and Monroe C. Beardsley, *Aesthetics: Problems in the Philosophy of Criticism* (1958), Chap. 3. For critiques of Richards' theory of emotive meaning in literature see, in addition to these two books, Max Black, "Questions about Emotive Meaning," in *Language and Philosophy* (1949).

CONVENTIONS. (1) In one sense of the term, conventions are necessary or convenient devices, widely accepted by the public, for solving the problems imposed by a particular artistic medium in representing reality. In watching a production of a Shakespearean play, for example, the audience accepts without question the convention by which a stage set with three walls (or if it is a theater in the round, with no walls) represents a room with four walls. It also accepts the convention of characters speaking in blank verse instead of prose, and uttering *soliloquies* and *asides*, as well as the convention by which actions presented on a single stage in less than three hours may represent events which take place in a great variety of places, and over a span of many years.

(2) In a second sense of the term, conventions are identifiable

elements of subject matter, form, or technique which recur repeatedly in works of literature. Conventions in this sense may be recurrent types of character, turns of plot, forms of versification, or kinds of diction and style. *Stock characters* such as the Elizabethan braggart soldier, or the languishing and fainting heroine of Victorian fiction, or the sad young men of the lost-generation novels of the 1920s, were conventions of their age. The abrupt reform of the villain at the end of the last act was a common convention of *melodrama. Euphuism* in prose, and the *Petrarchan* and *metaphysical conceits* in verse, were conventional modes of style. It is now just as much a literary convention to be utterly outspoken on sexual matters as it was to be utterly reticent in the age of Dickens.

There is nothing either good or bad in the degree to which a work conforms to preexisting conventions; all depends on how effective a use the individual writer makes of them. The *pastoral elegy*, for example, is one of the most convention-bound of literary forms, yet in "Lycidas" Milton achieved one of the greatest lyrics in the language. He did this by employing the ancient pastoral rituals with freshness and power, in order to absorb the individual death into the experience of the race and to add to his private voice a resonance from the many earlier pastoral laments for the death of a poet.

Invention was originally a term used in theories of *rhetoric*, and later in literary criticism, to signify the "finding" of the subject matter by the orator or the poet. Now "invention" is often opposed to "convention" to signify the inauguration by a writer of a new subject or form or style, and the resulting work is said to possess **originality.** The history of literature shows a repeated process in which innovative writers, such as Donne or Wordsworth or T. S. Eliot, break away from reigning conventions of their time to produce original works, only to have their inventions imitated by other writers, who thereby convert literary novelties into a new set of literary conventions.

See E. E. Stoll, *Poets and Playwrights* (1930); M. C. Bradbrook, *Themes and Conventions of Elizabethan Tragedy* (1935); Harry Levin, "Notes on Convention," in *Perspectives of Criticism* (1950). On convention and originality see John L. Lowes, *Convention and Revolt in Poetry* (1919); Graham Hough, *Reflections on a Literary Revolution* (1960).

COURTLY LOVE. A philosophy of love, including an elaborate code governing the relations of aristocratic lovers, which was widely represented in the lyric poems and *chivalric romances* of western Europe during the Middle Ages. The development of the conventions of courtly love is usually attributed to the troubadours (poets of Provence, in southern France), in the period from the latter eleventh century through the twelfth century. Love is regarded as the noblest passion this side of heaven. The courtly lover idealizes and idolizes his beloved, and subjects himself entirely to her every whim. (This love is usually that of a bachelor knight for another man's wife, as in the stories of Tristan and Isolde or of Lancelot and Guinevere; it must be remembered that marriage among the medieval upper classes was usually a kind of business contract, for utilitarian and political purposes.) The lover suffers agonies and sickness of body and spirit at the caprices of his imperious sweetheart, but remains devoted to her, and manifests his honor by his unswerving fidelity and his adherence to a rigorous code of behavior, both in knightly battles and in the complex ceremonies of courtly speech and conduct.

The origins of courtly love have been traced in part to a serious reading of Ovid's mock-serious book, *The Remedies of Love*; to an imitation in lovers' relations of the politics of feudalism (the lover is a vassal, and both his lady and the god of love are his lords); and to an importation into amatory situations, by a kind of serious parody, of Christian feeling and ritual, especially in the cult of the Virgin Mary. Thus, the lady is exalted and worshiped; the lover prays to the god of love; there are saints of love and lists of commandments; the lover sins and repents; and if his faith stays steadfast, he may be admitted at last into the lover's heaven through his lady's "gift of grace."

From southern France the literature of courtly love spread to Chrétien de Troyes and other poets and romance writers in northern France, to Dante (*La Vita Nuova*), Petrarch, and other writers in Italy, and to the love poetry of Germany and northern Europe. To the reader of English literature these conventions are best known in the medieval romance *Gawain and the Green Knight*, in Chaucer's *Troilus and Criseyde*, and in their later manifestation in the Petrarchan subject matter and the *Petrarchan conceits* of the Elizabethan sonneteers. There has long been a debate as to whether medieval courtly love was merely a literary convention and a topic for elegant conversation at courts, or whether, to some degree, it reflected the actual conditions of aristocratic life of the time. What is clear is that its views of the intensity and ennobling power of love as "the grand passion," of the special sensibility and spiritual status of women, and of the complex decorum governing relations between the sexes, have profoundly affected both the literature and the ways of feeling and acting in the Western world, through the nineteenth century and (though to an ever-diminishing extent) even into our own day of sexual candor, freedom, and the movement for total equivalence between the sexes.

See C. S. Lewis, *The Allegory of Love* (1936); A. J. Denomy,

The Heresy of Courtly Love (1947); M. J. Valency, *In Praise of Love* (1958). For a skeptical view of some commonly held opinions about the development of courtly love see Peter Dronke, *Medieval Latin and the Rise of European Love-Lyric* (1965–1966).

CRITICISM is the branch of study concerned with defining, classifying, expounding, and evaluating works of literature. **Theoretical criticism** undertakes to establish, on the basis of general principles, a coherent set of terms, distinctions, and categories to be applied to the consideration and interpretation of works of literature, as well as the "criteria" (the standards, or norms) by which these works and their writers are to be evaluated. The earliest great work of theoretical criticism was Aristotle's *Poetics*; recent influential books in English are I. A. Richards' *Principles of Literary Criticism* (1924) and Northrop Frye's *Anatomy of Criticism* (1957). **Practical criticism,** or "applied criticism," concerns itself with the discussion of particular works and writers; in an applied critique, the theoretical principles controlling the analysis and evaluation are left implicit, or brought in only as the occasion demands. Among the major works of applied criticism in England are the literary essays of Dryden, Dr. Johnson's *Lives of the Poets,* Coleridge's chapters on the poetry of Wordsworth in *Biographia Literaria* and his lectures on Shakespeare, Matthew Arnold's *Essays in Criticism,* and T. S. Eliot's *Selected Essays.*

Practical criticism is sometimes distinguished into impressionistic and judicial criticism:

Impressionistic criticism attempts to represent in words the felt qualities of a particular work, and to express the attitudes and feelingful responses (the "impression") which the work directly evokes from the critic as an individual. As Hazlitt put it in his essay "On Genius and Common Sense": "You decide from feeling, and not from reason; that is, from the impression of a number of things on the mind . . . though you may not be able to analyze or account for it in the several particulars." And Walter Pater later said that in criticism "the first step toward seeing one's object as it really is, is to know one's own impression as it really is, to discriminate it, to realise it distinctly" (Preface to *Studies in the History of the Renaissance*). At its extreme this mode of criticism becomes, in Anatole France's phrase, "the adventures of a sensitive soul among masterpieces."

Judicial criticism, on the other hand, attempts not merely to communicate, but to analyze and explain the effects of a work in terms of its subject, organization, and techniques, and to base the critic's individual judgments on general standards of literary excellence. Rarely are the two modes of criticism sharply distinct in practice, but good examples of primarily impressionistic commentary can be found in Longinus (see the characterization of the *Odyssey* in his essay *On the Sublime*), Hazlitt, Pater (the locus classicus of impressionism is his description of Leonardo's *Mona Lisa* in *The Renaissance*), and in the critical essays of E. M. Forster and Virginia Woolf.

Types of critical theory and practice can be discriminated according to whether, in explaining and judging a work of literature, they refer the work primarily to the outer world, or to the audience, or to the author, or else look upon the work as an entity in itself:

(1) **Mimetic criticism** views the literary work as an imitation, or reflection, or representation of the world and human life, and the primary criterion applied to a work is that of the "truth" of its representation to the objects it represents, or should represent. This mode of criticism, which first appeared in Plato and (in a qualified way) in Aristotle, is characteristic of modern theories of literary realism.

(2) **Pragmatic criticism** views the work as something which is constructed in order to achieve certain effects on the audience (effects such as aesthetic pleasure, instruction, or special feelings), and it tends to judge the value of the work according to its success in achieving that aim. This approach, which dominated literary discussion from Roman times through the eighteenth century, has been revived in recent *rhetorical criticism*, which emphasizes the artistic strategies by which an author engages and influences the responses of his readers to the matters represented in a literary work.

(3) **Expressive criticism** regards the work primarily in relation to the author himself. It defines poetry as an expression, or overflow, or utterance of feelings, or as the product of the poet's imagination operating on his perceptions, thoughts, and feelings; it tends to judge the work by its sincerity, or genuineness, or adequacy to the poet's individual vision or state of mind; and it often looks in the work for evidences of the particular temperament and experiences of the author who, consciously or unconsciously, has revealed himself in it. Such views were developed mainly by Romantic critics, and remain widely current in our own time.

(4) **Objective criticism** approaches the work as something which stands free from poet, audience, and the environing world. It describes the literary product as a self-sufficient object or integer, or as a world-in-itself, which is to be analyzed and judged by "intrinsic" criteria such as complexity, coherence, equilibrium, integrity, and the interrelations of its component elements. This is the characteristic approach of a number of important critics since the 1920s, including the *new critics* and the *Chicago school* of criticism.

A basic literary enterprise, which the ordinary reader takes for granted, is **textual criticism;** its aim is to establish as closely as possible what an author actually wrote, by assaying and correcting the sources of error and confusion in the various printings of a work.

It is also common to distinguish types of criticism which bring to bear upon literature various special areas of knowledge and theory, in the attempt to explain the influences which determined the particular characteristics of a literary work. Accordingly, we have "historical criticism," "biographical criticism," "sociological criticism" (an important subspecies is "Marxist criticism"), "psychological criticism" (a subspecies is "Freudian criticism"), and *archetypal* or *myth criticism* (which undertakes to explain literature by reference to the theories of myth and ritual in modern cultural anthropology).

On types of criticism and of critical approaches to literature, refer to René Wellek and Austin Warren, *Theory of Literature* (3d ed.; 1956), and M. H. Abrams, *The Mirror and the Lamp* (1953), Chap. 1. Histories of criticism: J. W. Atkins, *Literary Criticism in Antiquity* (2 vols.; 1934), and *English Literary Criticism: The Renascence* (1947); W. K. Wimsatt, Jr., and Cleanth Brooks, *Literary Criticism: A Short History* (1957); René Wellek, *A History of Modern Criticism, 1750–1950* (5 vols.; 1955 ff.). On criticism in the earlier nineteenth century see Abrams, *The Mirror and the Lamp*, and on recent criticism, S. E. Hyman, *The Armed Vision* (1948), and Murray Krieger, *The New Apologists for Poetry* (1956). Convenient anthologies of literary criticism are A. H. Gilbert and G. W. Allen, *Literary Criticism, Plato to Croce* (2 vols.; 1940–1941); W. J. Bate, *Criticism: The Major Texts* (1952); Walter Sutton and Richard Foster, *Modern Criticism: Theory and Practice* (1963); Lionel Trilling, *Literary Criticism: An Introductory Reader* (1970).

DECORUM,   as applied to literature, is the propriety or fittingness with which a literary kind, its characters and actions, and the style of its narration and its dialogue are matched to each other. The doctrine had its roots in classical theory, especially the versified essay on the *Art of Poetry* by Horace, and it achieved a highly elaborate form in the criticism and practice of literature in the Renaissance and the neoclassic age, when (as Milton put it in his essay *Of Education*) decorum became "the grand masterpiece to observe." In the strictest application of this concept, literary *genres*, characters, and style were all ordered in hierarchies, or "levels," from high through middle to low, and had to be matched to one another. Thus the highest and most serious genres (epic and tragedy) represented characters of the highest social classes (kings and nobility) speaking in the "high style." A number of critics in this period, however, especially in England, maintained the theory of decorum only in a qualified form.

See *Neoclassic and Romantic, Poetic diction,* and *Style.* Erich Auerbach's *Mimesis* (1953) describes the sustained conflict in postclassical Europe between the doctrines of literary decorum and the example of the Bible; in the Bible, the highest and most serious matters, including the sublime tragedy of Christ, are intermingled with base characters and humble narrative detail, and are treated with what seemed to a strict neoclassic taste a grotesque indecorum of style.

DEUS EX MACHINA   is Latin for "a god from a machine." It describes the practice of some Greek playwrights (especially Euripides) to end the drama with a god who was lowered to the stage by a mechanical apparatus and, by his judgment and commands, solved the problems of the human characters. The phrase is now used for any forced and improbable device—a telltale birthmark, an unexpected inheritance, the discovery of a lost will or letter—by which a hard-pressed author makes shift to resolve his plot. Notorious examples occur in novels as diverse as Dickens' *Oliver Twist* and Hardy's *Tess of the d'Urbervilles.* The German playwright Bertolt Brecht parodies the abuse of the device in the madcap conclusion of his *Threepenny Opera.*

DIDACTIC LITERATURE.   A didactic work of literature is one designed to expound a branch of theoretical or practical knowledge, or to present in an impressive and persuasive imaginative form a moral, religious, or philosophical thesis or doctrine. Such works are distinguished from purely imaginative works (sometimes called "mimetic" works) in which the materials are selected, ordered, and rendered not for the sake of presenting and enforcing knowledge or doctrine, but as ends in themselves, for their inherent human interest and appeal. The Roman Lucretius wrote his didactic poem *De Rerum Natura* to expound his naturalistic philosophy and ethics, and Vergil wrote his *Georgics* on the practical subject of how to manage a farm. Much of eighteenth-century English poetry is didactic. A number of poets wrote **georgics** (based on Vergil as model) on such practical arts as sheep-herding, running a sugar plantation, or making cider; and Pope's *Essay on Criticism* (modeled on Horace's verse letter *Ars Poetica*) and his *Essay on Man* are didactic poems.

Such works for the most part directly expound a branch of knowledge or art, or else argue an explicit doctrine by proofs and examples. Didactic literature, however, may also take on the aspect and attributes of imaginative works, by translating the doctrine into narrative or dramatic terms in order to add a dimension of aesthetic pleasure, and to enhance its interest and force. In the various forms of allegory, for example, including Spenser's *Faerie Queene* and Bunyan's *The Pilgrim's Progress,* the central doctrines constitute the principle that primarily determines the choice of characters and the development of the plot. The various forms of satire are didactic, in that they are designed, by various devices of ridicule, to alter the reader's attitudes toward certain types of people, institutions, and modes of conduct. As Dante's *Letter to Can Grande* shows, his *Divine Comedy* was designed to represent, in the mode of a visionary narrative, the major Christian truths and the way to avoid damnation and achieve salvation. And Milton's *Paradise Lost* can be called didactic, to the extent that the narrative is in fact organized, as Milton claimed in his opening invocation, around the "great argument" to "assert Eternal Providence, / And justify the ways of God to men." It will be seen from these examples that "didactic literature," as here defined, is a technical distinction, and in no way a derogatory term. Some literary masterpieces are didactic, and others (Shakespeare's *King Lear*, Jane Austen's *Emma*, Joyce's *Ulysses*) are essentially imaginative.

The term **propagandist literature** is sometimes used as the equivalent of didactic literature, but it is far more useful to reserve the term for that species of didactic work which undertakes to move the reader to take a position, or direct action, on a particular moral or political issue of the time at which the work is written. Examples of such works are Harriet Beecher Stowe's *Uncle Tom's Cabin* (on slavery in the South), Upton Sinclair's *The Jungle* (on the horrors of the unregulated slaughtering and meat-packing industry in Chicago in 1906), and Clifford Odets' *Waiting for Lefty* (1935; a play directed against the strong-arm tactics used to suppress a taxicab drivers' union).

See Dwight L. Durling, *The Georgic Tradition in English Literature* (1935); and on the distinction between didactic and imaginative, or purely "mimetic," literature, R. S. Crane, ed., *Critics and Criticism* (1952), especially pp. 63–68 and 589–594.

DISSOCIATION OF SENSIBILITY   was a phrase introduced into literary criticism by T. S. Eliot in his essay "The Metaphysical Poets" (1921). Eliot's claim was that the *metaphysical poets* of the earlier seventeenth century, like the Elizabethan and Jacobean dramatists, "possessed a mechanism of sensibility which could devour any kind of experience." They exhibited "a direct sensuous apprehension of thought," and felt "their thought as immediately as the odour of a rose. A thought to Donne was an experience; it modified his sensibility." But "in the seventeenth century a dissociation of sensibility set in, from which we have never recovered." This dissociation was greatly aggravated by the influence of Milton and Dryden; and most later poets in English either thought or felt, but did not think and feel as an act of unified sensibility.

Eliot's vaguely defined distinction has had a great vogue, and the supposed division between the unified mind and sensibility and the dissociated mind and sensibility was greatly expanded, and was referred to a variety of causes, but especially to the development in the seventeenth century of the scientific view of the world as a material universe stripped of human values and feeling. (See, for example, Basil Willey, *The Seventeenth-Century Background, 1934.) Especially since 1950, however, Eliot's doctrine of a sudden but persisting dissociation of sensibility has come in for strong criticism, as an unreal view of intellectual and poetic history which was contrived both to support Eliot's disapproval of the course that English history had taken after the Civil War of 1642, and to justify Eliot's particular poetic preferences.

See T. S. Eliot, "The Metaphysical Poets," Selected Essays (2d ed., 1960), and "Milton II," *On Poetry and Poets (1957). Important attacks on the validity of the doctrine are F. W. Bateson's "Dissociation of Sensibility," in the journal Essays in Criticism, I (1951) and II (1952); and Frank Kermode, *Romantic Image (1957), Chap. 8.

DISTANCE and INVOLVEMENT. Writing in 1912 Edward Bullough defined "psychical distance" as a sense of separation between "one's own self" and the object of aesthetic contemplation—a sense that permits an observer to experience the object in isolation from his personal concerns and from all "practical needs and ends." As early as 1790, in his Critique of Judgment, Immanuel Kant had put forward the view that we experience a beautiful object by an act of contemplation which is "disinterested" (independent of our personal interests) and free from all reference to its reality or utility. Bullough's related concept of psychical distance has proved useful because it emphasizes that in aesthetic experience there is always a felt distinction between the self and the work of art, yet one that permits us to distinguish variable degrees of this distance, along a scale of greater or lesser **involvement** with the matters that the work represents.

In literary criticism the term "psychical distance"—more commonly **aesthetic distance,** or simply **distance**—is frequently used not only to define a quality of literary experience in general, but also to distinguish the "distancing" effects of various literary techniques, and to analyze the way in which the reader's experience of distance varies in the course of a literary work. A number of dramatists, for example, have employed stylized stage sets, masks, and unrealistic costumes and manners of acting, in order to establish distance (or what Bertolt Brecht, the German dramatist, called "alienation effects") in place of the illusion of reality aimed at by the traditional theater. And recent critics have analyzed the many devices by which authors control the reader's distance or "detachment," as opposed to his involvement or "concern," with one or another character in a work of literature. It is instructive, for example, to observe in the first Canto of *Don Juan* (which narrates the course of the illicit love affair between Don Juan and Donna Julia) how Byron alternately distances us from the work as a whole by letting us in on his problems as the author of a palpable fiction—"I want a hero"; "My poem's epic, and is meant to be / Divided in twelve books"—and then involves us in the progress of his story. In the same Canto he also manipulates drastically our relation to Donna Julia: again and again he involves our concern and sympathy with her fortunes, only to jolt us into distance by evoking our mirth and detached judgment of her foibles, self-deception, and hypocrisies; at the end he leaves us entirely involved in a compassionate reading of the letter in which, as she is carried off to a convent, she bids a poignant farewell to her young lover.

See Edward Bullough, "Psychical Distance as a Factor in Art and an Aesthetic Principle," *British Journal of Psychology*, V (1912), reprinted in Melvin Rader, ed., *A Modern Book of Aesthetics* (rev. ed., 1952), and partially reprinted in Eliseo Vivas and Murray Krieger, eds., *The Problems of Aesthetics* (1963); W. C. Booth, **The Rhetoric of Fiction* (1961), Chap. 5 and Chap. 9 (a detailed analysis of "the control of distance in Jane Austen's *Emma*"); D. W. Harding, "Psychological Processes in the Reading of Fiction," *British Journal of Aesthetics*, II (1962).

DOGGEREL   is a term applied to rough, heavy-footed, and jerky versification. It may be the result of ineptitude on the part of the versifier, but is sometimes deliberately employed by very able poets for satiric, comic, or rollicking effect. John Skelton (1460?–1529) wrote in short (two- or three-stress), rough, variably metrical and rhymed lines which have come to be called **Skeltonics;** as he described his own versification in *Colin Clout*:

> For though my rhyme be ragged,
> Tattered and jagged,
> Rudely rain-beaten,
> Rusty and moth-eaten,
> If ye take well therewith,
> It hath in it some pith.

The tumbling, broken, and comically grotesque *octosyllabic couplets*, often using double, triple, and imperfect rhyme, which were developed by Samuel Butler for his satiric poem *Hudibras* (1663–1678), are a form of deliberate doggerel called **Hudibrastic verse:**

Besides, he was a shrewd philosopher,
And had read every text and gloss over;
Whate'er the crabbed'st author hath,
He understood b' implicit faith.

DRAMA   is the literary form designed for the theater, where actors take
the roles of the characters, perform the indicated action, and utter
the written dialogue. In **poetic drama** the dialogue is written in verse,
which in English is usually *blank verse*; almost all the *heroic dramas*
of the Restoration period, however, were written in heroic couplets
(iambic pentameter lines rhyming in pairs). A **closet drama** is written
in the form of a drama, but is intended to be read rather than to be
performed in the theater; examples are Milton's *Samson Agonistes*,
Shelley's *Prometheus Unbound*, and Byron's *Manfred*.

For types of drama, the elements composing a drama, and dramatic
devices, see the Index under the entry **Drama**.

DRAMATIC MONOLOGUE   designates a type of poem that was perfected by Robert Browning. In its complete form, as represented in
Browning's "My Last Duchess," "The Bishop Orders His Tomb,"
"Andrea del Sarto," and many other poems, the dramatic monologue
has the following characteristics: (1) A single person, who is *not* the
poet himself, utters the entire poem in a specific situation at a critical
moment: the Duke is negotiating with an emissary for a second wife;
the Bishop lies dying; Andrea once more attempts wistfully to believe
his wife's lies. (2) This person addresses and interacts with one or
more other people; but we know of the auditors' presence and what
they say and do only from clues in the discourse of the single speaker.
(3) The monologue is so organized that its focus is on the temperament and character that the dramatic speaker unintentionally reveals
in the course of what he says.

Even Browning, in monologues such as "Soliloquy of the Spanish
Cloister" and "Caliban upon Setebos," omits the second attribute, the
presence of a silent auditor; but attributes (1) and (3) are essential
distinctions between the dramatic monologue and the "dramatic lyric."
Thus John Donne's "The Canonization" and "The Flea," although very
close to the dramatic monologue, lack one essential feature: the focus
of interest is on the speaker's elaborately ingenious argument, rather
than on the character he inadvertently reveals in the course of arguing.
And although Wordsworth's "Tintern Abbey" is spoken by one person
to a silent auditor (his sister) in a specific situation at a significant
moment in his life, it is not properly a dramatic monologue, both
because we are invited to identify the speaker with the poet himself,

and because the organizing principle is not the revelation of the speaker's distinctive temperament but the evolution of his observation, thought, memory, and feelings.

Tennyson wrote "Ulysses" and other dramatic monologues, and the form has been used by Robert Frost, E. A. Robinson, Ezra Pound, Robert Lowell, and other poets of this century. The best known modern instance is T. S. Eliot's "The Love Song of J. Alfred Prufrock."

See Benjamin Fuson, *Browning and His English Predecessors in the Dramatic Monologue* (1948), and Robert Langbaum, *The Poetry of Experience: The Dramatic Monologue in Modern Literary Tradition* (1957).

DREAM VISION. A conventional narrative form widely employed by medieval poets: the narrator falls asleep, usually in a spring landscape, and dreams the events he goes on to relate; often he is led by a guide, human or animal, and the events which he dreams are at least in part an *allegory.* A very influential French example is the thirteenth-century *Roman de la Rose*; the greatest of medieval poems, Dante's *Divine Comedy*, is a dream vision; and in England, Langland employed the form in *Piers Plowman* and Chaucer used it in *The Book of the Duchess, The House of Fame*, and others of his earlier poems. After the Middle Ages the vogue of the dream allegory diminished, but it never died out, as Bunyan's *The Pilgrim's Progress* and Keats's *The Fall of Hyperion* bear witness. Lewis Carroll's *Alice in Wonderland* is a dream vision, and James Joyce's *Finnegans Wake* is an immense cosmic dream on the part of an archetypal dreamer.

See C. S. Lewis, *The Allegory of Love* (1938).

EDWARDIAN PERIOD. The literary period between the death of Victoria (1901) and the beginning of World War I (1914); it is named for King Edward VII, who reigned from 1901 to 1910. Poets writing at the time were Thomas Hardy, Alfred Noyes, W. B. Yeats, and Rudyard Kipling; dramatists included James Barrie, John Galsworthy, and playwrights of the *Celtic Renaissance* such as Lady Gregory, J. M. Synge, and G. B. Shaw. The major achievements were in prose fiction—works by Joseph Conrad, Ford Madox Ford, Galsworthy, H. G. Wells, Rudyard Kipling, and above all Henry James, who published his three great final novels, *The Wings of the Dove, The Ambassadors*, and *The Golden Bowl*, between 1902 and 1904.

ELEGY. In Greek and Roman literature, the elegy was any poem composed in a special elegiac meter (alternating hexameter and pentameter lines); and in England, until the seventeenth century and even later, the term was often applied to any poem of solemn meditation. In present critical usage, however, an elegy is a formal and sustained poem of lament for the death of a particular person, such as Tennyson's *In Memoriam* on the death of Arthur Hallam and W. H. Auden's "In Memory of W. B. Yeats." Sometimes the term is more broadly used for meditative poems, such as Gray's "Elegy Written in a Country Churchyard," which deal generally with the passing of men and the things they value.

The **dirge** also expresses grief on the occasion of death, but differs from the elegy in that it is short, less formal, and is usually represented as a text to be sung; examples are Shakespeare's "Full Fathom Five Thy Father Lies" and William Collins' "A Song from Shakespeare's *Cymbeline*." **Threnody** is now used mainly as an equivalent for "dirge," and **monody** for an elegy or dirge which is presented as the utterance of a single person. Milton describes his "Lycidas," in the subtitle, as a "Monody" in which "the Author bewails a learned Friend," and Matthew Arnold called his elegy on A. H. Clough "Thyrsis, A Monody."

An important species of the elegy is the **pastoral elegy,** which represents both the mourner and the one he mourns—who is usually also a poet—as shepherds (the Greek word for shepherd is *pastor*). This poetic form was originated by the Sicilian Greek poet Theocritus, was continued by the Roman Vergil, was developed in various European countries during the Renaissance, and remained current in English poetry through the nineteenth century. The most notable English pastoral elegies are Milton's "Lycidas," Shelley's "Adonais," and Arnold's "Thyrsis." The pastoral elegists, from the Greeks through the Renaissance, developed elaborate *conventions*, which are illustrated here by reference to "Lycidas." In addition to the representation of both mourner and subject as shepherds tending their flocks (lines 23–36 and elsewhere), there are these conventions:

(1) The lyric speaker begins by invoking the muses, and goes on to make frequent reference to other figures from classical mythology (line 15–22, and so on).

(2) All nature joins in mourning the shepherd's death (lines 37–49). (Recent critics who stress the mythic and ritual origins of poetic genres claim that this feature is a survival from primitive laments for the death of Thammuz, Adonis, or other vegetational deities who died in the autumn to be reborn in the spring.)

(3) The mourner charges with negligence the nymphs or other guardians of the dead shepherd (lines 50–63).

(4) There is a procession of appropriate mourners (lines 88–111).

(5) The poet raises questions about the justice of divine providence and adverts to the corrupt conditions of his own times (lines 64–84,

113–131). Such passages, though sometimes called "digressions," are entirely integral to the evolution of the mourner's thought in "Lycidas."

(6) Post-Renaissance elegies often include an elaborate passage in which appropriate flowers are brought to deck the hearse (lines 133–151).

(7) There is a closing consolation. In Christian elegies, the lyric reversal from grief and despair to joy and assurance occurs when the elegist suddenly realizes that death in this world is the entry to a higher life (lines 165–185).

In his *Life of Milton* Samuel Johnson, who disapproved both of pastoralism and mythology in modern poetry, decried "Lycidas" for "its inherent improbability," but in Milton and other major writers the ancient rituals are a source of strength. Some of the pastoral conventions, although adapted to an industrial age and a non-Christian world view, continue to be manifest in Walt Whitman's great elegy on Lincoln, "When Lilacs Last in the Dooryard Bloom'd."

See *Conventions* and *Pastoral*. On the elegy: Mary Lloyd, *Elegies, Ancient and Modern* (1903); T. P. Harrison, Jr., and H. J. Leon, eds., *The Pastoral Elegy: An Anthology* (1939). On "Lycidas": C. A. Patrides, ed., *Milton's "Lycidas": The Tradition and the Poem* (1961) —an anthology of recent critical essays; Scott Elledge, ed., *Milton's "Lycidas"* (1966).

ELIZABETHAN AGE   denotes the period of Queen Elizabeth's reign, 1558–1603. This was a time of great development in English commerce, maritime power, and nationalist feeling—the defeat of the Spanish Armada occurred in 1588. It was also a great (in drama the greatest) age of English literature; the age of Sidney, Marlowe, Spenser, Shakespeare, Raleigh, Bacon, Ben Jonson, and many other extraordinary writers of prose and of dramatic, lyric, and narrative poetry. See *Renaissance*.

EMPATHY and SYMPATHY.   Empathy (sometimes found in its German form **Einfühlung**—"feeling into") signifies an experience in which one identifies himself with an object of perception and seems to participate in its physical sensations, especially in sensations of bodily posture and motion. Empathy is often described as "an involuntary projection of ourselves into an object," and is commonly explained as the result of an "inner mimicry" on the part of the observer; that is, the observer undergoes incipient muscular movements which he does not experience as his own sensations, but as attributes of an outer object. The object may be human, or nonhuman, or even inanimate. In thoroughly absorbed contemplation we pirouette with a ballet dancer, soar with a hawk, bend with the movements of a tree in the wind, or share the strength, ease, and grace with which a well-proportioned arch supports a bridge. When Keats said that he becomes "a part of all he sees," and that "if a sparrow comes before my window I take part in its existence and pick about the gravel," he was describing an habitual experience of his intensely empathic nature, although long before the word was coined.

In literary criticism we call "empathic" a descriptive passage whose qualities conspicuously evoke such physical participation in the process of reading it. An example is Shakespeare's description, in *Venus and Adonis*, of

> the snail, whose tender horns being hit,
> Shrinks backward in his shelly cave with pain.

Another is the description of a wave in Keats's *Endymion*,

> when heav'd anew
> Old ocean rolls a lengthen'd wave to the shore,
> Down whose green back the short-liv'd foam, all hoar,
> Bursts gradual, with a wayward indolence.

Sympathy denotes fellow-feeling—not a feeling-into, but a feeling-along-with the state of mind and emotions of another human being, or of nonhuman beings to whom we attribute human emotions. We "sympathize," for example, with the emotional experience of a child in his first attempt to recite a piece in public; we may also "empathize" as he falters in his speech or makes an awkward gesture. Robert Burns's "To a Mouse" is an engaging expression of his quick sympathy with the "wee, sleekit, cow'rin, tim'rous beastie" whose nest he has turned up with his plough.

The engagement and control of a reader's sympathy with certain characters, and the establishment of his "antipathy" toward others, is essential to the literary artist. We sympathize with Cordelia, for example, and progressively with King Lear, but we feel unqualified horror and antipathy to his "pelican daughters," Goneril and Regan. Our attitude in the same play toward the villainous Edmund, the bastard son of Gloucester, as managed by Shakespeare, is more complex—antipathetic, yet with some slight element of sympathetic understanding. See *Distance and Involvement*.

Refer to H. S. Langfeld, *The Aesthetic Attitude* (1920)—the section on empathy is reprinted in the *Problems of Aesthetics* (1963), ed. Eliseo Vivas and Murray Krieger. On empathic passages in literature, see Richard H. Fogle, *The Imagery of Keats and Shelley* (1949), Chap. 4.

ENLIGHTENMENT.   The name applied to an intellectual movement and cultural atmosphere which developed in western Europe during the seventeenth century and reached its height in the eighteenth. The common element was the trust in man's reason as adequate to solve all the important problems and to establish all the essential norms in life, together with the belief that the application of reason was rapidly dissipating the darkness of superstition, prejudice, and barbarity, was freeing man from his earlier reliance on mere authority and un-examined tradition, and was preparing him to achieve an ideal exist-ence in this world. In some thinkers the model of "reason" was the inductive procedure of science: reasoning from the facts of experience to general laws; in others (especially Descartes and his followers), the model of "reason" was primarily geometrical: the deduction of particular truths from clear and distinct ideas which are known intuitively, by "the light of reason." Many thinkers relied on reason in both these senses.

In England, the thought and the world outlook of the Enlightenment are usually traced from Bacon through Locke to late eighteenth-century thinkers such as William Godwin; in France, from Descartes to Voltaire and to Diderot and other editors of the great 28-volume *Encyclopédie* (1751–1772); in Germany, from Leibniz to what is often described as the highest product of the Enlightenment, the "critical philosophy" of Immanuel Kant. In a famous essay of 1784 "What Is Enlightenment?" Kant defined it as "the liberation of mankind from his self-caused state of minority" and the achievement of a stage of maturity which is exemplified in his "determination and courage to use [his understanding] without the assistance of another."

A typical manifestation of the Enlightenment was the widespread mode of religious thought known as **deism.** Many thinkers simply assimilated elements of deism but remained professing Christians. The thoroughgoing deist, however, renounced, as violating reason, all "re-vealed religion"—that is, all particular religions, including Christianity, which are based on faith in the truths and mysteries revealed in special scriptures at a certain time and place and to a particular individual or group. The deist instead placed his reliance on those truths which prove their accord with universal human reason by the fact that they are to be found in all religions, everywhere, at all times. Therefore, the basic tenets of deism—for example, that there is a deity, discoverable by reasoning from the creation to the creator, who deserves our worship and sanctions all moral values—were, in theory, the common denominator of all particular, or "positive," religions. Alexander Pope, without renouncing his Catholicism, expressed suc-cinctly the basic tenets of deism in his poem "The Universal Prayer" (1738), which begins

Father of all! in every age,
In every clime adored,
By saint, by savage, and by sage,
Jehovah, Jove, or Lord!

See *Neoclassicism and Romanticism*; Ernst Cassirer, *The Philosophy of the Enlightenment* (1932); A. O. Lovejoy, *Essays in the History of Ideas* (1948); Basil Willey, *The Eighteenth Century Background* (1950); Peter Gay, *The Enlightenment: An Interpretation* (1966).

EPIC. In its strict use by literary critics the term **epic** or **heroic poem** is applied to a work that meets at least the following criteria: it is a long narrative poem on a great and serious subject, related in an elevated style, and centered on a heroic or quasi-divine figure on whose actions depends the fate of a tribe, a nation, or the human race. The "traditional epics" (also called "primary epics" or "folk epics") were shaped by a literary artist from historical and legendary materials which had developed in the oral traditions of his nation during a period of expansion and warfare. To this group are ascribed the *Iliad* and *Odyssey* of the Greek Homer, and the Anglo-Saxon epic *Beowulf*. The "literary" or "secondary" epics were composed by sophisticated craftsmen in deliberate imitation of the traditional form. Of this kind is Vergil's Latin poem *The Aeneid*, which later served as the chief model for Milton's literary epic *Paradise Lost*; and *Paradise Lost* in turn became a model for Keats's fragmentary epic *Hyperion*, as well as for Blake's several epics, or "prophetic books" (*The Four Zoas, Milton, Jerusalem*) which undertook to translate into Blake's own mythic terms the biblical design and materials which had served as Milton's subject matter.

The epic was ranked by Aristotle as second only to tragedy, and by Renaissance critics as the highest genre of all. The literary epic is certainly the most ambitious of poetic types, making immense demands on a poet's knowledge, invention, and skill to sustain the scope, grandeur, and variety of a poem that tends to encompass the world of its day and a large portion of its learning. Despite numerous attempts over nearly three thousand years, we possess no more than a half dozen epic poems of indubitable greatness. Literary epics are highly conventional poems which commonly share the following features, derived ultimately from the traditional epics of Homer:

(1) The hero is a figure of great national or even cosmic importance. In the *Iliad* he is the Greek warrior Achilles, who is the son of the Nereid, Thetis; and Vergil's Aeneas is the son of the goddess Aphrodite. In *Paradise Lost* Adam represents the entire human race,

or if we regard Christ as the hero, He is both God and man. Blake's primal figure is "the universal man" Albion who incorporates, before his fall, man and god and the cosmos as well.

(2) The setting of the poem is ample in scale, and may be world-wide, or even larger. Odysseus wanders over the Mediterranean basin (the whole of the world known to the author), and in Book XI he descends into the underworld (as does Vergil's Aeneas). The scope of *Paradise Lost* is cosmic, for it takes place on earth, in heaven, and in hell.

(3) The action involves superhuman deeds in battle, such as Achilles' feats in the Trojan War, or a long and arduous journey intrepidly accomplished, such as the wanderings of Odysseus on his way back to his homeland, despite the opposition of some of the gods. *Paradise Lost* includes the war in heaven, the journey of Satan through chaos to discover the newly created world, and his desperately audacious attempt to outwit God by corrupting mankind, in which his success is ultimately frustrated by the sacrificial enterprise of Christ.

(4) In these great actions the gods and other supernatural beings take an interest or an active part—the Olympian gods in Homer, and Jehovah, Christ, and the angels in *Paradise Lost*. These supernatural agents were in the neoclassic age called the **machinery,** in the sense that they were part of the literary contrivances of the epic.

(5) An epic poem is a ceremonial performance, and is narrated in a ceremonial style which is deliberately distanced from ordinary speech and proportioned to the grandeur and formality of the heroic subject matter and epic architecture. Hence Milton's "grand style"—his Latinate diction and stylized syntax, his sonorous lists of names and wide-ranging allusions, and his imitation of Homer's *epic similes* and *epithets.*

There are also commonly adopted conventions in the structure and in the choice of episodes of the epic narrative; prominent among them are these elements:

(1) The narrator begins by stating his **argument,** or theme, invokes a muse or guiding spirit to inspire him in his great undertaking, then addresses to the muse the **epic question,** the answer to which inaugurates the narrative proper (*Paradise Lost*, I, 1–49).

(2) This narrative starts **in medias res,** that is, "in the middle of the things," at a critical point in the action. *Paradise Lost* opens with the fallen angels in hell, gathering their forces and determining on revenge. Not until Books V–VII does the angel Raphael relate to Adam the events in Heaven which led to this situation; while in Books XI–XII, after the fall, Michael foretells to Adam future events

up to Christ's second coming. Thus Milton's epic, although its action focuses on the temptation and fall of man, encompasses all time from the creation to the end of the world.

(3) There are catalogues of some of the principal characters, introduced in formal detail, as in Milton's description of the procession of fallen angels in Book I of *Paradise Lost*. These characters are often given set speeches which reveal their diverse temperaments; an example is the debate in Pandemonium, Book II.

In addition to its strict use, the term "epic" is often applied to works which differ in many respects from this model, but manifest the epic spirit in the scale, the scope, and the profound human importance of their subjects; in such applications, as Brian Wilkie has remarked (*Romantic Poets and Epic Tradition*, 1965, Chap. 1), epics constitute a family, with variable physiognomic similarities, rather than a strictly definable genre. In this broad sense Dante's *Divine Comedy* and Spenser's *Faerie Queene* are often called epics, as are works of prose fiction such as Melville's *Moby-Dick* and Tolstoy's *War and Peace*; and Northrop Frye has described Joyce's *Finnegans Wake* as "the chief ironic epic of our time" (*Anatomy of Criticism*, p. 323).

See H. T. Swedenberg, *The Theory of the Epic in England, 1650–1800* (1944); C. M. Bowra, *From Vergil to Milton* (1945), and *Heroic Poetry* (1952); E. M. W. Tillyard, *The English Epic and Its Background* (1954); C. S. Lewis, *A Preface to Paradise Lost* (1942). For an archetypal theory of the epic, see Frye, *Anatomy of Criticism* (1957), pp. 315–326.

EPIC SIMILES   are formal and sustained similes in which the secondary subject, or "vehicle," is developed far beyond its specific points of parallel to the primary subject, or "tenor" (see *Figurative language*). This figure was imitated from Homer by Vergil, Milton, and other writers of literary epics, who employed it to enhance the ceremonial quality of the epic style. So in *Paradise Lost* I, lines 768 ff., Milton describes the fallen angels thronging toward their new-built palace of Pandemonium by an elaborate comparison to the swarming of bees:

> As Bees
> In spring time, when the Sun with Taurus rides,
> Pour forth their populous youth about the Hive
> In clusters; they among fresh dews and flowers
> Fly to and fro, or on the smoothed Plank,
> The suburb of their Straw-built Citadel,
> New rubb'd with Balm, expatiate and confer
> Their State affairs. So thick the aery crowd
> Swarm'd and were strait'n'd; . . .

EPIGRAM   originally meant, in Greek, an inscription, but was extended to encompass any very short poem—whether amorous, elegiac, meditative, complimentary, anecdotal, or satiric—which is polished, condensed, and pointed; often an epigram ends with a surprising or witty turn of thought. Martial, the Roman epigrammatist, established the enduring model for the caustically satiric epigram.

The epigram was much cultivated in England in the late sixteenth and seventeenth centuries by such poets as Donne, Jonson, and Herrick. The form flourished especially in the next century, during what Austin Dobson described as the age "of wit, of polish, and of Pope." Matthew Prior is one of the best English epigrammatists, and many of Alexander Pope's closed couplets are detachable epigrams. In that age, when the exiled Stuarts were still pretenders to the English throne, John Byrom proposed this toast:

> God bless the King—I mean the Faith's defender!
> God bless (no harm in blessing) the Pretender!
> But who pretender is or who is king—
> God bless us all! that's quite another thing.

And here is one of Coleridge's epigrams, to show that romanticism did not preclude wit:

> ON A VOLUNTEER SINGER
> Swans sing before they die—'twere no bad thing
> Should certain people die before they sing!

Many of the short poems of Walter Savage Landor (1775–1864) were fine examples of the nonsatirical epigram. The form has continued to be cultivated by W. B. Yeats, Ezra Pound, Roy Campbell, Ogden Nash, and other poets in our own time.

Since approximately the end of the eighteenth century, the term "epigram" has come to be applied to neat and witty statements in prose as well as verse; for prose examples see *Wit, humor, and the comic.* Refer to T. K. Whipple, *Martial and the English Epigram* (1925); E. B. Osborn, ed., *The Hundred Best Epigrams* (1928); W. H. Auden, ed., *The Oxford Book of Light Verse* (1938).

EPIPHANY   means "a manifestation," and by Christian thinkers was used to signify a manifestation of God's presence in the world. In the early draft of *A Portrait of the Artist as a Young Man*, entitled *Stephen Hero* (published posthumously in 1944), James Joyce adapted the term to secular experience, to signify a sense of sudden radiance and revelation while observing a commonplace object. "By an epiphany [Stephen] meant a sudden spiritual manifestation." "Its soul, its whatness, leaps to us from the vestment of its appearance. The soul of the commonest object . . . seems to us radiant. The object achieves its epiphany." Joyce's short stories and novels include a number of epiphanies; a climactic one is the revelation Stephen experiences at sight of the young girl wading on the strand in *A Portrait of the Artist*, Chap. 4.

"Epiphany" has become the standard term for the description, frequent in modern poetry and fiction, of the sudden flare into revelation of an ordinary object or scene. Joyce, however, merely substituted this word for what earlier secular authors had called "the **moment**." Thus Shelley, in his *Defense of Poetry*, described the "best and happiest moments . . . arising unforeseen and departing unbidden," "visitations of the divinity" which poetry "redeems from decay." William Wordsworth was a preeminent poet of what he called "moments," or alternatively, "spots of time." For instances of his short poems which represent a moment of revelation, see Wordsworth's "The Two April Mornings" and "The Solitary Reaper." Wordsworth's *Prelude*, like Joyce's narratives, is constructed as a sequence of such visionary encounters. Thus in Book VIII, lines 539–559, Wordsworth describes the occasion when he for the first time passed in a stagecoach over the "threshold" of London and the "trivial forms / Of houses, pavement, streets" suddenly manifested a profound power and significance:

> 'twas a moment's pause,—
> All that took place within me came and went
> As in a moment; yet with Time it dwells,
> And grateful memory, as a thing divine.

See Irene H. Chayes, "Joyce's Epiphanies," reprinted in *Joyce's "Portrait": Criticisms and Critiques*, ed. T. E. Connolly (1962); Robert Scholes, "Joyce and the Epiphany," *Sewanee Review*, LXII (1964). On the traditional "moment" and the modern epiphany see M. H. Abrams, *Natural Supernaturalism: Tradition and Revolution in Romantic Literature* (1970), Chaps. 7–8.

EPITHALAMION,   or in the Latin form, "epithalamium," is a poem written to celebrate a marriage. The name in Greek means "at the bridal chamber," for the verses were originally written to be sung outside the bedroom of the newly married couple. Sir Philip Sidney wrote the first English instance in about 1580, and fifteen years later Spenser wrote his great lyric, "Epithalamion," a celebration of his own marriage composed as a wedding gift to the bride. Spenser's poem follows the sequence of the hours during his wedding day and night and combines, with unfailing grace and dignity, the inherited pagan topics and mythology, Christian ritual and beliefs, and the local Irish setting. Donne, Jonson, Herrick, and many other Renaissance poets composed wedding poems, solemn or ribald, according to the intended audience and the poet's temperament. Sir John Suckling's "A Ballad Upon a Wedding" is an engaging parody of this upper-class poetic form, applied to a lower-class wedding. The tradition persists. Shelley composed an "Epithalamium"; Tennyson's *In Memoriam*, although it opens with a funeral, closes with an epithalamion; A. E. Housman spoke in the antique idiom of the bridal song in "He Is Here, Urania's Son"; and W. H. Auden wrote an "Epithalamion" in 1939.

See Robert H. Case, *English Epithalamies* (1896); Virginia J. Tufte, *The Poetry of Marriage* (1970); and (on Spenser's "Epithalamion") A. Kent Hieatt, *Short Time's Endless Monument* (1960).

EPITHET is derived from the Greek "epitheton," signifying "something added." As a term in criticism, it denotes an adjective or adjectival phrase used to define the special quality of a person or thing (Keats's *"silver snarling* trumpets"). The term is also applied to a characterizing phrase that stands in place of a noun (Pope's "the *glittering forfex*" for the scissors with which the Baron performs his heinous act in *The Rape of the Lock*). The frequent use of derogatory adjectives and phrases in *invective* has led to the mistaken notion that an "epithet" is always uncomplimentary.

Homeric epithets are adjectival terms—usually a compound of two words—like those which Homer used as formulas in referring to someone or something: *"fleet-footed* Achilles," *"bolt-hurling* Zeus," "the *wine-dark* sea." Buck Mulligan in Joyce's *Ulysses* parodied the formula in his reference to "the snot-green sea." We often use fixed, or "conventional," epithets in identifying historical or literary figures; for example, Charles *the Great*, Lorenzo *the Magnificent, Patient* Griselda.

ESSAY. Any brief composition in prose that undertakes to discuss a matter, express a point of view, or persuade us to accept a thesis on any subject whatever. The essay differs from a "treatise" or "dissertation" in its lack of pretension to be a systematic and complete exposition, and in being addressed to a general rather than a specialized audience; as a consequence, the essay discusses its subject in nontechnical fashion, and often with a liberal use of such devices as anecdote, striking illustration, and humor to augment its appeal.

A useful distinction is that between the formal and informal essay. The **formal essay** is relatively impersonal: the author writes as an authority, or at least as highly knowledgeable, on the subject and expounds it in an ordered and thorough fashion. Examples will be

found among the serious articles on current topics and issues in any
of the magazines addressed to a thoughtful audience—*Harper's, Commentary, Scientific American,* and so on. In the **informal essay** (or
"familiar" or "personal essay"), the author assumes a tone of intimacy
with his audience, tends to be concerned with everyday things rather
than with public affairs or specialized topics, and writes in a relaxed,
self-revelatory, and often whimsical fashion. Accessible modern examples are to be found in *The New Yorker*.

The Greeks, Theophrastus and Plutarch, and the Romans, Cicero
and Seneca, wrote essays long before the genre was given its standard
name by Montaigne's great French *Essais* in 1580. The title signifies
"attempts," and was meant to indicate the tentative and unsystematic
nature of Montaigne's discussions, in contrast to formal and technical
treatises on the same subjects. Francis Bacon, late in the sixteenth
century, inaugurated the English use of the term in his own series of
Essays, most of which are short comments on subjects such as "Of
Truth," "Of Adversity," "Of Marriage and the Single Life." Alexander
Pope adopted the term for his expository compositions in verse, the
Essay on Criticism and the *Essay on Man,* but the verse essay has had
few exponents after the eighteenth century. Addison and Steele's *Tatler*
and *Spectator,* with their many successors, gave to the prose essay its
standard modern vehicle, the literary periodical (earlier essays had
been published in books). In the early nineteenth century the founding
of new types of magazines, and their steady proliferation, gave great
impetus to the writing of essays, and made them a major department
of literature. This was the age when Hazlitt, De Quincey, and Charles
Lamb brought the essay—and especially the personal essay—to a level
that has remained unsurpassed. In our own time the many periodicals
pour out scores of essays every week. Most of them are formal in type;
George Orwell, E. M. Forster, James Thurber, and E. B. White,
however, are excellent modern practitioners of the informal essay.

See Hugh Walker, *The English Essay and Essayists* (1915); W. F.
Bryan and R. S. Crane, eds., *The English Familiar Essay* (1916).

EUPHEMISM   (from the Greek "to speak well") is the use—in place
of the blunt term for something disagreeable, terrifying, or offensive—
of a term that is vaguer, less direct, or less colloquial. Euphemisms are
frequently used in reference to death ("to pass away," "mortician");
in irreligious references to God (the Elizabethan "Zounds!" for "God's
wounds!" and the American "Gosh darn!" for "God damn!"); and in
discreet allusions to parts of the body, the bodily functions, and sex:
"comfort station," the Victorian use of "limb" for leg and "friend" for
an habitual sexual partner, and the traditional, but now diminishing,

use in mixed company and in literature of Latinate terms in place of the Anglo-Saxon four-letter words.

EUPHONY and CACOPHONY. **Euphony** is language which seems smooth, pleasant, and musical to the ear, as in Keats's

> And lucent syrops, tinct with cinammon;
> Manna and dates, in argosy transferred
> From Fez; and spicèd dainties, every one,
> From silken Samarcand to cedared Lebanon.

Analysis of the passage will show that what strikes us as a purely auditory agreeableness is due more to the meaning of the words, and to the ease of articulating the sound combinations, than to the inherent melodiousness of the speech sounds as such. Similarly, in **cacophony**—language which seems harsh, rough, and unmusical—the discordancy is the aggregate effect of difficulty in pronunciation, sense, and sound. Cacophony may be an inadvertent element, because of a lapse in the writer's attention or skill, as in the unfortunate line of Arnold's "Dover Beach": "Lay like the folds of a bright girdle furled." But cacophony may also be deliberate and functional: for humor, as in Browning's "Pied Piper,"

> Rats!
> They fought the dogs and killed the cats . . .
> Split open the kegs of salted sprats,
> Made nests inside men's Sunday hats;

or else for other effects, as in Hardy's attempt, in "In Tenebris I," to mimic, as well as describe, dogged endurance, by the difficulty of articulating the transition from one stressed monosyllable to the next:

> I shall not lose old strength
> In the lone frost's black length.
> Strength long since fled!

For other sound effects see *Alliteration* and *Onomatopoeia*; and refer to G. R. Stewart, *The Technique of English Verse* (1930), and Northrop Frye, ed., *Sound and Poetry* (1957).

EUPHUISM   was a formal and elaborate prose style which had a great vogue in the 1580s. It takes its name from the moralistic prose romance *Euphues: The Anatomy of Wit*, which John Lyly wrote in 1578. In the dialogues of this work and of *Euphues and His England* (1580), as well as in his stage comedies, Lyly exaggerated and used persistently a kind of prose which other writers had developed earlier. The style is sententious (that is, full of moral maxims), relies constantly on balanced and antithetical constructions, reinforces the structural parallels by heavy and elaborate patterns of *alliteration* and *assonance*, and is addicted to long similes and learned allusions which are often drawn from mythology and the habits of legendary animals. Here is an example from *Euphues*; the character Philautus is speaking:

> I see now that as the fish *Scolopidus* in the flood Araris at the waxing of the Moon is as white as the driven snow, and at the waning as black as the burnt coal, so Euphues, which at the first encreasing of our familiarity, was very zealous, is now at the last cast become most faithless.

Shakespeare good-humoredly parodied this self-consciously elegant style in *Love's Labour's Lost* and other plays, but he, like other authors of the day, had profited from Lyly's explorations of the formal and rhetorical possibilities of English prose.

See *Style*; also Jonas A. Barish, "The Prose Style of John Lyly," *English Literary History*, XXIII (1956), and G. K. Hunter, *John Lyly* (1962).

EXPRESSIONISM   was an artistic movement which began in Germany at the start of this century, under the strong influence of the Swedish dramatist Strindberg (1849–1912), and reached its height in the decade 1915–1925. It manifested itself in painting and music, as well as in literature, where its most persistent influence has been in the theater. The central feature of expressionism is a radical revolt against realism. Instead of representing the world as it objectively is, the author undertakes to express inner experience by representing the world as it appears to his state of mind, or to that of one of his characters—an emotional, troubled, or abnormal state of mind. Often the work implies that this mental condition is representative of anxiety-ridden modern man in an industrial and technological society which is drifting toward chaos.

Expressionist dramatists dislocated the time-sequence, wrote a stylized dialogue, used masked characters and violently distorted stage sets, and exploited such modern devices as the revolving stage and special effects in lighting and sound. German expressionists included George Kaiser (*Gas, From Morn to Midnight*), Ernst Toller (*Mass Man*), and Bertolt Brecht. This mode of German drama had an important influence on the American theater. Eugene O'Neill's *The Emperor Jones* (1920) projected, in a sequence of symbolic scenes, the individual and racial memories and the recurrent fantasies of a terrified modern Negro; and Elmer Rice's *The Adding Machine* (1923) used a variety of nonrealistic means to represent the mechanical, sterile, and terrifying world which is experienced by Mr. Zero, a small and helpless cog in the impersonal system of big business.

Though expressionism as a concerted dramatic movement did not endure, it has had an important effect on the writing and staging of such plays as Thornton Wilder's *The Skin of Our Teeth* and Arthur Miller's *Death of a Salesman,* as well as on more recent nonrealistic enterprises such as the "theater of the *absurd.*" The extraordinarily flexible possibilities of its medium has made the motion picture an important vehicle of expressionism. The early German expressionist film *The Cabinet of Dr. Caligari* (Austria, 1920) is often revived, and the techniques of expressionism are being exploited to manifest the distorted perceptions, dreams, and fantasies of distressed, disturbed, or psychotic characters in the current films of Ingmar Bergman, Federico Fellini, and Michelangelo Antonioni.

See Richard Samuel and R. H. Thomas, *Expressionism in German Life, Literature and the Theater, 1910–1924* (1939); Siegfried Kracauer, *From Caligari to Hitler* (1947); Mordecai Gorelik, *New Theatres for Old* (1962).

FABLIAU. The fabliau was a medieval form: a short comic or satiric tale in verse dealing realistically with middle-class or lower-class characters and delighting in the ribald and the obscene. (Professor Douglas Bush neatly characterized the type as "a short story broader than it is long.") The fabliau flourished in France in the twelfth and thirteenth centuries, and became popular in England during the fourteenth century. Chaucer, who wrote one of the greatest serious stories in verse, the account of Death and the rioters in "The Pardoner's Tale," also wrote one of the best fabliaux, the wildly comic "The Miller's Tale."

See Joseph Bédier, *Les Fabliaux* (5th ed., 1928).

FANCY and IMAGINATION. The distinction between fancy and imagination was a key element in Coleridge's theory of poetry, as well as in his general theory of the mental processes. In earlier discussions of literature "fancy" and "imagination" had for the most part been used synonymously to denote a faculty of the mind which is distinguished from "reason" and "judgment," and which receives "images" from the senses and reorders them into new combinations. In the thirteenth chapter of *Biographia Literaria* (1817), Coleridge attributes this function to the lower-order faculty he calls **fancy:** "Fancy . . . has no other counters to play with, but fixities and definites. The Fancy is indeed no other than a mode of Memory emancipated from the order of time and space." To Coleridge, that is, the fancy is a mechanical process which receives the elementary images—the "fixities and definites" which come to it ready-made from the senses—and, without altering the parts, reassembles them into a different spatial and temporal order from that in which they were originally perceived. The **imagination** operative in producing a higher order of poetry, however,

> dissolves, diffuses, dissipates, in order to re-create; or where this process is rendered impossible, yet still at all events it struggles to idealize and unify. It is essentially *vital*, even as all objects (*as objects*) are essentially fixed and dead.

The imagination, that is, is able to "create" rather than merely reassemble, by dissolving the fixities and definites—the mental pictures, or images, received from the senses—and unifying them into a new whole. And while the fancy is merely mechanical, the imagination is "vital"; that is, it is an organic faculty which operates not like a machine, but like a living and growing plant. As Coleridge says elsewhere, the imagination "generates and produces a form of its own," while its rules are "the very powers of growth and production." And in the fourteenth chapter of the *Biographia* Coleridge adds his famous statement that the "synthetic" power which is the "imagination . . . reveals itself in the balance or reconcilation of opposite or discordant qualities: of sameness, with difference; of the general, with the concrete; the idea, with the image. . . ." The faculty of imagination, in other words, assimilates and synthesizes the most disparate elements into an organic whole—that is, a newly generated unity, constituted by a living interdependence of parts whose identity cannot survive their removal from the whole. (See *organic form*.)

Most critics after Coleridge who distinguished fancy from imagination tended to make fancy simply the faculty that produces a lesser, lighter, or humorous kind of poetry, and to make imagination the faculty that produces a higher, more serious, and more passionate poetry. And the concept of "imagination" itself is as various as the modes of psychology that critics have adopted (associationist, Gestalt, Freudian, Jungian) and the ways in which they conceive the essential nature of a poem (as essentially realistic or essentially visionary, as "object" or as "myth," as "pure poetry" or as a work designed to produce effects on an audience).

See I. A. Richards, *Coleridge on Imagination* (1934); M. H. Abrams, *The Mirror and the Lamp* (1953), Chap. 7; R. H. Fogle, *The Idea of Coleridge's Criticism* (1962).

FICTION, in the inclusive sense, is any narrative which is feigned or invented rather than historically or factually true. In most present-day discussion, however, the term "fiction" is applied primarily to prose narratives (the *novel* and the *short story*), and is sometimes used simply as a synonym for the novel. Literary forms in which fiction takes off from fact are often denoted by compound names, such as "historical fiction," "fictional biography," "fictional autobiography."

In his comprehensive reclassification of all the standard genres, Northrop Frye applies the name "fiction" to any "work of art in prose," and subdivides this capacious genre into four main forms: (1) The "novel," which in Frye's usage is equivalent to what is usually known as the realistic novel, or the novel of manners. (2) The *prose romance,* which is related to forms of folklore; the romancer, Frye says, "does not attempt to create 'real people' so much as stylized figures which expand into psychological archetypes," with the hero, heroine, and villain reflecting "Jung's libido, anima, and shadow." (3) The **confession,** or prose autobiographical form, which includes the *Confessions* of St. Augustine and of Rousseau, and Cardinal Newman's *Apologia.* (4) The **anatomy** (named after Robert Burton's *Anatomy of Melancholy,* 1621), which is a mixed or encyclopedic form that satirizes various kinds of intellectual types and attitudes, usually by means of long comic dialogues; this form was traditionally called *Menippean satire.*

See Frye, *Anatomy of Criticism (1957), pp. 303–314; Robert Scholes and Robert Kellog, *The Nature of Narrative (1966); and the useful collections of essays: *Discussions of the Novel (1960), ed. Roger Sale, and *Theory of the Novel (1967), ed. Philip Stevick (which includes a comprehensive bibliography).

FIGURATIVE LANGUAGE   deviates from what we apprehend as the standard significance or sequence of words, in order to achieve special meaning or effect. **Literal language,** in its broadest sense, is distinguished from all figurative language, and signifies entire accordance with standard usage; in a more limited sense, "literal language" is distinguished only from the use of metaphors and other "tropes" (see below). Figures were for long characterized as "ornaments" of literal language, but they are entirely integral to the functioning of language, and in fact indispensable, not only to poetry, but to all modes of fluid discourse.

Since classical times figurative language has often been divided into two classes: (1) "figures of thought," or **tropes** (meaning "turns," "conversions"), in which words are used in a way that effects a decided change or extension in their standard meaning; and (2) "figures of speech," or "rhetorical figures," in which the departure from standard usage is not, primarily, in the meaning but in the order and rhetorical effect of the words. This distinction is not a sharp one, nor do all critics agree in its application. For convenience, however, the most commonly identified "figures of thought" are listed here; other figures are collected under the heading "rhetorical figures"; still others are discussed in individual articles (see the entries under *Figurative language* in the Index).

In a **simile** a comparison between two distinctly different things is indicated by the word "like" or "as." A simple example is Burns's "O my love's like a red, red rose." The following simile from Wordsworth's "Ode: Intimations of Immortality" differs from Burns's, in that it specifies the aspects in which custom is similar to frost ("heavy") and to life ("deep"):

> And custom lie upon thee with a weight
> Heavy as frost, and deep almost as life.

In a **metaphor** a word which in standard (or literal) usage denotes one kind of thing, quality, or action is applied to another, in the form of a statement of identity instead of comparison. For example, if Burns had said "O my love is a red, red rose" he would have used, technically speaking, a metaphor instead of a simile. Here is a more complex metaphor, from Stephen Spender:

> Eye, gazelle, delicate wanderer,
> Drinker of horizon's fluid line.[1]

It should be noted that these metaphors can be analyzed into two elements. In a usage now widely adopted, I. A. Richards introduced the term **tenor** for the subject to which the metaphoric word is applied ("my love" in the altered line from Burns, and "eye" in Spender), and the term **vehicle** for the metaphoric word itself ("rose" in Burns, and the three words, "gazelle," "wanderer," and "drinker" in Spender). See I. A. Richards, *Philosophy of Rhetoric* (1936), Chaps. 5–6. In an **implicit metaphor** the tenor is not stated, but is implied by the verbal context; thus, if one says "That reed was too frail to survive the storm of its sorrows," the context indicates that "reed" is the vehicle for an unstated tenor, a human being. All the metaphoric words cited so far have been nouns, but other parts of speech may also be used metaphorically. The metaphoric use of a verb occurs in Shakespeare's *Merchant of Venice* (V. i. 54), "How sweet the moonlight *sleeps* upon this bank"; and the metaphoric use of an adjective occurs in Andrew Marvell's "The Garden":

> Annihilating all that's made
> To a *green* thought in a green shade.

---

[1] From "Not palaces, an era's crown." Copyright 1934 and renewed 1962 by Stephen Spender. Reprinted from *Collected Poems, 1928–1953*, by Stephen Spender, by permission of Random House, Inc., and Faber and Faber Ltd.

A **mixed metaphor** combines two or more diverse metaphoric vehicles. When used inadvertently, without adequate sensitivity to the possible incongruity of the vehicles, the effect can be ludicrous: "Girding up his loins, the chairman ploughed through the mountainous agenda." Densely figurative poets such as Shakespeare, however, often mix metaphors in a functional way. Examples are Hamlet's expression of his troubled mind in his soliloquy (III. i. 59–60), "to take arms against a sea of troubles, / And by opposing end them," and the intricate involvement of metaphor within metaphor in Shakespeare's Sonnet LXV:

> O, how shall summer's honey breath hold out
> Against the wrackful siege of battering days?

A **dead metaphor** is one which, like "the leg of a table" or "the heart of the matter," has become so common a usage that we have ceased to be aware of the discrepancy between vehicle and tenor. A dead metaphor, however, is only moribund, and can readily be brought back to life. Someone asked Groucho Marx, "Are you a man or a mouse?" He answered, "Throw me a piece of cheese and you'll find out."

Some species of "implicit metaphor" (above) are frequently given names of their own:

In **metonymy** (Greek for "a change of name"), the term for one thing is applied to another with which it has become closely associated in experience. Thus "the crown" or "the scepter" can stand for a king; "Milton" can signify the writings of Milton ("I have read all of Milton"); and typical attire can signify the male and female sexes: "doublet and hose ought to show itself courageous to petticoat" (*As You Like* It, II. iv. 6).

In **synecdoche** (Greek for "taking together"), a part of something is used to signify the whole, or (more rarely) the whole is used to signify a part. We use the term "ten *hands*" for ten workmen, and Milton refers to the corrupt clergy in "Lycidas" as "blind *mouths*."

Another figure related to metaphor is **personification,** or in the Greek term, **prosopopeia,** in which either an inanimate object or an abstract concept is spoken of as though it were endowed with life or with human attributes or feelings (compare *pathetic fallacy*). Milton wrote in *Paradise Lost* (IX, 1002–1003), as Adam bit into the fatal apple,

> Sky lowered, and muttering thunder, some sad drops
> Wept at completing of the mortal sin.

The second stanza of Keats's "To Autumn" finely personifies the abstraction, autumn, as a woman carrying on the rural chores of that season. The personification of abstractions was standard in eighteenth-century *poetic diction,* where it sometimes became stereotyped. Coleridge remembered reading an eighteenth-century ode celebrating the invention of inoculation against smallpox which began

Inoculation! heavenly Maid, descend!

In recent years figures have come in for close and repeated consideration, and have been classified and analyzed in many diverse ways; for a summary of recent discussions, with bibliography, see René Wellek and Austin Warren, *Theory of Literature* (rev. ed., 1966), Chap. 15. A full and useful treatment of the conventional classification of figures in the Renaissance is Sister Miriam Joseph, *Shakespeare's Use of the Arts of Language* (1947). See also Isabel C. Hungerland, *Poetic Discourse* (1958), Chap. 4, and Max Black, "Metaphor," in *Models and Metaphors* (1962).

FOLKLORE, since the mid-nineteenth century, has been the collective name applied to traditional verbal materials and social rituals that have been handed down solely, or at least primarily, by word of mouth and by example rather than in written form. Folklore developed and continues to flourish best in communities where few if any people can read or write. It includes, among other things, legends, superstitions, songs, tales, proverbs, riddles, spells, nursery rhymes; pseudo-scientific lore about the weather, plants, and animals; customary activities at births, marriages, and deaths; and traditional dances and forms of drama which are performed on holidays or at communal gatherings. Elements of folklore have at all times entered into sophisticated written literature. For example, the choice among the three caskets in Shakespeare's *Merchant of Venice* (II. ix), and the superstition about a maiden's dream which is central to Keat's *Eve of St. Agnes,* are both derived from folklore.

Certain forms of folklore are listed here because they have been of special importance for written literature:

Folk drama originated in primitive rites of song and dance, especially in connection with agricultural activities at the various seasons, that centered on vegetational deities and goddesses of fertility. It is widely believed that Greek *tragedy* developed from such rites, celebrating the life, death, and rebirth of the vegetational god Dionysus. Folk dramas survive in England in such forms as the St. George play and the mummers' play (a "mummer" is a masked actor). Thomas Hardy's *The Return of the Native* (Book II, Chap. 5) describes the performance of a mummers' play, and a type of this drama is still performed in America in the Kentucky mountains. See Edmund K. Chambers, *The English Folk-Play* (1933).

Folk songs include love songs, Christmas carols, work songs, sea chanties, religious songs, drinking songs, children's game-songs, and many other types, in addition to their most important form, the narrative song, or traditional *ballad*. All forms of folk song have been assiduously collected since the late eighteenth century, and they have inspired many imitations by major writers of lyric poetry. Robert Burns collected and edited Scottish folk songs, restored or rewrote them, and imitated them in his own songs. His "A Red, Red Rose" and "Auld Lang Syne," for example, both derive from one or more folk songs, and his "Green Grow the Rashes, O" is a tidied-up version of a bawdy folk song. See J. C. Dick, *The Songs of Robert Burns* (1903); Cecil J. Sharp, *Folk Songs of England* (5 vols.; 1908–1912); and Alan Lomax, *The Folk Songs of North America* (1960).

The **folktale,** strictly defined, is a short narrative in prose, of unknown authorship, which has been transmitted orally. The term, however, is usually extended to include stories by a known author (such as Robert Southey's story of *The Three Bears* and Parson Mason L. Weems's story of George Washington and the cherry tree) which, after they were printed, were adopted and transmitted orally by the people. Folktales are found among peoples all over the world. They include *myths, fables,* tales of heroes (whether historical like Johnny Appleseed, or legendary like Paul Bunyan), and fairy tales. Many so-called fairy tales (the German word **märchen** is frequently used) are not stories of fairies, but of various kinds of marvels; examples are "Snow White" and "Jack and the Beanstalk." Another type of folktale, the set "joke," or comic (often bawdy) *anecdote,* is the most prolific and persistent of all; new jokes, or new versions of very old jokes, continue to be a staple of the conversation wherever men—and now men and women—congregate in a relaxed mood.

The same, or closely similar, oral stories have turned up in Europe, the Orient, and even in Africa, and have been embodied in the narratives of many sophisticated writers. Chaucer's *Canterbury Tales* includes a number of folktales; "The Pardoner's Tale" of death and the three rioters, for example, was Oriental in its origin. See Benjamin A. Botkin, *A Treasury of American Folklore* (1944), and the standard catalogue of the recurrent *motifs* in the folktales of the world, Stith Thompson's *Motif-Index of Folk-Literature* (1932–1937).

FORM and STRUCTURE. "Form" is one of the most frequently discussed—and variously interpreted—terms in literary criticism. It is often used in limited senses for a literary genre or type ("the lyric form," "the short story form"), or for patterns of meter, lines, and rhymes ("the verse form," "the stanza form"). It is also, however, the common term for a central critical concept. The "form" of a work, in this central sense, is its essential organizing principle; and here we find great diversity in critical formulations. All critics agree that "form" is not simply a fixed container, like a bottle, into which the "content" or "subject matter" of a work is poured; but beyond this, a critic's definition of form varies according to his particular premises and orientation (see *Criticism*).

Many neoclassic critics, for example, thought of the form of a work as a combination of component parts, put together according to the principle of *decorum*, or mutual fittingness. Coleridge and other Romantic organicists distinguished between **mechanic form,** which is a preexistent shape such as we impose on wet clay by a mold, and **organic form,** which, as Coleridge says, "is innate; it shapes as it develops itself from within, and the fullness of its development is one and the same with the perfection of its outward form." To Coleridge, in other words, a good poem is like a growing plant which evolves, by an internal energy, into the organic unity which constitutes its achieved form. (See *Fancy and Imagination*.) Many *New Critics* of our own time prefer the word **structure,** which they use interchangeably with form, and which they regard as primarily an equilibrium, or an interaction, or an ironic and paradoxical tension, of diverse words and images in a stable totality of "meanings." And various exponents of *archetypal* theory regard the form of a literary work as one of a limited number of plot-shapes which it shares with myths, rituals, dreams, and other elemental and recurrent patterns of human experience.

In an increasingly influential critical mode R. S. Crane, a leader of the **Chicago School** of criticism, has revived and developed the concept of form in Aristotle's *Poetics*. Crane distinguishes between "form" and "structure." The form of a literary work is (in the Greek term) the "dynamis," the particular "working" or "emotional 'power'" that the work is designed to effect, and that functions as its "shaping principle." This formal principle controls and synthesizes the "structure" of a work—the order, emphasis, and rendering of all its component materials and parts—into "a beautiful and effective whole of a determinate kind." See R. S. Crane, *The Languages of Criticism and the Structure of Poetry* (1953), Chaps. 1 and 4; also his edition of essays by various Chicago critics, *Critics and Criticism* (1952).

FORMAT OF A BOOK. Format signifies the size, shape, and other physical features of a book. The printer begins with a large "sheet"; if the sheet is folded once so as to form two "leaves" of four pages, the book is a **folio** (the Latin word for "leaf"). When we refer to "the first Shakespeare folio," for example, we mean a volume published in 1623, the first edition of Shakespeare's collected plays, the leaves of which were made by a single folding of the printer's sheets. A sheet folded twice into four leaves makes a **quarto;** a sheet folded a third time into eight leaves makes an **octavo.** A **duodecimo** volume is made by folding a sheet so that it makes twelve leaves. The more leaves into which a single sheet is divided, the smaller the leaf, so that these terms indicate the dimensions of a book; but only approximately, because the size of the full sheet varies, especially in modern printing. It can be said, however, that a folio is a very large book; a quarto is the next in size, with a leaf that is nearly square. The third in size, the octavo, is the one most frequently used in modern printing.

As this book is open in front of you, the page on the right is called a **recto,** and the page on the left is called a **verso.**

The **colophon** (Greek for "summit") in older books was a note at the end stating such facts as the title, author, printer, and date of issue. In modern books the colophon is usually in the front, on the title page. With reference to modern books, "colophon" has come to mean, usually, the publisher's emblem, such as a torch (Harper), an owl (Holt), or a ship (Viking).

The term **incunabula** (Latin for "swaddling clothes") signifies books published in the infancy of printing. The terminal date is 1500, about fifty years after the German printer, Johann Gutenberg, invented movable printing types.

The word **edition** now designates the total copies of a book that are printed from a single setting of type; the various "printings" or "reprints" of this edition—sometimes with a few minor changes in the text—may be spaced over a period of years. We identify as "a new edition" a printing in which substantial changes have been made in the text. A book may be revised and reprinted in this way many times; hence the terms "second edition," "third edition," and so on.

A **variorum edition** designates either (1) an edition of a work that lists all the textual variants in the author's manuscripts and in his revised editions; a recent example is *The Variorum Edition of the Poems of W. B. Yeats*, ed. Peter Allt and Russell K. Alspach (1957); or (2) an edition of a text that includes a collection of the annotations and commentaries on the text by earlier editors. *The New Variorum Shakespeare*, still in progress, is a variorum edition in both senses of the word.

The classic work on bookmaking and printing is Ronald B. Mc-Kerrow, *An Introduction to Bibliography* (1928).

FREE VERSE, or in the French term **vers libre,** is printed in short lines instead of with the continuity of prose, and it has a more controlled rhythm than ordinary prose; but it lacks the regular stress-pattern, organized into recurrent feet, of traditional versification. Most free verse also has irregular line lengths and lacks rhyme. Within these broad confines, there are a great variety of measures labeled as "free verse." Something close to one modern form of free verse is to be found in the King James translation (reflecting the original Hebrew parallelism and cadences) of the Psalms and the Song of Solomon; Blake and Matthew Arnold experimented with free measures; and Walt Whitman startled the literary world in his *Leaves of Grass* (1855) by using lines of variable length which depended for their rhythmic effect on the repetition, balance, and variation of phrases, instead of on recurrent metric feet.

The French Symbolist poets, toward the end of the nineteenth century, and American and English poets of this century, especially after World War I, began the period of the intensive use of free verse. It has been employed by T. S. Eliot (see, for example, "Ash Wednesday"), Ezra Pound, William Carlos Williams, and numberless other poets. The writer of free verse surrenders the rhythmic power and song of traditional versification in order to exploit other effects. The opening section of a poem by E. E. Cummings will demonstrate the kind of effects, in the suspension of syntax and the increased control of pace, pause, and time, that become available when the verse is released from the necessity of a recurrent beat and regular line:

CHANSON INNOCENTE [1]

in Just-
spring   when the world is mud-
luscious the little
lame balloonman

whistles   far   and wee

and eddieandbill come
running from marbles and
piracies and it's
spring

See *Meter*; and refer to Percy Mansell Jones, *The Background of Modern French Poetry* (1951), and Graham Hough, "Free Verse," *Proceedings of the British Academy*, XLIII (1957).

GENRE, a term taken from the French, is used in literary criticism to signify a literary species or, as we now often say, a "literary form."

[1] From *Poems 1923–1954.* Copyright 1923, 1951 by E. E. Cummings. Reprinted by permission of Harcourt, Brace & World, Inc., and Granada Publishing Limited.

The genres into which literary works have been classified are numerous, and the criteria for classification have been highly variable; but the most common names still are such ancient ones as tragedy, comedy, epic, satire, and lyric, plus some relative newcomers like novel, essay, and biography. From the Renaissance through much of the eighteenth century the recognized poetic genres—or poetic "kinds" as they were usually called—were widely thought to be fixed artistic types, somewhat like species in the biological order, and a number of critics applied *rules* which specified the proper subject matter, structure, style, and effect in each kind. At that time the genres were also commonly ranked in a hierarchy ranging from epic and tragedy at the top to the short lyric, epigram, and other minor types at the bottom. Shakespeare lampooned pedantic genre-critics in Polonius' catalogue (*Hamlet* II. ii) of dramatic types: "tragedy, comedy, history, pastoral, pastoral-comical, historical-pastoral, tragical-historical, tragical-comical-historical-pastoral. . . ."

The development of new literary forms—such as the novel and the miscellaneous poem that combined description, philosophy, and narrative (James Thomson's *The Seasons*, 1726–1730)—together with the extraordinary rise, in the latter eighteenth century, in the prominence and esteem of the short lyric poem, and the concurrent shifts in the bases of critical theory, effected a drastic alteration both in the conception and the ranking of the genres. Since the Romantic period, genres have frequently been conceived as convenient but rather arbitrary ways to classify works of literature, and the major criteria for evaluating literature have not been specific to one genre, but applicable to all kinds of works: "sincerity," "intensity," "organic unity," "high seriousness," "maturity," "ironically qualified attitudes," and so on. In much of the recent *new criticism*, the distinction between the genres has all but ceased to play an essential function in critical analysis and evaluation.

See René Wellek and Austin Warren, *Theory of Literature* (rev. ed., 1966), Chap. 5. For a defense of the utility to practical criticism of the distinction between genres see R. S. Crane, ed., *Critics and Criticism* (1952), pp. 12–24, 546–563. A new mode of generic theory, in which the four major genres (comedy, romance, tragedy, and satire) are held to reflect the archetypal myths correlated with the four seasons, has been proposed by Northrop Frye, *Anatomy of Criticism* (1957), pp. 158–239.

GEORGIAN   is applied both to the reigns of the four successive Georges (1714–1830) and to the reign of George V (1910–1936). **Georgian poets** usually designates a group of writers in the latter era who loomed

large in four anthologies entitled *Georgian Poetry*, which were published by Edward Marsh between 1912 and 1922. Marsh favored
writers we now regard as minor poets, such as Rupert Brooke, Walter
de la Mare, Ralph Hodgson, W. H. Davies, and John Masefield, and
the term "Georgian poetry" has come to connote verse which is mainly
rural in subject matter, deft and delicate rather than bold and passionate in manner, and traditional rather than experimental in technique
and form.

GOTHIC NOVEL.   The term "Gothic" originally referred to the Goths,
a Germanic tribe, then came to signify "Germanic," then "medieval."
"Gothic architecture" now denotes the medieval type of architecture,
characterized by the use of the pointed arch and vault, which spread
through western Europe between the twelfth and sixteenth centuries.
The **Gothic novel,** or "Gothic romance," is a type of fiction which was
inaugurated by Horace Walpole's *Castle of Otranto, a Gothic Story*
(1764)—the subtitle refers to its medieval setting—and which flourished through the early nineteenth century. Following Walpole's
example, authors of such novels set their stories in the medieval
period, often in a gloomy castle replete with dungeons, subter-
ranean passages, and sliding panels, and made plentiful use of
ghosts, mysterious disappearances, and other sensational and supernatural occurrences (which in some writers turned out to have natural
explanations); their principal aim was to evoke chilling terror by
exploiting mystery, cruelty, and a variety of horrors. Most of the novels
are now enjoyed mainly as period pieces, but the best of them opened
up to fiction the realm of the irrational and of the perverse impulses
and the nightmarish terrors that lie beneath the orderly surface of the
civilized mind. Examples of Gothic novels are William Beckford's
Vathek (1786)—of which the setting is both medieval and Oriental
and the subject both erotic and sadistic—Ann Radcliffe's *The Mysteries
of Udolpho* (1794) and Matthew Gregory Lewis' *The Monk* (1797).
   The term "Gothic" has also been extended to denote a type of
fiction which lacks the medieval setting but develops a brooding atmosphere of gloom or terror, represents events which are uncanny, or
macabre, or melodramatically violent, and often deals with aberrant
psychological states. In this sense "Gothic" has been applied to Mary
Shelley's *Frankenstein* (1817), the terror tales of Poe, the romances
of Scott and Hawthorne, Dickens' *Bleak House* (for example, Chaps.
11, 16, and 47) and *Great Expectations* (see the Miss Havisham
episodes), William Faulkner's *Sanctuary* and *Absalom, Absalom!*, and
the fiction of Truman Capote.
   See Eino Railo, *The Haunted Castle* (1927); Montagu Summers,

The Gothic Quest (1938); Lowry Nelson, Jr., "Night Thoughts on the Gothic Novel," *The Yale Review*, LII (1963), reprinted in part in *Pastoral and Romance*, ed. Eleanor T. Lincoln (1969). On "American Gothic"—and especially the "Southern Gothic"—see Chester E. Eisinger, "The Gothic Spirit in the Forties," *Fiction in the Forties* (1963), reprinted in part in *Pastoral and Romance*.

GRAVEYARD POETS. A term applied to eighteenth-century poets who wrote meditative poems, usually set in a graveyard, on the theme of human mortality and in moods which range from elegiac pensiveness to profound gloom. Examples are Thomas Parnell's "Night-Piece on Death" (1721), Edward Young's long *Night-Thoughts* (1742), and Robert Blair's "The Grave" (1743). The vogue resulted in one masterpiece, Gray's "Elegy Written in a Country Churchyard" (1751).

See Amy Louise Reed, *The Background of Gray's Elegy* (1924). Edith M. Sickels, in *The Gloomy Egoist* (1932), follows the evolution of graveyard and other melancholy verse through the Romantic period.

GREAT CHAIN OF BEING. The concept is grounded in ideas about the nature of God, or the first cause, found in Plato, Aristotle, and Plotinus, and was developed by later thinkers into an inclusive world view. This view was already prevalent in the Renaissance, but was given further philosophical refinement by Leibniz early in the eighteenth century, and was adopted by many thinkers of the *Enlightenment*. In its comprehensive eighteenth-century form it held that the essential "excellence" of God consists in His illimitable creativity, an unstinting overflow into the fullest possible variety of beings. From this premise were deduced three consequences:

(1) Plenitude. The universe is absolutely full of every possible kind and variety of life; no conceivable species of being can remain unrealized.

(2) Continuity. Each species differs from the next by the least possible degree, and so merges all but imperceptibly into its nearest related kinds.

(3) Gradation. The existing species exhibit a hierarchy of status and so compose a great chain, or ladder, of being, extending from the lowliest condition of the merest existence up to God Himself. In this chain man occupies the middle position between the animal kinds and the angels, or purely spiritual beings.

On these concepts Leibniz and other thinkers also grounded what is called the doctrine of **philosophical optimism**—the view that this is the best of all possible worlds, but only in the special sense that this is the best world that is logically *capable* of being brought into existence. Since God's bountifulness consists in His creation of the greatest possible variety of graded beings, what seems to a limited point of view to be deficiency and evil follows necessarily from the very excellence of the divine nature, which logically entails that there be a progressive set of limitations, hence increasing "evils," as we move farther down along the scale of being.

With his incomparable precision and economy, Alexander Pope compresses all these ideas into a half dozen or so heroic couplets, in Epistle I of his *Essay on Man*:

> Of systems possible, if 'tis confessed
> That Wisdom Infinite must form the best,
> Where all must full or not coherent be,
> And all that rises rise in due degree;
> Then in the scale of reasoning life, 'tis plain,
> There must be, somewhere, such a rank as man. . . .
> See, through this air, this ocean, and this earth,
> All matter quick, and bursting into birth. . . .
> Vast Chain of Being! which from God began,
> Natures ethereal, human, angel, man,
> Beast, bird, fish, insect, what no eye can see,
> No glass can reach! from Infinite to thee,
> From thee to nothing. . . .

See A. O. Lovejoy's classic in the history of ideas, *The Great Chain of Being* (1936); also E. M. W. Tillyard, *The Elizabethan World Picture* (1943), Chaps. 4–5.

HEROIC COUPLET. Lines of iambic pentameter which rhyme in pairs: *aa, bb*, and so on. The adjective was applied in the latter seventeenth century, because of the frequent use of such couplets in "heroic" (that is, epic) poems and plays. This verse form was introduced into English poetry by Geoffrey Chaucer (in *The Legend of Good Women* and most of *The Canterbury Tales*), and has been in constant employment ever since. From the age of Dryden through that of Dr. Johnson, the heroic couplet became the predominant English measure for all the poetic kinds; some poets, including Alexander Pope, used it almost to the exclusion of other meters.

In this *neoclassic period*, the poets wrote in **closed couplets**; that is, the end of each couplet tends to coincide with the end either of a sentence or of a self-contained unit of syntax. The sustained employment of the closed heroic couplet meant that two lines had to serve something of the function of a stanza. In order to maximize the interrelations of the component parts, neoclassic poets often used an end-stopped first line (that is, made the end of the line coincide with a pause in the syntax), and also broke each single line into subunits by balancing it around a strong *caesura*, or medial pause in the syntax.

The following passage from John Denham's *Cooper's Hill* (added in the version of 1655) is an early instance of the artful management of the closed couplet which fascinated later neoclassic poets; they quoted it and commented upon it again and again, and used it as a model for exploiting the possibilities of this verse form. Note how Denham achieves diversity and emphasis within the straitness of his couplets by shifts in the position of the caesuras; the use of rhetorical balance and *antithesis* between the single lines, and between the two halves within a single line; the variable positioning of the adjectives in the second couplet; and the manipulation of similar and contrasting vowel and consonant sounds. The poet is addressing the River Thames:

> O could I flow like thee, and make thy stream
> My great example, as it is my theme!
> Though deep, yet clear; though gentle, yet not dull;
> Strong without rage, without o'erflowing full.

And here is a passage from Alexander Pope, the greatest master of the metrical, syntactical, and rhetorical possibilities of the closed couplet ("Of the Characters of Women," lines 243–248):

> See how the world its veterans rewards!
> A youth of frolics, an old age of cards;
> Fair to no purpose, artful to no end,
> Young without lovers, old without a friend;
> A fop their passion, but their prize a sot;
> Alive, ridiculous, and dead, forgot!

Compare these closed neoclassic couplets with the "open couplets" quoted from Keats's *Endymion* in the entry *meter*, in which the pattern of stresses varies often from the iambic norm, the syntax is unsymmetrical, and the couplets run on freely, with the rhyme serving to color rather than to stop the verse.

See George Williamson, "The Rhetorical Pattern of Neoclassical Wit," *Modern Philology*, XXXIII (1935); W. K. Wimsatt, Jr., "One Relation of Rhyme to Reason (Alexander Pope)," in *The Verbal Icon* (1954).

HEROIC DRAMA   was a form mainly specific to the Restoration period, though instances continued to be written in the earlier eighteenth century. As Dryden defined it: "An heroic play ought to be an imitation, in little, of an heroic poem; and consequently . . . love and valour ought to be the subject of it." (Preface to *The Conquest of Granada*, 1672.) By "heroic poem" he meant epic, and the plays attempted to emulate the *epic* by including a large-scale warrior as hero, an action involving the fate of an empire, and an elevated and elaborate style, usually cast in the epigrammatic form of the closed *heroic couplet*. A noble hero and heroine are typically represented in a situation in which their passionate love conflicts with the demands of honor and the hero's patriotic duty to his country; if the conflict ends in disaster, the play is called an **heroic tragedy**. Often the central dilemma is patently contrived and the characters are statuesque and unconvincing, while the attempt to sustain a high epic style swells irresistibly into *bombast*. Thus in Dryden's *Love Triumphant* (1693): "What woods are these? I feel my vital heat / Forsake my limbs, my curdled blood retreat."

Dryden's *Conquest of Granada* is one of the better heroic tragedies, but his highest achievement is his adaptation (which he called *All for Love*) of Shakespeare's *Antony and Cleopatra* to the heroic formula. Other heroic dramatists were Nathaniel Lee (*The Rival Queens*) and Thomas Otway, whose *Venice Preserved* is a fine tragedy that transcends the limits of the form. We also owe indirectly to heroic tragedy two of the most diverting of dramatic parodies: the Duke of Buckingham's *The Rehearsal* and Henry Fielding's *The Tragedy of Tragedies, or the Life and Death of Tom Thumb the Great*.

See Bonamy Dobrée, *Restoration Tragedy* (1929); Allardyce Nicoll, *Restoration Drama* (1955); Arthur C. Kirsch, *Dryden's Heroic Drama* (1965).

HUMANISM.   In the sixteenth century the word "humanist" was coined to signify one who taught or worked in the "studia humanitatis," or **humanities**—that is, grammar, rhetoric, history, poetry, and moral philosophy, as distinguished from fields less concerned with the moral and imaginative aspects and activities of man, such as mathematics, natural philosophy, and theology. Scholarly humanists recovered, edited, and expounded many ancient texts in Greek and Latin, and so contributed greatly to the store of materials and ideas of the European *Renaissance*. These humanists also wrote many works concerned with educational, moral, and political problems, based largely on classical writers such as Aristotle, Plato, and above all, Cicero. In the nineteenth century a new word, **humanism,** came to be applied to the view of man, the general values, and the educational ideas common to many Renaissance humanists, as well as to later writers in the same tradition.

Typically, Renaissance humanism assumed the dignity and central position of man in the universe; emphasized the study of classical imaginative and philosophical literature, as against natural science, but with emphasis on its moral and practical rather than purely aesthetic values; and insisted on the primacy of reason (considered

the distinctively human faculty), as opposed to the instinctual appe-
tites and the "animal" passions, in ordering human life. Many
humanists also stressed the need for a rounded development of man's
diverse powers, physical and mental, artistic and moral, as opposed to
merely technical or specialized training.

In our time, "humanist" often connotes a man who bases truth on
human experience and bases values on human nature, rejecting the
truths and sanctions of a supernatural creed. With few exceptions,
however, Renaissance humanists were pious Christians, who incorporated the concepts and ideals inherited from pagan antiquity into the
frame of the Christian creed. The result was that they emphasized
the values achievable in this world, and minimized earlier Christian
emphasis on man's innate corruption and on the ideals of extreme as-
ceticism and of withdrawal from this world in a preoccupation with
the world hereafter. It has recently become standard to refer to this
structure of classical and Christian views, typical of writers such as
Sir Philip Sidney, Spenser, and Milton, as **Christian humanism.**

The rapid advance in the achievements and prestige of natural
science and technology after the Renaissance sharpened, in later heirs
of the humanistic tradition, the need to defend the role of the humanities in a liberal education against the encroachments of natural
philosophy and the practical arts. As Dr. Johnson, the eighteenth-
century humanist who had once been a schoolmaster, wrote in his
Life of Milton:

> The truth is, that the knowledge of external nature, and the
> sciences which that knowledge requires or includes, are not the
> great or the frequent business of the human mind. . . . We are
> perpetually moralists, but we are geometricians only by chance.
> . . . Socrates was rather of opinion that what we had to learn
> was, how to do good, and avoid evil.

Matthew Arnold, the great proponent of humanism in the Victorian
period, strongly defended the predominance of humane studies in
general education. Many of Arnold's leading ideas are adaptations of
the tenets of the older humanism—his view, for example, that culture
is a perfection "of our humanity proper, as distinguished from our
animality," and consists of "a harmonious expansion of *all* the powers
which make the beauty and worth of human nature"; his emphasis on
knowing "the best that is known and thought in the world" and his
assumption that much of what is best is in the classical writers; and
his conception of poetry as essentially "a criticism of life."

In our own century the American movement of 1910–1933 known
as the **New Humanism,** under the leadership of Irving Babbitt and
Paul Elmer More, argued strongly for a return to a primarily humanistic

education, and to a view of moral and literary values based largely on classical literature. But in the present age of proliferating demands for specialists in the sciences, technology, and the practical arts, the broad humanistic base for a general education has been greatly eroded. In most colleges the earlier humanistic theory of education survives only in the requirement that all students in the liberal arts must take six hours in "the humanities."

See Douglas Bush, *The Renaissance and English Humanism* (1939); P. O. Kristeller, *The Classics and Renaissance Thought* (1955); H. I. Marrou, *A History of Education in Antiquity* (1956); R. S. Crane, *The Idea of the Humanities* (2 vols., 1967). For the New Humanism see Irving Babbitt, *Literature and the American College* (1908), and Norman Foerster, ed., *Humanism and America* (1930).

HYPERBOLE and UNDERSTATEMENT.   The figure of speech called **hyperbole** (Greek for "overshooting") is bold overstatement, or extravagant exaggeration of fact, used either for serious or comic effect. Iago says gloatingly of Othello (III. iii. 330 ff.):

> Not poppy nor mandragora,
> Nor all the drowsy syrups of the world,
> Shall ever medicine thee to that sweet sleep
> Which thou ow'dst yesterday.

See also Ben Jonson's gallantly hyperbolic compliments to his lady in "Drink to me only with thine eyes," and the ironic hyperboles in "To His Coy Mistress," by which Marvell attests how slow his "vegetable love should grow"—if he had "but world enough and time." The "tall talk" and "tall tale" of the American West is a form of comic hyperbole. (There is the story of a cowboy in an Eastern restaurant who ordered a steak well done. "Do you call this well done?" he roared at the waitress. "I've seen critters hurt worse than that get well!")

The contrary figure is **understatement** (the Greek term is **meiosis,** "lessening") which deliberately represents something as much less in magnitude or importance than it really is. The effect is usually ironic— savagely ironic in Swift's *A Tale of a Tub*, "Last week I saw a woman flayed, and you will hardly believe how much it altered her person for the worse," and comically ironic in Mark Twain's comment: "The reports of my death are greatly exaggerated." (See *Irony.*) Some critics extend "meiosis" to the use in literature of an utterly simple, unemphatic statement to enhance the effect of a pathetic or tragic event; an example is the line at the close of the narrative in Wordsworth's *Michael*: "And never lifted up a single stone."

A special form of understatement is **litotes** (Greek for "plain" or "simple"), which is the assertion of an affirmative by negating its contrary: "He's not the brightest man in the world" meaning "He is stupid." The figure is frequent in Anglo-Saxon poetry. In *Beowulf*, after Hrothgar has described the ghastly mere where dwells the monster Grendel, he comments, "That is not a pleasant place."

IMAGERY.   This term is one of the most common in modern criticism, and one of the most ambiguous. Its applications range all the way from the "mental pictures" which, it is claimed, are experienced by the reader of a poem, to the totality of the elements which make up a poem. An example of this latter usage is C. Day Lewis' statement, in his *Poetic Image* (1948), pp. 17–18, that an image "is a picture made out of words," and that "a poem may itself be an image composed from a multiplicity of images." Three uses of the word, however, are especially frequent:

(1) "Imagery" (that is, "images" taken collectively) is used to signify all the objects and qualities of sense perception referred to in a poem or other work of literature, whether by literal description, by allusion, or in the analogues (the *vehicles*) used in its similes and metaphors. In Wordsworth's "She Dwelt among the Untrodden Ways," the imagery in this broad sense includes the literal objects the poem refers to ("ways," "maid," "grave"), as well as the "violet" and "stone" of the metaphor and the "star" and "sky" of the simile in the second stanza. The term "image" should not be taken to imply a visual reproduction of the object referred to; some readers of the passage experience visual images and some do not; and among those who do, the explicitness and detail of the mind-pictures vary greatly. Also, imagery includes auditory, tactile (touch), olfactory (smell), gustatory (taste), or kinesthetic (sensations of movement), as well as visual qualities. In his *In Memoriam*, number 101, for example, Tennyson's references are to qualities of smell and hearing, as well as sight, in the lines

> Unloved, that beech will gather brown, . . .
> And many a rose-carnation feed
> With summer spice the humming air. . . .

(2) Imagery is used, more narrowly, to signify only descriptions of visible objects and scenes, especially if the description is vivid and particularized, as in Coleridge's "Ancient Mariner":

> The rock shone bright, the kirk no less,
> That stands above the rock:
> The moonlight steeped in silentness
> The steady weathercock.

(3) Most commonly, imagery is used to signify *figurative language,* especially the vehicles of metaphors and similes. Recent criticism, and especially the *new criticism,* has gone far beyond older criticism in stressing imagery, in this sense, as the essential component in poetry, and as a major clue to poetic meaning, structure, and effect.

Caroline Spurgeon, in her very influential book, *Shakespeare's Imagery and What It Tells Us* (1935), made statistical counts of the subjects of this type of imagery in Shakespeare, and used the results as clues to Shakespeare's personal experience, interests, and temperament. She also pointed out the frequent occurrence in Shakespeare's plays of "image-clusters" (recurrent groupings of metaphors and similes), and presented evidence that a number of the individual plays have characteristic image motifs (for example, animal imagery in *King Lear,* and the figures of disease, corruption, and death in *Hamlet*); these elements she viewed as establishing the overall tonality of a play. Many critics have joined Miss Spurgeon in the search for images, image patterns, and "thematic imagery" in works of literature. By some critics the implicit interaction of the imagery, rather than the explicit statements, or the overt speeches and actions of the characters, is held to constitute the working out of the primary subject, or "theme," of many plays, poems, and novels. See, for example, the critical writings of G. Wilson Knight, Cleanth Brooks on *Macbeth* in *The Well-Wrought Urn* (1947), Chap. 2, and Robert B. Heilman, *This Great Stage: Image and Structure in "King Lear"* (1948).

On imagery in general see also H. W. Wells, *Poetic Imagery* (1924); June E. Downey, *Creative Imagination* (1929); R. H. Fogle, *The Imagery of Keats and Shelley* (1949); Norman Friedman, "Imagery: From Sensation to Symbol," *Journal of Aesthetics and Art Criticism,* XII (1953).

IMAGISM   was a poetic movement that flourished in England, and even more vigorously in America, between the years 1912 and 1917. It was organized by a group of English and American writers in London, partly under the influence of the poetic theory of T. E. Hulme, as a revolt against what Ezra Pound called the "rather blurry, messy . . . sentimentalistic mannerish" poetry at the turn of the century. Ezra Pound, the first leader of the movement, was soon succeeded by Amy Lowell; other leading participants in the movement were H[ilda] D[oolittle], D. H. Lawrence, William Carlos Williams, John Gould Fletcher, and Richard Aldington. The Imagist claims, as voiced by Amy Lowell in her Preface to the first of three anthologies called *Some Imagist Poets* (1915–1917), declared for a poetry which (abandoning conventional poetic materials and versification) is free to choose any subject and to create its own rhythms, is expressed in common speech, and presents an image that is hard, clear, and concentrated.

The typical Imagist poem is written in *free verse*, and undertakes to render as exactly and tersely as possible, without comment or generalization, the writer's response to a visual object or scene; often the impression is rendered by means of metaphor, or by juxtaposing a description of one object with that of a second and diverse object. This famed example by Ezra Pound exceeds all Imagist poems in the degree of its concentration:

IN A STATION OF THE METRO
The apparition of these faces in the crowd;
Petals on a wet, black bough.[1]

In this poem Pound, like a number of other Imagists, was influenced by the Japanese **haiku** (or **hokku**), a lyric form that represents the poet's impression of a natural object or scene, viewed at a particular season or month, in exactly seventeen syllables.

Imagism was too restrictive to endure long as a concerted movement, but it proved to be the beginning of modern poetry. Almost every major poet up to this day, including W. B. Yeats, T. S. Eliot, and Wallace Stevens, has felt strongly the influence of the Imagist experiments with precise, clear images, juxtaposed without expressed connection.

See T. E. Hulme, *Speculations, ed. Herbert Read (1924); Stanley K. Coffman, *Imagism* (1951); *The Imagist Poem*, introduction by William Pratt (1963).

IMITATION.   In literary criticism the word **imitation** has two distinct applications: (1) to define the nature of literature and the other arts, and (2) to indicate the relation of one literary work to another literary work which served as its model.

(1) In his *Poetics* Aristotle defines poetry as an imitation (in Greek, "mimesis") of human actions. By "imitation" he means something like "representation," in its root sense: the poem imitates by taking a type of human action and re-presenting it in a new "medium," or material— that of words. By distinguishing differences in the artistic media, in the kind of actions imitated, and in the manner of imitation (for example, dramatic or narrative), Aristotle first discriminates poetry from the other arts, and then discriminates among the various poetic kinds, such as drama and epic, tragedy and comedy. The term "imitation" continued to be an indispensable word in discussing the nature

[1] Ezra Pound, *Personae*. Copyright 1926 by Ezra Pound. Reprinted by permission of New Directions Publishing Corporation, and Faber and Faber Ltd.

of poetry through the eighteenth century; critics differed radically, however, in their concept of the nature of the mimetic relationship, and of the kinds of things in the external world that works of literature imitate, or ought to imitate. With the emergence in the early nineteenth century of the Romantic theory that poetry is essentially an expression of the poet's feelings or imaginative process, imitation tended to drop out of its central place in literary theory (see *criticism*). In recent decades, however, the use of the term has been strongly revived, especially by R. S. Crane and the other *Chicago Critics*, who ground their theory on the method and basic distinctions of Aristotle's *Poetics*.

(2) Ancient rhetoricians and critics often recommended that a poet should "imitate" in a work the established models, or "classic" works, in that literary genre. The notion that the proper procedure for poets, with the very rare exception of an "original genius," was to imitate the normative forms and styles of the ancient masters continued to be influential well into the eighteenth century; although all the major critics also insisted that mere copying was not enough—that a good work imitated the form and spirit rather than the detail of the classic models, and could be achieved only by a poet who possessed an innate individual talent.

In a specialized use of the term in this second sense, "imitation" was also used to describe a literary work which deliberately echoed an older work but adapted it to subject matter in the writer's own age. In the poems that Alexander Pope called *Imitations of Horace*, for example, an important part of the intended effect depends on the reader's recognition of the resourcefulness, subtlety, and wit with which Pope accommodated to contemporary circumstances the structure, details, and even the wording of one or another of Horace's satires.

On "imitation" as a term used to define literature see R. S. Crane, ed., *Critics and Criticism* (1952), and M. H. Abrams, *The Mirror and the Lamp* (1953), Chaps. 1–2. On Pope's imitations of Horace and other ancient masters see R. A. Brower, *Alexander Pope: The Poetry of Allusion* (1959).

INTENTIONAL FALLACY identifies what is held to be the error of interpreting or evaluating a work by reference to the intention—the design or plan—of the author in writing the work. The term was proposed by W. K. Wimsatt, Jr., and H. C. Beardsley in "The Intentional Fallacy" (1946), reprinted in Wimsatt's *The Verbal Icon* (1954). It is claimed that whether the author has himself stated his intention in commenting on his work, or whether his intention is simply inferred from the work itself, the intention is irrelevant, because the meaning and value resides in the actual text—the made object—which is the finished and free-standing work itself. Any reference to the author's avowed or supposed purpose and general state of mind is in fact misleading, for it distracts us from the text to "external" matters about the author's biography and his psychological condition or creative process, which we tend to substitute for the "internal" constitution of the work as such.

This concept has been widely adopted by modern exponents of *objective criticism*, and has been much debated by critical theorists. A reasonable view is that if we possess an author's statement about his intention in writing a work of literature, that statement has a special status as evidence, since the maker of a work has direct access to data about what went into its making which may be highly relevant to our own interpretation and evaluation. But though the author's stated intention has a privileged status, it does not have a determinative one as evidence, for it must be validated by reference to the text itself, and it must be qualified, or even rejected, if an alternative reading provides a better fit to the order and details of the work before us. As for an "intention" which is entirely inferred from the text of the work—that is simply a synonym for the internal organizing principle of the poem itself.

See René Wellek and Austin Warren, *Theory of Literature* (rev. ed., 1966), Chap. 12; Isabel C. Hungerland, *Poetic Discourse* (1958), Chap. 6; E. D. Hirsch, Jr., "Objective Interpretation," in *Validity in Interpretation* (1967).

IRONY. In Greek comedy the character called the *eiron* was a "dissembler," who characteristically spoke in understatement and deliberately pretended to be less intelligent than he was, yet triumphed over the *alazon*—the self-deceiving and stupid braggart. In most of the diverse critical uses of the term "irony" there remains the root sense of dissimulation, or of a difference between what is asserted and what is actually the case.

Verbal irony is a statement in which the implicit meaning intended by the speaker differs from that which he ostensibly asserts. Such an ironic statement usually involves the explicit expression of one attitude or evaluation, but with the implication of a very different attitude or evaluation. Thus in Canto IV of Pope's *Rape of the Lock* after Sir Plume, egged on by the ladies, has stammered out his incoherent request for the return of the stolen lock of hair, the Baron answers him:

"It grieves me much," replied the Peer again,
"Who speaks so well should ever speak in vain."

This is a straightforward case of an ironic reversal of the surface statement, because there are patent clues in the circumstances that the Peer is not in the least aggrieved, and that poor Sir Plume has not spoken at all well. Another justly famed instance of irony is the opening sentence of Jane Austen's *Pride and Prejudice*: "It is a truth universally acknowledged that a single man in possession of a good fortune must be in want of a wife"; the implication is that a single woman wants a rich husband. Sometimes the use of irony by Pope and other masters is very complex; the meaning and evaluations may be subtly qualified rather than simply reversed, and the clues to the ironic countermeaning under the surface statement may be indirect and unobtrusive. That is why recourse to irony by an author carries an implicit compliment to the intelligence of the reader, who is associated with the author and the knowing minority who are not taken in by the ostensible meaning. That is also why many ironists are misinterpreted and sometimes (like Defoe and Swift) get into serious trouble with the obtuse authorities. Following the intricate and shifting maneuvers of a great ironist like Plato, Swift, or Henry James is an ultimate test of skill in reading between the lines.

Some literary works exhibit **structural irony,** in that they are persistently, or even totally, ironic. In such works the author, instead of using an occasional verbal irony, introduces a structural feature which serves to sustain the duplicity of meaning. One common device of this sort is the invention of a **naive hero,** or else a naive narrator or spokesman, whose invincible simplicity leads him to persist in putting an interpretation on affairs which the knowing reader—who penetrates to, and shares, the implicit point of view of the authorial presence behind the naive *persona*—just as persistently is able to alter and correct. (Note that verbal irony depends on knowledge of the speaker's intention shared by the speaker and his audience; structural irony depends on a knowledge of the author's intention shared by the audience, but unknown to the speaker.) One example of the naive spokesman is Swift's well-meaning but insanely rational economist who makes the "Modest Proposal" to convert the children of the oppressed and poverty-stricken Irish into a financial and gastronomical asset. Other examples are Swift's stubbornly credulous Gulliver, the self-deceiving and paranoid monologuist in Browning's "Soliloquy of the Spanish Cloister," and the insane editor, Kinbote, in Vladimir Nabokov's *Pale Fire.* A related device for sustaining ironic qualification is the use of the *fallible narrator*, in which the teller of the story is himself a participant in it but, although he may be neither foolish nor demented, nevertheless manifests a failure of insight, viewing and appraising his own motives, and the motives and actions of other characters, through the distorting perspective of his prejudices and private interests. (See *Point of view.*)

Irony can be discriminated from some related uses of language:

Invective is direct denunciation by the use of derogatory *epithets*; so Prince Hal, in *Henry IV, 1,* calls the rotund Falstaff "this sanguine coward, this bed-presser, this horseback-breaker, this huge hill of flesh. . . ." (In the dramatic context there is in this instance of invective an ironic undertone of affection, as often when friends, secure in an intimacy which guarantees that they will not be taken literally, resort to name-calling in the exuberance of their esteem.) In his *Discourse Concerning Satire* Dryden described the difference in efficacy between direct invective and the indirectness of irony, in which the ironist is able to maintain the advantage of detachment by leaving it to the circumstances to convert his bland compliments into insults:

> How easy is it to call rogue and villain, and that wittily! But how hard to make a man appear a fool, a blockhead, or a knave, without using any of those opprobrious terms. . . . There is . . . a vast difference between the slovenly butchering of a man, and the fineness of a stroke that separates the head from the body, and leaves it standing in its place.

Sarcasm in ordinary parlance is sometimes used for all irony, but it is better to restrict it to the crude and blatant use of apparent praise for dispraise: "Oh, you're God's great gift to women, you are!" Sarcasm is the common form of irony in dormitory persiflage.

The term "irony," qualified by an adjective, is also used in a number of specialized senses for literary devices and modes of organization:

Socratic irony takes its name from Socrates' characteristic assumption, in philosophical dialogue, of the pose of ignorance, an eagerness to be instructed, and a modest readiness to entertain points of view which, upon his continued questioning, invariably turn out to be ill-grounded or to lead to absurd consequences.

Dramatic irony involves a situation in a play or a narrative in which the audience shares with the author knowledge of which a character is ignorant: the character acts in a way grossly inappropriate to the actual circumstances, or expects the opposite of what fate holds in store, or says something that anticipates the actual outcome, but not at all in the way that he means it. Writers of Greek tragedy, who based their plots on legends whose outcome was already known to their audience, made frequent use of this device. Sophocles' *Oedipus,* for example, is a complex instance of **tragic irony,** for the king ("I, Oedipus, whom all men call great") engages in a hunt for the evil-doer who has brought a plague upon Thebes; the object of the hunt turns out (as the audience has known right along) to be the hunter himself, and the king, having achieved a vision of the terrible truth, penitently blinds himself. Dramatic irony is also possible in comedy. An example is the scene in *Twelfth Night* (II. v) in which Malvolio struts and preens in anticipation of a good fortune which the audience knows is based on a fake letter; the dramatic irony is heightened by Malvolio's ignorance, but our knowledge, of the presence of the hoaxers, who gleefully observe and comment on his speech and actions.

Cosmic irony (or "the irony of fate") refers to literary works in which God, or destiny, or the universal process, is represented as though deliberately manipulating events to frustrate and mock the protagonist. This is a favorite structural device of Thomas Hardy. In his *Tess of the d'Urbervilles* the heroine, having lost her virtue because of her innocence, then loses her happiness because of her honesty, finds it again only by murder, and having been briefly happy, is hanged. Hardy concludes: "The President of the Immortals, in Aeschylean phrase, had ended his sport with Tess."

Romantic irony is a term invented by German writers of the late eighteenth and early nineteenth centuries to designate a mode of dramatic or narrative writing in which the author builds up artistic illusion, only to break it down by revealing that he, as artist, is the arbitrary creator and manipulator of his characters and their actions. The concept owes much to Lawrence Sterne's use of a self-conscious and willful narrator in his *Tristram Shandy*. Byron's great narrative poem *Don Juan* constantly employs this device for ironic effect, letting the reader into the author's confidence, and revealing him as an inventor who is often at a loss for matter to sustain his plot and undecided about how to continue it.

A number of writers associated with the *new criticism* use "irony" in a greatly extended sense, as a general criterion of literary value. This use is based largely on two literary theorists. T. S. Eliot praised a kind of "wit," absent in the Romantic poets, which is an "internal equilibrium" that implies the "recognition," in dealing with any one kind of experience, "of other kinds of experience which are possible." ("Andrew Marvell," 1921, in *Selected Essays*, 1960.) And I. A. Richards defined irony as an equilibrium of oppositions (*Principles of Literary Criticism*, 1924, Chap. 32):

> Irony in this sense consists in the bringing in of the opposite, the complementary impulses; that is why poetry which is exposed to it is not of the highest order, and why irony itself is so constantly a characteristic of poetry which is.

Such observations were developed by Robert Penn Warren, Cleanth Brooks, and others, into the claim that poems in which the writer commits himself unreservedly to an exclusive attitude or outlook, such as love or admiration or idealism, are of an inferior order, and vulnerable to the reader's irony; the greatest poems, on the other hand, are invulnerable to external irony because they incorporate the poet's own "ironic" awareness of opposite and complementary attitudes. See R. P. Warren, "Pure and Impure Poetry" (1943), in *Critiques and Essays in Criticism*, ed. R. W. Stallman (1949); Cleanth Brooks, "Irony as a Principle of Structure" (1949), in *Literary Opinion in America*, ed. M. W. Zabel (1951).

On the traditional use of the term see J. A. K. Thomson, *Irony: An Historical Introduction* (1926); A. R. Thompson, *The Dry Mock: A Study of Irony in Drama* (1948); W. C. Booth, *The Rhetoric of Fiction* (1961); A. E. Dyson, *The Crazy Fabric, Essays in Irony* (1965). A suggestive earlier treatment of the subject was Søren Kierkegaard's *The Concept of Irony* (1841), trans. Lee M. Capel (1965).

JACOBEAN AGE.   The reign of James I (in Latin, "Jacobus"), 1603–1625, which followed the Elizabethan Age. This was the period in prose writings of Bacon, Donne's sermons, Burton's *Anatomy of Melancholy*, and the King James translation of the Bible. It was the period also of Shakespeare's greatest tragedies and tragicomedies, and of major writings by other notable poets and playwrights, including Donne, Ben Jonson, Drayton, Beaumont and Fletcher, Webster, Chapman, Middleton, and Massinger.

See Basil Willey, *The Seventeenth Century Background* (1934); Douglas Bush, *English Literature in the Earlier Seventeenth Century* (1945); C. V. Wedgewood, *Seventeenth Century English Literature* (1950).

LAI.   The term is applied to a variety of poems by medieval French writers in the latter twelfth and thirteenth centuries. Some *lais* were lyric, but most of them were short romantic narratives written in octasyllabic couplets. Marie de France, who wrote in French, although at the English court of King Henry II, composed a number of charming poems of this sort; they are called "Breton lais" because their narratives are for the most part drawn from Arthurian and other Celtic legends. ("Breton" refers to Brittany, which was a Celtic part of France.) The Anglicized term "Breton lay" was applied in the fourteenth century to English poems written in imitation of the narratives of Marie de France; they included *Sir Orfeo*, the *Lay of Launfal*, and Chaucer's *Franklin's Tale*. Later still, "lay" was used by English poets simply as a synonym for song, or for a fairly short narrative poem (for example, Scott's *Lay of the Last Minstrel*).

See Roger S. Loomis, ed., *Arthurian Literature in the Middle Ages* (1959).

LIGHT VERSE uses the ordinary speaking voice and a relaxed manner to treat its subjects gaily, or comically, or whimsically, or with good-natured satire. Its subjects may be serious as well as trivial; the defining quality is the attitude of the lyric or narrative speaker toward the subject. Thomas Love Peacock's "The War Song of Dinas Vawr" (1829) begins

> The mountain sheep are sweeter,
> But the valley sheep are fatter;
> We therefore deemed it meeter
> To carry off the latter.

And it ends

> We brought away from battle,
> And much their land bemoaned them,
> Two thousand head of cattle,
> And the head of him who owned them:
> Ednyfed, king of Dyfed,
> His head was borne before us;
> His wine and beasts supplied our feasts,
> And his overthrow, our chorus.

The dispassionate attitude, brisk language, and pat rhymes convert what might have been matter for epic or tragedy into a comic narrative.

Vers de société ("society verse") is the species of light verse that deals with the relationships, concerns, or events of polite society. It is often satiric, but in the mode of badinage rather than severity; and when it deals with love it does so as a sexual game, or flirtatiously, or in the mode of elegant and witty compliment, rather than with passion or high seriousness. The tone is urbane, the style deft, and the form polished and sometimes very elaborate; most poems using intricate French stanza forms, such as the *vilanelle*, are society verse.

Nursery rhymes and other children's verses are another type of light verse. Edward Lear ("The Jumblies," "The Owl and the Pussy Cat") and Lewis Carroll ("Jabberwocky," *The Hunting of the Snark*) made children's nonsense verses into a Victorian specialty. Lear also popularized the limerick, which is a form of light verse everyone knows and most of us have practiced.

Some other fine artificers of light and society verse are the *cavalier poets* of the early seventeenth century, and John Dryden, Matthew Prior, Alexander Pope, and W. S. Gilbert; modern practitioners include

Ezra Pound, W. H. Auden, E. E. Cummings, Ogden Nash, and John Betjeman.

See *An Anthology of Light Verse*, ed. Louis Kronenberger (1935); *The Oxford Book of Light Verse*, ed. W. H. Auden (1938); *Worldly Muse: An Anthology of Serious Light Verse*, ed. A. J. M. Smith (1951).

LITERATURE OF THE ABSURD.   The name is applied to a number of works in drama and prose fiction which have in common the sense that the human condition is essentially and ineradicably absurd, and that this condition can only be adequately represented in works of literature that are themselves absurd. This literature has its roots in the movements of *expressionism* and *surrealism*, as well as in the fiction of James Joyce and of Franz Kafka (*The Trial, Metamorphosis*). The current movement, however, emerged after World War II as a rebellion against the essential beliefs and values both of traditional culture and traditional literature. Central to this earlier tradition had been the assumptions that man is a rational creature who lives in an at least partially intelligible universe, that he is part of an orderly social structure, and that he is capable of heroism and dignity even in defeat. In the last thirty years or so, however, there has been a widespread tendency, especially prominent in the **existentialist philosophy** of men of letters such as Jean-Paul Sartre and Albert Camus, to view each man as an isolated being who is cast ignominiously into an alien universe, to conceive the universe as possessing no inherent human truth, value, or meaning, and to represent man's life, as it moves from the nothingness whence it came toward the nothingness where it must end, as an existence which is both anguished and absurd. As Camus said in *The Myth of Sisyphus*,

> In a universe that is suddenly deprived of illusions and of light, man feels a stranger. His is an irremediable exile. . . . This divorce between man and his life, the actor and his setting, truly constitutes the feeling of Absurdity.

Or as Eugène Ionesco, a leading writer of the drama of the absurd, has put it in an essay on Kafka: "Cut off from his religious, metaphysical, and transcendental roots, man is lost; all his actions become senseless, absurd, useless."

Samuel Beckett, the most influential of all writers in this movement, is an Irishman living in Paris who writes in French and then translates many of his own works into English. His plays project the senseless irrationalism and absurdity of life, in dramatic forms that reject realistic settings, logical reasoning, or a consistently evolving plot. *Waiting for Godot* presents two tramps in a waste place, fruitlessly and all but hopelessly waiting for an unidentified person, Godot, who may or may not exist and with whom they sometimes think they remember that they may have an appointment; as one of them remarks, "Nothing happens, nobody comes, nobody goes, it's awful." Like most works in this mode, the play is "absurd" in the double sense that it is grotesquely comic as well as irrational; it is a deliberate parody of the traditional assumptions of Western culture, of traditional drama, and even of its own inescapable participation in the dramatic medium. The lucid but eddying and pointless dialogue is often funny, and pratfalls and other modes of slapstick are used to project the sense of metaphysical alienation and anguish. Beckett's prose fiction, such as *Molloy* and *The Unnamable*, present an antihero who plays out the absurd moves of the end game of civilization in a non-work which tends to destroy the logical and syntactical coherence of its own medium, language itself.

Another important French playwright of the absurd is Jean Genêt (who combines absurdism and diabolism); some of the dramatic work of the Englishman Harold Pinter and the American Edward Albee are in a similar mode. There are also affinities with this movement in the numerous recent works which exploit **black humor:** baleful or inept characters in a fantastic or nightmarish modern world play out their roles in what Ionesco called a "tragic farce," in which the events are simultaneously comic, brutal, horrifying, and absurd. See, for example, Joseph Heller's *Catch-22*, Thomas Pynchon's *V*, and the novels of the German Gunter Grass and the American Kurt Vonnegut, Jr.

Refer to Martin Esslin, *The Theatre of the Absurd* (rev. ed., 1969), David Grossvogel, *The Blasphemers: The Theatre of Brecht, Ionesco, Beckett, Genêt* (1965), and Arnold P. Hinchliffe, *The Absurd* (1969). See also Lionel Trilling's discussion of the movement of "anti-culture" in modern literature, in *Beyond Culture* (1965).

LITERATURE OF SENSIBILITY. When a modern critic talks of a poet's **sensibility,** or of the *dissociation of sensibility* that set in, according to T. S. Eliot, with the poetry of Milton and Dryden, he signifies a person's characteristic emotional and intellectual responsiveness to experience. When a literary historian, however, talks of the **literature of sensibility,** he refers to a particular cultural phenomenon of the eighteenth century. The background was the moral theory that developed as a reaction to seventeenth-century Stoicism (which emphasized reason and the unemotional will as the sole motives to virtue), and even more importantly, as a reaction against Thomas Hobbes's theory that man is innately selfish, and that the mainsprings of his behavior are self-interest and the drive for power and status. Many sermons, philosophical writings (notably the Earl of Shaftesbury's *Characteristicks*, 1711), and popular tracts and essays proclaimed that "benevolence"—wishing other persons well—is an innate human sentiment; that virtue is mainly spontaneous action in response to this instinctive tendency; and that central to moral experience is sympathy and "sensibility": a hair-trigger responsiveness to another man's distresses and joys. It became a commonplace in popular morality that constant readiness to shed a sympathetic tear was the sign both of polite breeding and a virtuous heart, and also that sympathy with another's grief, unlike personal grief, was a pleasurable emotion in itself. Common phrases in the cult of sensibility were "the luxury of grief," "pleasurable sorrow," and "the sadly pleasing tear." A late eighteenth-century mortuary inscription in Dorchester Abbey says:

> Reader! If thou hast a Heart fam'd for Tenderness and Pity, Contemplate this Spot. In which are deposited the Remains of a Young Lady. . . . When Nerves were too delicately spun to bear the rude Shakes and Jostlings which we meet with in this transitory world, Nature gave way; She sunk and died a Martyr to Excessive Sensibility.

In literature these tendencies were reflected in the **drama of sensibility,** or **sentimental comedy,** that replaced the tough amorality and the representation of aristocratic sexual license in *Restoration Comedy.* In these plays, Oliver Goldsmith wrote in his "Comparison between Sentimental and Laughing Comedy" (1773), "the virtues of private life are exhibited rather than the vices exposed, and the distresses rather than the faults of mankind make our interest in the piece"; the characters, "though they want humor, have abundance of sentiment and feeling"; with the result, he added, that the audience "sit at a play as gloomy as at the tabernacle." Plays such as Richard Steele's *The Conscious Lovers* (1722) and Richard Cumberland's *The West Indian* (1771) present monumentally benevolent heroes and heroines of the middle class, whose dialogue consists largely in the exchange of elevating sentiments and who, prior to the manipulated happy ending, suffer tribulations designed to evoke the maximum in tears from the audience.

The **novel of sensibility,** or **sentimental novel,** of the eighteenth century similarly emphasized the tearful distresses of the virtuous, either at their own sorrows or those of their friends. Richardson's *Pamela, or Virtue Rewarded* (1740) exploits sensibility in some of its scenes; and Lawrence Sterne, in *Tristram Shandy* and *A Sentimental Journey,* gives us his own inimitable compound of sensibility, irony, and innuendo. An extreme instance is Henry MacKenzie's *The Man of Feeling* (1771), which represents a hero of such exquisite sensibility that he goes into a decline from excess of tenderness toward a young lady, and dies in the perturbation of declaring his emotion. "If all his tears had been tears of blood," declares an editor of the novel, Hamish Miles, "the poor man could hardly have been more debile."

See Ernest Bernbaum, *The Drama of Sensibility* (1915); Herbert Ross Brown, *The Sentimental Novel in America* (1940); C. A. Moore, *Backgrounds of English Literature, 1700–1760* (1953); Arthur Sherbo, *English Sentimental Drama* (1957); R. P. Utter and G. B. Needham, *Pamela's Daughters* (1963); R. S. Crane, "Suggestions toward a Genealogy of the 'Man of Feeling,' " in *The Idea of the Humanities* (2 vols.; 1967).

LOCAL COLOR. The detailed representation in fiction of the setting, dialect, customs, dress, and ways of thinking and feeling which are characteristic of a particular region, such as Thomas Hardy's "Wessex" or Kipling's India. After the Civil War a number of American writers exploited the possibilities of local color in various parts of America; for example, the West (Bret Harte), the Mississippi region (Mark Twain), the South (George Washington Cable), the Midwest (E. W. Howe, Hamlin Garland), and New England (Sarah Orne Jewett). The term "local color writing" is usually applied to works which, like O. Henry's or Damon Runyon's stories about New York City, rely for their interest mainly on a sentimental or comic representation of the surface peculiarities of a region, without penetrating to universal human characteristics and problems.

LYRIC. Greek writers identified the lyric as a song rendered to the accompaniment of a lyre. The term is now used for any fairly short, nonnarrative poem presenting a single speaker who expresses a state of mind or a process of thought and feeling. The lyric speaker may be musing in solitude; in a "dramatic lyric," however, he is represented in a particular situation, addressing himself to another person, as in Donne's "Canonization" and Wordsworth's "Tintern Abbey." Although the lyric is uttered in the first person, we should be wary about identifying the "I" in the poem with the poet himself. In some lyrics, such as Milton's sonnet "When I consider how my light is spent" and Coleridge's "Frost at Midnight," the relation to the known circumstances of the author's life invites us to read the poem as the personal utterance of the writer. Even in such poems, however, the character of the lyric speaker is adapted to the particular lyric situation and effect, and the utterance is artistically ordered into a whole which is independent of outside biographical information. In many lyrics the speaker is an invented character, and one who may be very different from the actual poet. (See *Persona.*)

A lyric poem may be simply a brief expression of a mood or state of feeling; for example, Shelley's "To Night," or this fine medieval song:

> Fowles in the frith,
> The fisshes in the flood,
> And I mon waxe wood:
> Much sorwe I walke with
> For best of bone and blood.

But the genre also includes extended expressions of a complex evolution of mind, such as in the long elegy and ode. The process of observation, thought, memory, and feeling in a lyric may be organized in a variety of ways. For example, in "love lyrics" the speaker may simply express his state of mind in an ordered form, as in Burns's "O my love's like a red, red rose"; or he may gallantly elaborate a compliment to his lady (Ben Jonson's "Drink to me only with thine eyes"); or he may deploy an argument to persuade his mistress to take advantage of opportunity and fleeting youth (Marvell's "To His Coy Mistress"). In other kinds of lyric the speaker manifests and justifies his particular disposition and values (Milton's "L'Allegro" and "Il Penseroso"); or he expresses a sustained process of observation and meditation, in which he analyzes and tries to resolve an emotional problem (Wordsworth's "Intimations Ode," Arnold's "Dover Beach"); or he is exhibited as making and justifying the choice of a way of life (Yeats's "Sailing to Byzantium").

For subclasses of the lyric see *Dramatic monologue, Elegy, Ode,* and *Sonnet.* Refer to Ernest Rhys, *Lyric Poetry* (1913); C. M. Ing, *Elizabethan Lyrics* (1951); Norman Maclean, "From Action to Image: Theories of the Lyric in the 18th Century," in *Critics and Criticism,* ed. R. S. Crane (1952). In the present century the lyric has become by far the preponderant form of poetry; see, for example, M. L. Rosenthal, *The Modern Poets* (1960), and *The New Poets* (1967).

MASQUE.   The masque was developed in Renaissance Italy and flourished in England during the reigns of Elizabeth, James I, and Charles I. It was an elaborate form of court entertainment, combining poetic drama, music, song, dance, splendid costuming, and stage spectacle. A plot—often slight, and mainly mythological and allegorical—served to hold together these diverse elements. The characters, who wore masques, were played by ladies and gentlemen of the court, including royalty itself. The play concluded with a dance of the players, who doffed their masques and took members of the audience for partners.

In the early seventeenth century the masque drew upon the finest artistic talents of the day, including Ben Jonson for the poetic script (for example, *The Masque of Blacknesse* and *The Masque of Queens*) and Inigo Jones, the architect, for the elaborate stage machinery. Each lavish production cost a fortune; it was literally the sport of kings and queens until both court and drama were abruptly ended by the Puritan triumph of 1642. The two examples best known to modern readers are the masque-within-a-play in the fourth act of Shakespeare's *The Tempest* and Milton's sage and serious revival of the form, *Comus*, which was presented at Ludlow Castle in 1634.

The **antimasque** was a form developed by Ben Jonson. In it the characters were grotesque and unruly, the action ludicrous, and the humor broad; it served as a foil to the elegance, order, and ceremony of the masque proper, with which it was juxtaposed.

See Enid Welsford, *The Court Masque* (1927); Allardyce Nicoll, *Stuart Masques and the Renaissance Stage* (1937).

MELODRAMA. "Melos" is Greek for song, and the term "melodrama" was originally applied to all musical plays, including opera. In early nineteenth-century London, many plays were put on which used musical accompaniment simply to fortify the emotional tone of the various scenes; the procedure was developed in part to circumvent the Licensing Act, which allowed "legitimate" plays only as a monopoly of the Drury Lane and Covent Garden theaters, but permitted musical entertainments elsewhere. "Melodrama" is now applied to some typical products of this period; it can be said to bear the relation to tragedy that farce does to comedy. The protagonists are flat types; the hero and heroine are pure as the driven snow and the villain is a monster of malignity (the good guys and bad guys of the movie western are modern derivatives of character types in the older melodramas). The plot revolves around malevolent intrigue and violent action, while credibility both of character and plot is sacrificed for violent effect and emotional opportunism. Nineteenth-century melodramas, such as *Sweeney Todd, The Demon Barber of Fleet Street* (1842), *Under the Gaslight* (1867), and the temperance play *Ten Nights in a Barroom* (1858), are still sometimes produced—no longer for thrills, however, but for laughs. The adjective "melodramatic" is applied to any literary work or episode that relies on improbable events and sensational action.

See M. W. Disher, *Blood and Thunder: Mid-Victorian Melodrama and Its Origins* (1949), and *Plots That Thrilled* (1954); Frank Rahill, *The World of Melodrama* (1967); R. B. Heilman, *Tragedy and Melodrama* (1968).

METAPHYSICAL POETS. Dryden said in his *Discourse of Satire* (1693) that John Donne in his poetry "affects the metaphysics"—that is, employs the terminology and abstruse arguments of the medieval

Scholastic philosophers; and in 1779 Dr. Johnson extended the term "metaphysical" from Donne to a school of poets, in the acute and balanced critique which he incorporated in his "Life of Cowley." The name is now applied to a group of seventeenth-century poets who, whether or not directly influenced by Donne, employ a similar poetic manner and imagery, both in secular poetry (Cleveland, Marvell, Cowley) and in religious poetry (Herbert, Vaughan, Crashaw).

Attempts have been made to demonstrate that these poets had in common a philosophical world view. The term "metaphysical," however, fits these very diverse writers only if it is used, as Johnson used it, to indicate a common poetic style and way of organizing the thought. Donne set the metaphysical pattern by writing poems which are sharply opposed to the rich mellifluousness, the sense of human dignity, and the idealized view of sexual love, which had constituted a central tradition in Elizabethan poetry, especially in the writings of Spenser and the Petrarchan sonneteers. Instead, Donne wrote in a diction and meter modeled on the rough give-and-take of actual speech, and usually organized his poems in the dramatic and rhetorical form of an urgent or heated argument—with a reluctant mistress, or an intruding friend, or God, or Death, or with himself. He employed a subtle and often deliberately outrageous logic; he was realistic, ironic, and sometimes cynical in his treatment of the complexity of human motives, especially in the sexual relation; and whether playful or serious, and whether writing the poetry of love or of intense religious experience, he was persistently "witty," making ingenious use of *paradox, pun,* and startling parallels and distinctions. (See *metaphysical conceit.*) The beginnings of four of Donne's poems will illustrate the shock tactics, the dramatic form of direct address, the rough idiom, and the rhythms of the living voice which are characteristic of his metaphysical style:

> Go and catch a falling star,
> Get with child a mandrake root. . . .
>
> For God's sake hold your tongue, and let me love. . . .
>
> Busy old fool, unruly sun. . . .
>
> Batter my heart, three-personed God. . . .

The metaphysical poets have had a few admirers in every age, but beginning with the *neoclassic period* of the later seventeenth century, they were for the most part regarded as interesting but perversely ingenious and obscure eccentrics, until an astonishing revaluation after World War I elevated Donne high in the rank of English poets. This reversal owed much to H. J. C. Grierson's Introduction to *Meta-

physical Lyrics and Poems of the Seventeenth Century (1912), was given strong impetus by T. S. Eliot's essays on "The Metaphysical Poets" and "Andrew Marvell" (1921), and has been continued by a great number of commentators, including the *New Critics,* who tended to elevate the metaphysical style into the very model of the poetry of a "unified sensibility."

See George Williamson, **The Donne Tradition* (1930); Helen C. White, **The Metaphysical Poets* (1936); Cleanth Brooks, **Modern Poetry and the Tradition* (1939); Alfred Alvarez, **The School of Donne* (1961); Helen Gardner, ed., **John Donne: A Collection of Critical Essays* (1962).

METER. In all sustained spoken English we feel a **rhythm,** in the sense of a recognizable though variable pattern in the beat of the stresses in the stream of sound. If this rhythm is structured into a recurrence of regular—that is, approximately equal—units, we call it **meter.** Compositions written in meter are known as **verse.**

There is considerable dispute about the best way to analyze and classify English meters. This article will present a traditional stress-and-syllable analysis which has the virtue of being simple, widely accepted, and applicable to by far the greater part of English versification from Chaucer to the present day. Some major departures from this stress-and-syllable meter will be described at the end.

The meter of a line of verse is determined by the pattern of stronger and weaker stresses in its component syllables. (What the ear detects as a strong stress is not an absolute quantity, but is relative to the degree of stress in the adjacent syllables; the degree of perceived stress is determined primarily by the relative loudness of the pronunciation of the syllable, and to a lesser extent, by its relative pitch and duration.) There are three factors that determine where the **stresses** (in the sense of the relatively stronger stresses, or "accents") will fall in a line of verse: (1) Most important is the "word accent" in polysyllabic words; in the noun "accent" itself, for example, the stress falls on the first syllable. (2) There are also many monosyllabic words in the language, and on which of these—in a sentence or a phrase—the stress will fall depends on the grammatical function of the word (we normally put stronger stress on nouns, verbs, and adjectives, for example, than on articles or prepositions), and also on the "rhetorical accent," or the emphasis we give a word because we want to enhance its importance in a particular utterance. (3) Another determinant of stress is the "metrical accent," which is an expected pulsation, in accordance with the stress-pattern which was established earlier in the metrical line or passage.

If the metrical accent enforces an alteration of the normal word accent, we get a **wrenched accent.** Wrenching may be the result of a lack of metrical skill; it was, however, conventional in the *folk ballad* (for example, "fair ladié," "far countreé"), and is sometimes deliberately used, as in Byron's *Don Juan* and in the verses of Ogden Nash, for comic effects.

It is possible to distinguish various degrees of relative stress in English speech, but the most common and generally useful fashion of analyzing and classifying the standard English meters is to distinguish only two categories of stress in syllables—weak stress and strong stress—and to group the syllables into metric feet according to the patterning of these two stresses. A **foot** is the combination of a strong stress and the associated weak stress or stresses which make up the recurrent metric unit of a line. The relatively stronger-stressed syllable is called, for short, "stressed"; the relatively weaker-stressed syllables are called "light," or "slack," or simply "unstressed."

The four standard feet distinguished in English are:

(1) **Iambic** (the noun is "iamb"): a light followed by a stressed syllable.

The cúr few tólls the knéll of pár ting dáy.

> (Gray, "Elegy in a Country Churchyard")

(2) **Anapestic** (the noun is "anapest"): two light syllables followed by a stressed syllable.

The Ás sŷr ian cáme dówn like a wólf on the fóld.

> (Byron, "The Destruction of Sennacherib")

(3) **Trochaic** (the noun is "trochee"): A stressed followed by a light syllable.

Thére they áre, mý fíf tý mén and wó men.

> (Browning, "One Word More")

Most trochaic lines lack the final syllable—in the technical term, such lines are **catalectic.** So in Blake's "The Tiger":

Tí ger ! tí ger ! burn ing bríght

In the fó rest of the níght.

(4) **Dactylic** (the noun is "dactyl"): a stressed syllable followed by two light syllables.

/ ◡ ◡ / | / ◡ ◡ / |
Éve, with her ' bás ket, wás

/ ◡ ◡ / | / ◡ ◡ / |
Deép in the ' bélls and gráss.

(Ralph Hodgson, "Eve")

Iambs and anapests, since the strong stress is at the end, constitute a "rising meter"; trochees and dactyls, with the strong stress at the beginning, constitute a "falling meter." Iambs and trochees, with two syllables, are called "duple meter"; anapests and dactyls, with three syllables, are called "triple meter." It should be noted that the iamb is by far the commonest English foot.

Two other feet, often distinguished, occur only as occasional variants from standard feet:

(5) **Spondaic** (the noun is "spondee"): two successive syllables with approximately equal strong stresses, as in the first two feet of this line:

/ / | / / | ◡ / | ◡ / | ◡ / |
Good strong ' thick stu pe fy ing in cense smoke.

(Browning, "The Bishop Orders His Tomb")

(6) **Pyrrhic** (the noun is also "pyrrhic"): two successive syllables with approximately equal light stresses, as in the second and fourth feet in this line:

/ ◡ | ◡ ◡ | ◡ / | ◡ ◡ | ◡ / ◡ |
My way ' is to ' be gin ' with the ' be gin ning

(Byron, *Don Juan*)

(Some traditional metrists do not admit the existence of a true pyrrhic, on the grounds that the prevailing metrical accent—in this instance, iambic—always imposes a slightly stronger stress on one of the two syllables.)

A metric line is named according to the number of feet composing it:

monometer: one foot
dimeter: two feet
trimeter: three feet
tetrameter: four feet
pentameter: five feet
hexameter: six feet (an **Alexandrine** is a line of six iambic feet)
heptameter: seven feet (a **fourteener** is a line of seven iambic feet; it tends to break into a unit of four feet followed by a unit of three feet)
octameter: eight feet

To describe the meter of a line we name (a) the predominant foot and (b) the number of feet it contains. In the illustrations above, for example, the line from Gray's "Elegy" is "iambic pentameter," and the line from Byron's "The Destruction of Sennacherib" is "anapestic tetrameter."

To **scan** a passage of verse is to go through it line by line, analyzing the component feet, and also indicating where any major pauses fall within a line. Here is a **scansion,** signified by conventional symbols, of the first five lines from Keats's *Endymion*: the passage was chosen because it exemplifies a flexible and variable rather than a highly regular metrical pattern.

1) Ă thíng │ ŏf beaú tў │ ĭs │ ă jŏy │ fŏr ĕ vĕr:

2) Ĭts lóve │ lĭ nĕss │ ĭn creás ĕs; ∥ ĭt │ wĭll név ĕr

3) Páss ĭn tŏ nóth │ĭng nĕss, │ ∥ bŭt stíll │ wĭll keép

4) Ă bów ĕr quí et fŏr ŭs, ∥ ănd │ ă sleép

5) Fúll ŏf │ swĕet dreáms, │ ănd heálth, │ ănd quí et breáth ĭng.

The prevailing meter is clearly iambic, and the lines are iambic pentameter. As in all fluent verse, however, there are "variations" upon the basic iambic foot:

(a) The closing feet of lines 1, 2, and 5 end with an extra light syllable, and are said to have a **feminine ending.** Lines 3 and 4, in which the closing feet, since they are standard iambs, end with a stressed syllable, are said to have **masculine endings.**

(b) In lines 3 and 5, the opening iambic feet have been "inverted" to form trochees. (These initial positions are the most common place for such inversions in iambic verse.)

(c) I have marked the second foot in line 2, and the third foot of line 3 and line 4, as pyrrhics (two light stresses). This is a procedure with which competent readers often disagree: some will feel enough of a metric beat in all these feet to mark them as iambs; others will mark still other feet (for example, the third foot of line 1) as pyrrhics also. And some metric analysts prefer to use symbols measuring two degrees of strong stress, and will indicate a difference in the feet, as follows:

Ĭts lóve lĭ nĕss ĭn creás es.

Notice, however, that these are differences in nuance rather than in essentials: the readers agree that the prevailing pulse of Keats's versification is iambic throughout.

Two other elements are important in the metric movement of Keats's passage: (1) In lines 1 and 5, the pause in the reading—which occurs naturally at the end of a syntactic phrase or clause—coincides with the end of the line; such lines are called **end-stopped.** Lines 2 through 4, on the other hand, are called **run-on lines** (or in a French term, they exhibit **enjambement**—"a striding-over"), because the pressure of the incompleted syntactic unit toward closure carries on over the end of the verse-line. (2) When a strong phrasal pause falls within a line, as in lines 2, 3, and 4, it is called a **caesura**—indicated in the quoted passage by the conventional symbol, //. The management of these internal pauses is important for giving variety and for providing rhetorical emphases in the long pentameter line.

To understand the function of such scansion, we must realize that it is an abstract scheme which deliberately omits notation of ˙many physical attributes of the actual reading of a poem that contribute to its movement and total impression. It does not specify, for example, whether the component words in a metric line are short words or long words, or whether the strong stresses fall on short vowels or long vowels; nor does it give any indication of the "intonation," or voice melody—the overall rise and fall of the pitch and loudness of the voice—which we use to bring out the meaning and rhetorical effect of these poetic lines. We deliberately omit such details in order to lay bare the essential metric skeleton; that is, the fall of the stronger stresses in the syllabic sequence. Moreover, an actual reading of a poem, if it is a skillful reading, will not accord mechanically with the scansion. That is, there is a difference between the scansion, as an abstract metrical paradigm or norm, and the oral "performance" of a poem; and in fact, no two readers will perform the same lines in precisely the same way. But the metric norm indicated by the scansion is sensed as an implicit understructure of pulses, and the interplay of an expressive performance, sometimes with and sometimes against this underlying structural pattern, helps to give tension and vitality to our experience of a poem.

We should note, finally, that various kinds of English versification differ from the syllable-and-stress type already described:

(1) **Strong-stress meters.** In this native English meter only the strong stresses count in the scanning, and the number of intervening light syllables is indeterminate and variable. There are usually four stressed syllables in a line. This was the meter of Old English poetry and of many Middle English poems, until Chaucer popularized the syllable-and-stress meter. In the opening passage, for example, of *Piers Plowman* (latter fourteenth century) the four strong stresses (always divided by a medial caesura) are often reinforced by allitera-

tion (see *alliterative meter*); the light syllables, which vary in number, are recessive and do not assert their individual presence:

> In a sómer séson, // whan sóft was the sónne,
>
> I shópe me in shroúdes, // as Í a shépe were,
>
> In hábits like an héremite, // unhóly of wórkes,
>
> Went wýde in this wórld, // wónders to hére.

This type of meter still survives in traditional children's rhymes, and was revived as an artful literary meter by Coleridge in *Christabel*, in which each line has four strong stresses and the number of syllables in a line may vary from four to twelve.

What G. M. Hopkins called his **sprung rhythm** is a variant of strong-stress meter: each foot, as he describes it, begins with a stressed syllable, which may stand alone, or else be associated with from one to three (occasionally even more) light syllables. Two six-stress lines from Hopkins' "The Wreck of the *Deutschland*" indicate the variety of the rhythms in this meter, and also exemplify its most striking feature: the great weight of the strong stresses, and the frequent juxtaposition of strong stresses at any point in the line. The stresses in the second line were marked in a manuscript by Hopkins himself; they indicate that in complex instances, his metric decisions may be rather arbitrary:

> The sóur scythe crínge, and the bléar sháre cóme.
>
> Our héarts' charity's héarth's fíre, our thóughts' chivalry's
>
> thróng's Lórd.

(See Elisabeth Schneider, "Sprung Rhythm," *PMLA*, LXXX, 1965). A number of modern metrists, such as T. S. Eliot and Ezra Pound, skillfully interweave both strong-stress and syllable-and-stress meters in some of their versification.

(2) **Quantitative meters** in English are written in imitation of Greek and Latin versification, in which the metrical pattern is not determined by the stress but by the "quantity" (duration of pronunciation) of a syllable, and the foot consists of a combination of "long" and "short" syllables. Sidney, Spenser, and other Elizabethan poets experimented with this meter in English, as did Coleridge, Tennyson, Longfellow, and Robert Bridges later on. The strong accentual character of English, however, as well as the indeterminateness of the syllabic duration,

makes it impossible to sustain a purely quantitative meter in that language.

(3) In *free verse*, the component lines have no (or at least only occasional) units of recurrent stress-patterns.

George Saintsbury, *Historical Manual of English Prosody* (1910), and R. M. Alden, *English Verse* (1930), are well-illustrated treatments of traditional syllable-and-stress metrics. For later discussions of this and alternative metric theories see George R. Stewart, *The Technique of English Verse* (1930); Seymour Chatman, *A Theory of Meter* (1965); Karl Shapiro and Robert Beum, *A Prosody Handbook* (1965); and W. K. Wimsatt, Jr., and M. C. Beardsley, "The Concept of Meter" (1959). This last essay is reprinted in W. K. Wimsatt, *Hateful Contraries* (1965), and in Harvey Gross, ed., *The Structure of Verse* (1966)—an anthology which reprints other essays, including Northrop Frye, "The Rhythm of Recurrence," and Yvor Winters, "The Audible Reading of Poetry."

MIDDLE ENGLISH PERIOD. The four and one-half centuries between the Norman Conquest in 1066, which effected radical changes in both the language and culture of England, and about 1500, when the standard literary language (deriving from the dialect of the London area) had become recognizably "modern English"—that is, the language we speak and write today.

The span from 1100 to 1350 is sometimes discriminated as the **Anglo-Norman period,** because the non-Latin literature of that time was written mainly in Anglo-Norman, the French dialect spoken by the new ruling class of England. When the native vernacular, descended from Anglo-Saxon and known as "Middle English," came into general literary use, it was at first the vehicle mainly for religious and homiletic writings. The first great age of primarily secular literature was the second half of the fourteenth century—the age of Chaucer and John Gower, of William Langland's great religious and satirical poem *Piers Plowman,* and of the anonymous master who wrote four fine poems in complex alliterative measures, including the elegy *Pearl* and *Gawain and the Green Knight.* This last poem is by far the best of the English metrical romances; the best prose romance was Thomas Malory's *Morte d'Arthur,* written a century later. The outstanding poets of the fifteenth century were the "Scottish Chaucerians," who included King James I of Scotland and Robert Henryson. The fifteenth century was more important for popular literature than for the artful literature written for the upper classes: it was the age of many excellent songs, secular and religious, and of many of the best folk ballads, as well as the flowering time of the popular medieval drama, the *miracle* and *morality plays.*

See W. L. Renwick and H. Orton, *The Beginnings of English Literature to Skelton* (rev. ed., 1952); H. S. Bennett, *Chaucer and the Fifteenth Century* (1947); Edward Vasta, ed., *Middle English Survey: Critical Essays* (1965).

MIRACLE PLAYS, MORALITY PLAYS, and INTERLUDES were all types of late medieval drama, written in a variety of verse forms.

The **miracle play** had as its subject a story from the Scriptures, or else the life and martyrdom of a saint. (In the usage of some historians of drama "miracle play" denotes only dramas based on saints' lives, and the term **mystery play** is applied to dramas based on the Old and New Testaments.) The biblical plays originated within the church in about the tenth century, in dramatizations of brief parts of the Latin liturgical service; gradually these evolved into complete plays which were written in the vernacular, produced under the auspices of the trade guilds, and acted on stages outside the church. The miracle plays written in England are of unknown authorship. In the fourteenth century there developed the practice, on the feast of Corpus Christi (sixty days after Easter), of putting on great "cycles" of such plays, representing in chronological order crucial events in the biblical history of mankind, from the Creation and Fall of man, through the Nativity, Crucifixion, and Resurrection of Christ, to the Last Judgment. Each scene was played on a separate "pageant wagon," which was drawn, in its proper sequence, to the various fixed "stations" in a city where the entire cycle was enacted. The biblical subject matter was greatly expanded in these plays, and the author often added comic scenes of his own invention. For examples of the variety, vitality, and power of these dramas, see the Wakefield "Noah" and "Second Shepherd's Play," and the Brome "Abraham and Isaac."

Morality plays were dramatized *allegories* of the life of man, his temptation and sinning, his quest for salvation, and his confrontation by death. The hero represents Mankind, or Everyman; among the other characters are personifications of virtues, vices, and Death, as well as angels and demons who contest the possession of the soul of man. A character known as **the Vice** often played the role of the tempter in a fashion both sinister and comic; he is regarded by some literary historians as a predecessor both of the cynical and ironic villain and of some of the comic figures in Elizabethan drama, including Falstaff. The best-known morality play is the fifteenth-century *Everyman*; another fine example, written early in the same century, is *The Castle of Perseverance*.

Interlude (Latin, "between the play") is a term applied to a variety of short entertainments, including secular farces and witty dialogues with a religious or political point. In the late fifteenth and early sixteenth centuries, these little dramas were performed by bands of professional actors; it is believed that they were often put on between the courses of a feast or between the acts of a longer play. Among the better-known interludes are John Heywood's farces, especially *The Four PP* (that is, the Palmer, the Pardoner, the 'Pothecary, and the Pedler, who engage in a lying contest), and *Johan Johan the Husband, Tyb His Wife, and Sir John the Priest.*

See A. W. Pollard, *English Miracle Plays, Moralities, and Interludes* (1890); A. P. Rossiter, **English Drama from Early Times to the Elizabethans* (1950); Hardin Craig, *English Religious Drama of the Middle Ages* (1955); Arnold Williams, *The Drama of Medieval England* (1961); T. W. Craik, *The Tudor Interlude* (1962); V. A. Kolve, *The Play Called Corpus Christi* (1966). On the relation of "the Vice" in the morality plays to figures in Shakespearean drama, see Bernard Spivak, *Shakespeare and the Allegory of Evil* (1958).

MODERN PERIOD.   The term "modern" is, of course, highly variable in its temporal reference, but it is frequently applied to the literature written since the beginning of World War I in 1914. This half-century has been one of the outstanding periods in English and American literature. It has been marked by persistent and multidimensioned experiments in subject matter and form, and has produced major achievements in all the literary genres. The poets include Yeats, Frost, Eliot, Wallace Stevens, Auden, Robert Graves, Robert Lowell, and Dylan Thomas; the novelists, Conrad, Joyce, Lawrence, Virginia Woolf, E. M. Forster, Ernest Hemingway, F. Scott Fitzgerald, and William Faulkner; the dramatists, G. B. Shaw, Sean O'Casey, Eugene O'Neill, Tennessee Williams, and Samuel Beckett; and the critics, T. S. Eliot, I. A. Richards, F. R. Leavis, Lionel Trilling, and the American *New Critics.*

MOTIF and THEME.   A **motif** is an element—a type of incident, device, or formula—which recurs frequently in literature. The "loathly lady" who turns out to be a beautiful princess is a common motif in *folklore.* The man fatally bewitched by a fairy lady is a motif adopted from folklore in Keats's "La Belle Dame sans Merci." Common in lyric poems is the **ubi sunt motif,** or "where-are" formula for lamenting the vanished past ("Where are the snows of yesteryear?"); another is the *carpe diem* motif, whose nature is sufficiently indicated by Robert Herrick's title, "To the Virgins, to Make Much of Time." An older term for such recurrent poetic concepts or formulas is the **topos** (Greek for "a commonplace"). The term "motif," or the German

leitmotif (a guiding motif), is also applied to the frequent repetition of a significant phrase or set description in a single work, as in the operas of Richard Wagner, or in novels by Thomas Mann, James Joyce, Virginia Woolf, and William Faulkner.

Theme is sometimes used interchangeably with motif, but the term is more usefully applied to a thesis or doctrine which an imaginative work is designed to incorporate and make persuasive to the reader. Milton states as the theme of *Paradise Lost* to "assert Eternal Providence, / And justify the ways of God to men"; see *Didactic Literature*. In modern criticism it is often claimed that all nontrivial works of literature, including lyric poems, involve an implicit conceptual "theme" which is embodied and dramatized in the evolving meanings and imagery; see, for example, Cleanth Brooks, *The Well-Wrought Urn* (1947).

MYTH.   In classical Greek, "mythos" signified any story or plot, whether true or false. In its central modern significance, a myth is one story in a **mythology**—a system of hereditary stories which were once believed to be true by a particular cultural group, and which served to explain (in terms of the intentions and actions of supernatural beings) why the world is as it is and things happen as they do, and to establish the rationale for social customs and observances and the sanctions for the rules by which men conduct their lives. Most myths involve rituals—prescribed forms of sacred ceremonials—but social anthropologists disagree as to whether rituals generated myths or myths generated rituals. If the protagonist is a man rather than a supernatural being, the story is usually not called myth but **legend;** if the story concerns supernatural beings, but is not part of a systematic mythology, it is usually classified as a *folktale*.

A mythology, we can say, is any religion in which we no longer believe. Poets, however, long after having ceased to believe in them, have persisted in using the myths of Jupiter, Venus, Prometheus, Wotan, Adam and Eve, and Jonah for their plots, episodes, or allusions; as Coleridge said, "still doth the old instinct bring back the old names." The term has also been extended to denote supernatural tales which are deliberately invented by their authors. Plato used such myths in order to project philosophical speculation beyond the point at which certain knowledge is possible; see, for example, his "Myth of Er" in Book X of *The Republic*. The German Romantic writers, F. W. J. Schelling and Friedrich Schlegel, proposed that to write great literature, modern poets must develop a new unifying mythology which will synthesize the insights of the myths of the Western past with the new discoveries of philosophy and physical science. In the same period in England William Blake, who felt "I must create a system or be enslaved by another man's," incorporated in his poems a mythology he had himself created by fusing hereditary myths with his own intuitions and visions. A number of modern writers have also asserted that an integrative mythology, whether inherited or invented, is essential to literature. Joyce in *Ulysses* and *Finnegans Wake*, Eliot in *The Waste Land*, O'Neill in *Mourning Becomes Electra*, and many other writers have deliberately woven their modern materials on the pattern of ancient myths; while Yeats, like Blake, undertook to construct his own systematic mythology, which he expounded in *A Vision* (1926) and embodied in a number of great lyric poems.

Myth has become one of the most prominent terms in contemporary literary analysis. A large group of writers, the **myth critics**—including Robert Graves, Francis Fergusson, Richard Chase, Philip Wheelwright, Leslie Fiedler, and (now the most influential) Northrop Frye —view the genres and individual plot patterns of all (or almost all) literature, including what on the surface are highly sophisticated and realistic works, as recurrences of certain *archetypes* and essential mythic formulas. As Northrop Frye puts it, "the typical forms of myth become the conventions and genres of literature." According to Frye's theory, there are four main narrative genres—comedy, romance, tragedy, and irony (satire)—and these are "displaced" modes of the four elemental forms of myth, associated with the seasonal cycle of spring, summer, autumn, and winter. (See *Genre*.)

The student should be alert to the bewildering variety of applications of the term "myth" in contemporary criticism. In addition to the meanings already described, its uses range all the way from a widely held fallacy ("the myth of progress," "the American success myth") to the solidly imagined realm in which a work of fiction is enacted ("Faulkner's myth of Yoknapatawpha County," "the mythical world of *Moby Dick*").

On classical mythology consult H. J. Rose, *A Handbook of Greek Mythology* (1939), and G. M. Kirkwood, *A Short Guide to Classical Mythology* (1959). Among studies of myths especially influential for modern literature and criticism are Sir J. G. Frazer, *The Golden Bough* (rev. ed., 1911); Jessie Weston, *From Ritual to Romance* (1920); Jane E. Harrison, *Themis* (2d ed., 1927); F. R. R. S. Raglan, *The Hero* (1936). For the theory and practice of myth criticism see Francis Fergusson, *The Idea of a Theater* (1949); Richard Chase, *Quest for Myth* (1949); Philip Wheelwright, *The Burning Fountain* (1954); Leslie Fiedler, *Love and Death in the American Novel* (1960); Northrop Frye, *Anatomy of Criticism* (1957), and "Literature and Myth" in *Relations of Literary Study*, ed. James Thorpe (1967). This last essay has a useful bibliography both of the theory and history of myths and of the exponents of myth criticism.

NEOCLASSIC and ROMANTIC. The simplest use of these troublesome terms is as noncommittal names for periods of English literature. In this application, the "neoclassic period" spans the hundred and forty years or so after the Restoration (1660), and the "romantic period" extends from the outbreak of the French Revolution in 1789— or alternatively, from the publication of *Lyrical Ballads* in 1798— through the first three decades of the nineteenth century. Historians, however, have often tried to "define" neoclassicism or romanticism, as though each term denoted a single essence which was shared, to varying degrees, by all the major writings of an age. But literary history does not seem to have formed itself around such simple entities, and the numerous and conflicting single definitions of neoclassicism and romanticism are either so vague as to be next to meaningless or so specific as to fall far short of equating with the great range and variety of the literary facts.

A more useful undertaking is to specify certain salient attributes of literary theory and practice, common to a number of the important writers of the neoclassic period, which serve to distinguish them from major writers of the romantic period. The following list of ideas and characteristics, largely shared by such authors as Dryden, Pope, Addison, Swift, Johnson, Goldsmith, and Edmund Burke may serve as an introductory sketch of **neoclassic** literature:

(1) These authors manifested a strong traditionalism, which was often joined to a distrust of radical innovation, and was evidenced above all in their immense respect for classical writers (especially Roman writers), who were thought to have established the enduring models, and to have achieved an unapproachable level of excellence, in most of the major literary *genres.* Hence the term "neoclassic."

(2) Literature was conceived to be primarily an "art"; one which, though it requires innate talents, must be perfected by long study and practice, and which consists mainly in the deliberate adaptation of known and tested means to the achievement of foreseen ends upon the audience of readers. The neoclassic ideal, founded especially on Horace's *Ars Poetica*, is the craftsman's ideal, demanding the utmost finish, correction, and attention to detail. Special allowances were often made for the unerring freedom of "natural geniuses," and also for happy strokes, available even to some less gifted poets, which occur without premeditation and achieve, as Pope said, "a grace beyond the reach of art." But the natural genius like Homer or Shake-

speare is a rarity, and probably a thing of the past, and to even the best of artful poets, literary "graces" come only occasionally. The neoclassic writer strove, therefore, for "correctness," was careful to observe the complex demands of stylistic *decorum*, and for the most part respected the established "rules" of his art. The **rules of poetry** were, in theory, the essential properties of the various genres (such as epic, tragedy, comedy, pastoral) that have been abstracted from classical works whose long survival has proved their excellence. These properties, such as the *three unities*, many believed, must be embodied in modern works if they too are to be excellent and to survive.

(3) Man, and especially man as an integral part of an organized society, was regarded as the primary source of poetic subject matter. Poetry is an imitation of human life—"a mirror held up to nature." And by the human actions it imitates, and the artistic form it gives to the imitation, poetry was designed to yield both instruction and aesthetic pleasure to the men who read it. Not art for art's sake, but art for *man's* sake was the ideal of neoclassic humanism.

(4) Both in the subject matter and the appeal of art, emphasis was placed on what men possess in common—representative characteristics, and widely shared experiences, thoughts, feelings, and tastes. "True wit," Pope said in a much quoted passage, is "what oft was thought but ne'er so well expressed." That is, a primary aim of poetry is to give new and perfect expression to the great commonplaces of human wisdom, whose prevalence and durability are the best warrant of their importance and truth. There was also insistence, it should be noted, on the need to balance or enhance the typical and the familiar with the opposing qualities of novelty, particularity, and invention. Johnson substituted for Pope's definition of true wit the statement that wit "is at once natural and *new*," and praised Shakespeare because, while his characters are all species, they are all "discriminated" and "distinct." But there was wide agreement that the general nature of mankind is the basic source and test of art; and also, that the fact of universal consent, everywhere and always, is the best test of moral and religious, as well as aesthetic, truth. (See *Deism.*)

(5) Neoclassic writers, like the philosophers of the time, viewed man as an essentially limited being who ought to address himself to accessible goals. Many of the great works of the period, satiric and didactic, attack man's "pride," or presumption beyond the natural limits of his species, and enforce the lesson of the golden mean (the avoidance of extremes) and of man's need to submit to his restricted position in the order of things—an order often envisioned as a natural hierarchy, or *great chain of being.* In art, as in life, there prevailed the law of measure and the acceptance of strict limits upon one's

freedom. The poets admired extremely the great genres of epic and tragedy, but wrote their own masterpieces in admittedly lesser forms such as the essay in verse and prose, the comedy of manners, and especially satire, in which they felt they had more chance to equal or surpass their English predecessors. They gladly submitted to at least some rules and other limiting conventions in their subjects, structure, and diction. Typical was their election, in many of their poems, to write within the extremely tight restrictions of the *closed couplet*. But the essence of the urbane and civilized poetry of the neoclassic period is "the art that hides art"; that is, the seeming freedom and triumphant ease with which, at its best, it meets the challenge set by traditional and drastically restrictive patterns.

Here are some aspects in which **romantic** ideals and writings in the first three decades of the nineteenth century differ most conspicuously from the neoclassic:

(1) The prevailing attitude favored innovation instead of traditionalism in the materials, forms, and style of literature, without regard to classical precedent. Romantic poetry began with a kind of "manifesto," or statement of revolutionary aims, in the Preface to the second edition of Wordsworth and Coleridge's *Lyrical Ballads* (1800). This Preface, written by Wordsworth, denounced the poetic diction of the preceding century and proposed to deal with materials from "common life" in "a selection of language really used by men." The serious or tragic treatment of lowly subjects in common language violated the basic neoclassic rule of decorum, which asserted that the serious genres should deal with high subjects in an appropriately elevated style. Other innovations in the period were the exploitation by Coleridge, Keats, and others of the realm of the supernatural and of "the far away and the long ago"; the assumption by Blake, Wordsworth, and Shelley of the persona of a poet-prophet who writes a visionary mode of poetry; and the use of poetic *symbolism* (especially by Blake and Shelley) deriving from a world view in which objects are charged with a significance beyond their physical qualities. "I always seek in what I see," as Shelley said, "the likeness of something beyond the present and tangible object."

(2) In his Preface to *Lyrical Ballads* Wordsworth repeatedly described good poetry as "the spontaneous overflow of powerful feelings." According to this point of view poetry is not a mirror of men in action; its essential element, on the contrary, is the poet's own feelings, while the process of composition, being "spontaneous," is the opposite of the artful manipulation of means to foreseen ends stressed by the neoclassic critics. (See *expressive criticism*.) Wordsworth care-

fully qualified this radical doctrine by describing his poetry as "emotion recollected in tranquillity," and by specifying that a proper spontaneity is the result of a prior process of deep reflection, and may be followed by second thoughts and revisions. But the immediate act of composition, if a poem is to be genuine, must be spontaneous—that is, unforced, and free of what Wordsworth decried as the "artificial" rules and conventions of his neoclassic predecessors. "If poetry comes not as naturally as the leaves to a tree," Keats wrote, "it had better not come at all." The philosophical-minded Coleridge opposed to neoclassic rules, imposed by the poet from without, the concept of the organic "laws" of the *imagination*: each poetic work, like a growing plant, evolving according to its inherent principles into its final form.

(3) To an extraordinary degree external nature—the landscape, together with its flora and fauna—became a persistent subject of poetry, and was described with an accuracy and sensuous nuance unprecedented in earlier writers. It is a mistake, however, to describe romantic poets as simply "nature poets." While many major poems by Wordsworth and Coleridge—and to a lesser extent by Shelley and Keats—set out from and return to an aspect or change of aspect in the landscape, the outer scene is not presented for its own sake, but only as a stimulus for the poet to engage in the most characteristic human activity, that of thinking. The important romantic poems are in fact poems of feelingful meditation about an important human problem. Wordsworth said that it is "the Mind of Man" which is "my haunt, and the main region of my song."

(4) Neoclassic poetry was about other men, but much of romantic poetry represented the poet himself, either directly, as in Wordsworth's *Prelude* and a number of romantic lyric poems, or in altered but recognizable form, as in Byron's *Childe Harold*. In prose we find a parallel vogue in the revealingly personal essays of Lamb and Hazlitt and in a number of spiritual and intellectual autobiographies—De Quincey's *Confessions of an English Opium Eater*, Coleridge's *Biographia Literaria*, and Carlyle's fictionalized *Sartor Resartus*. And whether the romantic subject was the poet himself or someone else, he was no longer part of an organized society but, typically, a solitary figure engaged in a long—and sometimes infinitely elusive—quest; often he was a social nonconformist or outcast. Many important romantic works had as protagonist the rebel, whether for good or ill: Prometheus, Cain, the Wandering Jew, the Satanic hero-villain, or the great outlaw.

(5) What seemed the infinite promise of the French Revolution fostered the sense in writers of the romantic period that theirs was a great age of new beginnings and high possibilities. Many writers viewed man as a being of limitless aspiration toward the infinite good

envisioned by the poet's faculty of imagination. "Our destiny," Wordsworth says in a moment of insight in *The Prelude*, "our being's heart and home, / Is with infinitude, and only there," and with the desire for "something evermore about to be." "Less than everything," Blake announced, "cannot satisfy man." Man's unquenchable aspiration beyond his limits, which to the neoclassic moralist had been his tragic error, now became man's glory and his triumph over the pettiness of circumstance. In a parallel way, the earlier judgment that the highest art is the perfect achievement of limited aims gave way to a dissatisfaction with inherited rules and imposed restrictions. According to a number of romantic writers, the highest art consists in the intrepid attempt beyond possibility; as a result, neoclassical satisfaction in the perfectly accomplished, because limited, enterprise was replaced by a preference for the glory of the imperfect, in which the artist's very failure attested the grandeur of his aim. Romantic writers once more entered into competition with their greatest predecessors in audacious long poems in the most exacting genres: Wordsworth's *Prelude* (a personal re-rendering of the themes of Milton's *Paradise Lost*); Blake's visionary and prophetic epics; Shelley's *Prometheus Unbound* (emulating Greek drama); Keats's Miltonic epic, *Hyperion*; and Byron's ironic conspectus of all modern European civilization, *Don Juan*.

See *Enlightenment*, and refer to: R. S. Crane, "Neoclassical Criticism," in *Dictionary of World Literature*, ed. Joseph T. Shipley (1943); A. O. Lovejoy, *Essays in the History of Ideas* (1948); James Sutherland, *A Preface to Eighteenth Century Poetry* (1948); W. J. Bate, *From Classic to Romantic* (1948); Harold Bloom, *The Visionary Company: A Reading of English Romantic Poetry* (1961); René Wellek, "The Concept of Romanticism in Literary History" and "Romanticism Re-examined," in *Concepts of Criticism* (1963); Northrop Frye, ed., *Romanticism Reconsidered* (1963); and Frye, *A Study of English Romanticism* (1968); M. H. Abrams, *The Mirror and the Lamp: Romantic Theory and the Critical Tradition* (1953), and *Natural Supernaturalism: Tradition and Revolution in Romantic Literature* (1970). A useful collection of essays that define or discuss romanticism is Robert F. Gleckner and Gerald E. Enscoe, eds., *Romanticism: Points of View* (2d ed., 1970).

NEW CRITICISM.   This term became current after the publication of John Crowe Ransom's book, *The New Criticism* (1941). It has come to be applied to a widespread tendency in recent American criticism, deriving in part from various elements in I. A. Richards' *Principles of Literary Criticism* (1924) and *Science and Poetry* (1926), and from the critical essays of T. S. Eliot. Notable critics in this mode are

Cleanth Brooks and Robert Penn Warren; their textbook, *Understanding Poetry*, first published in 1938, did much to make the new criticism the reigning point of view in American colleges, and even in high schools. Other prominent writers often identified as new critics are Allen Tate, R. P. Blackmur, J. C. Ransom, and William K. Wimsatt, Jr. An important English writer who shares some critical tenets and practices with these Americans is F. R. Leavis.

The new critics differ from one another in many ways, but the following points of view and procedures are common to many of them: (1) A poem, it is held, should be treated *qua* poem, as an object in itself—or in Eliot's words, "primarily as poetry and not another thing." The first law of criticism, John Crowe Ransom said, "is that it shall be objective, shall cite the nature of the object" and shall recognize "the autonomy of the work itself as existing for its own sake." (See *objective criticism*.) New critics warn the reader against such temptations to lose sight of the object itself as the *intentional fallacy* and the *affective fallacy*; and in analyzing and evaluating a particular work, they usually eschew recourse to the biography of the author, to the social conditions at the time of its production, or to its psychological and moral effects on the reader; they also tend to minimize recourse to the history of literary genres and subject matter. (2) The distinctive procedure of the new critic is **explication,** or **close reading:** the detailed and subtle analysis of the complex interrelations and *ambiguities* (multiple meanings) of the component elements within a work. "Explication de text" has long been a formal procedure for teaching literature in French schools, but the distinctive explicative procedure of the new criticism derives from such books as I. A. Richards' *Practical Criticism* (1929) and William Empson's *Seven Types of Ambiguity* (1930). (3) The principles of the new criticism are basically verbal. That is, literature is conceived to be a special kind of language whose attributes are defined by systematic opposition to the language of science and of logical discourse, and the key concepts of this criticism deal with the meanings and interactions of words, figures of speech, and symbols. There is great emphasis on the "organic unity" of structure and meaning, and warnings against separating the two by what Cleanth Brooks has called "the heresy of paraphrase." (4) The distinction between literary *genres*, although casually recognized, is not essential in the new criticism. The basic components of any work of literature, whether lyric, narrative, or dramatic, are conceived to be words, images, and symbols rather than character, thought, and plot. These linguistic elements are often said to be organized around a central *theme*, and to manifest "tension," "irony," and "paradox" within a structure which is a "reconciliation of diverse impulses" or an "equilibrium of opposed forces." The form of a work, whether or not it has characters and plot, is said to be primarily a "structure of meanings," and to develop mainly through a play and counterplay of evolving "thematic imagery" and "symbolic action."

The revolutionary thrust of the new criticism had lost much of its force by the late 1950s, when a number of new critics began to re-assay and broaden their critical premises and procedures, but it has left a permanent mark on the criticism of literature, in the primary emphasis on the individual work as such, and in the variety and subtlety of the devices made available for literary analysis.

Central instances of the theory and practice of the new criticism are Cleanth Brooks, *The Well-Wrought Urn* (1947), and W. K. Wimsatt, Jr., *The Verbal Icon* (1954). Robert W. Stallman's *Critiques and Essays in Criticism, 1920–1948* (1949) is a convenient collection of essays, most of which are in this critical mode; the literary journal, *The Explicator* (1942 ff.), devoted to close reading, is a characteristic product of its approach to literary texts. See also Wimsatt, ed., *Explication as Criticism* (1963); and, for critiques of the theory and method of the new criticism, R. S. Crane, ed., *Critics and Criticism, Ancient and Modern* (1952), and his *The Languages of Criticism and the Structure of Poetry* (1953).

NOVEL.   The term **novel** is now applied to a great variety of writings that have in common only the attribute of being extended works of prose *fiction*. As an extended narrative, the novel is distinguished from the *short story* and from the work of middle length called the "novelette"; its magnitude permits a greater variety of characters, greater complication of plot (or plots), an ampler development of milieu, and a more sustained and subtle exploration of character than do the shorter, hence necessarily more concentrated, modes. As a prose narrative, the novel is distinguished from the long verse nar-ratives of Chaucer, Spenser, and Milton which, beginning with the eighteenth century, it has increasingly supplanted. Within these limits the novel includes such diverse works as Richardson's *Pamela* and Sterne's *Tristram Shandy*; Dickens' *Pickwick Papers* and Henry James's *The Wings of the Dove*; Hemingway's *The Sun Also Rises* and Joyce's *Ulysses*; C. P. Snow's *Strangers and Brothers* and Nabokov's *Ada or Ardor*.

The term for the novel in most European languages is "roman," which is a derivative from the medieval "romance." The English name for the form, however, is derived from the Italian **novella** (meaning "a little new thing"), which was a short tale in prose. In fourteenth-century Italy there was a great vogue for collections of *novelle*, some serious and some scandalous; the best known of these collections is Boccaccio's *Decameron*, which is still available in English translation at any well-stocked bookstore.

Another important predecessor of the novel was the **picaresque narrative,** which emerged in sixteenth-century Spain, although the most popular instance, *Gil Blas* (1715), was written by the Frenchman Le Sage. "Picaro" is Spanish for "rogue," and the typical story has for its subject the escapades of an insouciant rascal who lives by his wits, and shows little if any alteration of character through the long succession of his adventures; picaresque fiction is realistic in manner, episodic in structure, and usually satiric in aim. We recognize the survival of the type in many later novels such as Mark Twain's *Huckleberry Finn* and Saul Bellow's *The Adventures of Augie March.* The development of the novel owes much to works which, like the picaresque story, were written to deflate romantic or idealized fictional forms. Many *novelle* were of this sort, and Cervantes' great *Don Quixote* (1605)—in which an engaging madman who tries to live by the ideals of chivalric romance is used to explore the role of illusion and reality in life—was the single most important progenitor of the modern novel.

After these precedents and many others, including the seventeenth-century *character* (a brief sketch of a typical personality or way of life), the novel as we now think of it emerged in England in the early eighteenth century. In 1719 Daniel Defoe wrote *Robinson Crusoe,* and in 1722 *Moll Flanders.* Both of these are picaresque in type, in the sense that they are a sequence of episodes held together largely because they happened to one person; and Moll is herself a colorful female version of the old *picaro*—"twelve Year a Whore, five times a Wife (whereof once to her own Brother), Twelve Year a Thief, Eight Year a Transported Felon in Virginia," as the title page resoundingly informs us. But *Robinson Crusoe* is given an enforced unity of action by its focus on the problem of surviving on an uninhabited island, while both stories present so convincing a central character, set in so solid and factually realized a world, that Defoe is often credited with writing the first true "novels of incident."

The credit for having written the first English "novel of character" is nearly unanimously given to Samuel Richardson for his *Pamela; or, Virtue Rewarded* (1740). *Pamela* is the story of a sentimental but shrewd young woman who, by prudently safeguarding her chastity, succeeds in becoming the wife of a wild young gentleman instead of becoming a debauched servant girl. The distinction between the novel of incident and the novel of character cannot be drawn sharply; but in the novel of incident the greater weight of interest is on what the character will do next and on how the story will come out; in the novel of character, it is on his motives for what he does, and on how he as a person will turn out.

Pamela, like its greater and tragic successor, Richardson's *Clarissa* (1747–1748), is an **epistolary novel;** that is, the narrative is conveyed entirely by an exchange of letters. Later novelists have preferred alternative devices for limiting the narrative *point of view* to one or another single character, but the epistolary technique is still occasionally revived—for example, in Mark Harris' hilarious novel, *Wake Up, Stupid* (1959).

Novels may have any kind of plot form—tragic, comic, satiric, or romantic. A distinction—which was introduced by Hawthorne (for example, in his Preface to *The House of the Seven Gables*) and has been adopted and expanded by a number of recent critics—is that between two basic types of prose fiction: the novel proper and the "romance." The novel is characterized as the fictional attempt to give the effect of realism, by representing complex characters with mixed motives who are rooted in a social class, operate in a highly developed social structure, interact with many other characters, and undergo plausible and everyday modes of experience. The **prose romance** has as its ancestors the *chivalric romance* of the Middle Ages and the *Gothic novel* of the latter eighteenth century. It typically deploys simplified characters, larger than life, who are sharply discriminated as heroes and villains, masters and victims; the protagonist is often solitary, and isolated from a social context; the plot emphasizes adventure, and is often cast in the form of the quest for an ideal, or the pursuit of an enemy; and the nonrealistic and occasionally melodramatic events are sometimes claimed to project in symbolic form the primal desires, hopes, and terrors in the depths of the human mind, and to be therefore analogous to the materials of dream, myth, ritual, and folklore. Examples of romance novels (as distinct from the realistic novels of Jane Austen, George Eliot, or Henry James) are Walter Scott's *Rob Roy*, Emily Brontë's *Wuthering Heights*, and the mainstream of American fiction, from Poe, Cooper, Hawthorne, Melville, and Mark Twain to William Faulkner and Saul Bellow. See Richard Chase, **The American Novel and Its Tradition* (1957); Northrop Frye, "The Mythos of Summer: Romance," in **Anatomy of Criticism* (1957); and the essays on romance in **Pastoral and Romance*, ed. Eleanor T. Lincoln (1969).

Other common classifications of novel types are based on differences in subject matter, emphasis, and artistic purpose:

Bildungsroman and **Erziehungsroman** are German terms signifying "novels of formation" or "novels of education." The subject of these novels is the development of the protagonist's mind and character, as he passes from childhood through varied experiences—and usually through a spiritual crisis—into maturity and the recognition of his identity and role in the world. The vogue was begun by Goethe's *Wilhelm Meister's Apprenticeship* (1795–1796) and includes Thomas Mann's *The Magic Mountain* and Somerset Maugham's *Of Human Bondage*. An important subtype of the Bildungsroman is the **Künstlerroman** ("artist-novel"), which represents the development of a novelist or other artist into the stage of maturity in which he recognizes his artistic destiny and achieves mastery of his artistic craft. Instances of this type include some of the major twentieth-century novels: Proust's *Remembrance of Things Past*, Joyce's *A Portrait of the Artist as a Young Man*, Mann's *Tonio Kröger* and *Dr. Faustus*, Gide's *The Counterfeiters*. See Susanne Howe, *Wilhelm Meister and His English Kinsmen* (1930); Maurice Beebe, *Ivory Towers and Sacred Founts: The Artist as Hero in Fiction* (1964).

The **sociological novel** emphasizes the influence of social and economic conditions on characters and events; often it also embodies an implicit or explicit thesis recommending social reform: H. B. Stowe's *Uncle Tom's Cabin*, Upton Sinclair's *The Jungle*, John Steinbeck's *The Grapes of Wrath*.

The **historical novel** takes its setting and some of its characters and events from history; the term is usually applied only if the historical milieu and events are fairly elaborately developed, and important to the central narrative: Scott's *Ivanhoe*, Dickens' *A Tale of Two Cities*, Kenneth Roberts' *Northwest Passage*. See Georg Lukacs, °*The Historical Novel* (1962).

The **regional novel** emphasizes the setting, speech, and customs of a particular locality, not merely as *local color*, but as important conditions affecting the temperament of the characters, and their ways of thinking, feeling, and acting: "Wessex" in Hardy's novels, and "Yoknapatawpha County," Mississippi, in Faulkner's.

Since its flowering time in the second half of the nineteenth century, the novel has displaced all other literary forms in popularity, and has replaced long verse narratives almost entirely. The novelistic art has received the devoted attention of some of the supreme craftsmen of modern literature—Flaubert, Henry James, Proust, Mann, and Joyce. There has been constant experimentation with new fictional techniques and procedures, such as the control of the *point of view* so as to minimize the apparent role of the author-narrator, the use of *symbolist* and *expressionist* techniques and of devices adopted from the art of the cinema, the dislocation of time-sequence, the adaptation of forms and motifs from myths and dreams, and the exploitation of the *stream of consciousness* method in a way that converts the narrative of outer action and events into a drama of the life of the mind. Henry James's Prefaces, gathered into one volume as *The Art of the Novel* (1934), exemplify the care and subtlety lavished on the craft of fiction, while the novels of Proust, Joyce, Virginia Woolf, and Faulkner show how drastic—and successful—have been modern innovations in narrative methods, form, and the interrelations of the novelistic parts.

In recent decades such experimentation has reached a radical extreme. Vladimir Nabokov is a supreme technician who writes "involuted fiction" (a work whose subject involves its own author, genesis, and development—for example, his *Pale Fire*), employs multilingual puns and jokes, incorporates strategies from chess, crossword puzzles, and other games, parodies other novels (and his own as well), and sets elaborate traps for the unwary reader. This is also the era of what is sometimes called the **anti-novel**—that is, a work which is deliberately constructed in a negative fashion, relying for its effects on omitting or annihilating traditional elements of the novel, and on playing against the expectations established in the reader by the novelistic methods and conventions of the past. Thus Alain Robbe-Grillet, a leader among the exponents of the *nouveau roman,* the **new novel,** in France, has written a work, *Jealousy* (1957), in which he leaves out such standard novelistic elements as plot, characterization, descriptions of states of mind, normal relations of time and space, and some frame of reference for the guidance of the reader. We are simply presented in this work with a sequence of perceptions, mainly visual, from which we eventually infer that we are occupying the physical space and sharing the hyperacute observations of a jealous husband, and from which we are left to infer also the tortured state of his disintegrating mind.

In addition to the books already mentioned, refer to the following. Histories of the novel: E. A. Baker, *History of the English Novel* (12 vols.; 1924 ff.); Arnold Kettle, *An Introduction to the English Novel* (2 vols.; 1951); Dorothy Van Ghent, *The English Novel: Form and Function* (1953); Walter Allen, *The English Novel* (1954); Frank O'Connor, *The Mirror in the Roadway* (1956); Ian Watt, *The Rise of the Novel* (1957). The art of the novel: Percy Lubbock, *The Craft of Fiction* (1921); E. M. Forster, *Aspects of the Novel* (1927); Edwin Muir, *The Structure of the Novel* (1928); John W. Aldridge, ed., *Critiques and Essays on Modern Fiction* (1952); W. C. Booth, *The Rhetoric of Fiction* (1961); Laurent Le Sage, *The French New Novel* (1962).

OBJECTIVE and SUBJECTIVE. John Ruskin complained in 1856 that "German dullness and English affectation have of late much multiplied among us the use of two of the most objectionable words that were ever coined by the troublesomeness of metaphysicians—namely, 'objective' and 'subjective'." Ruskin was at least in part right. The words were imported into English criticism from the post-Kantian German critics of the later eighteenth century, and they have certainly been troublesome. Amid the endless variety of ways in which this opposition has been applied, one is sufficiently widespread to be worth specifying. A **subjective** work is one in which the author incorporates his own experiences or projects his personal disposition, judgments, values, and feeling. An **objective** work is one in which the author simply presents his invented situation or his fictional characters and their thoughts, feelings, and actions, himself seemingly remaining detached, and non-commital. Thus a subjective lyric is one in which we seem clearly invited to associate the "I," or lyric speaker, with the poet himself (Coleridge's "Frost at Midnight," Wordsworth's "Tintern Abbey," Shelley's "Ode to the West Wind"); in an objective lyric the speaker is obviously an invented character (Browning's "My Last Duchess," Eliot's "Love Song of J. Alfred Prufrock," Wallace Stevens' "Sunday Morning"). A subjective novel is one in which the author intervenes to comment and deliver judgments about the characters and actions he represents; an objective novel is one in which the author effaces himself, and seemingly leaves the story to tell itself. See *Persona* and *Point of view.*

On the introduction of these terms into English criticism, and something of the variousness of their application, see M. H. Abrams, *°The Mirror and the Lamp* (1953), pp. 235–244. For their application to modern criticism of the novel, see W. C. Booth, *°The Rhetoric of Fiction* (1961), Chap. 3.

OBJECTIVE CORRELATIVE is a term rather casually introduced by T. S. Eliot in an essay on "Hamlet and His Problems" (1919) whose subsequent vogue in literary criticism, Eliot has confessed, astonished its inventor. "The only way of expressing emotion in the form of art is by finding an 'objective correlative'; in other words, a set of objects, a situation, a chain of events which shall be the formula of that *particular* emotion," and which will evoke the same emotion from the reader. Eliot's formulation has been often criticized for falsifying the way a poet actually composes, since no object or situation is in itself a "formula" for an emotion, but depends for its emotional significance and effect on the way it is rendered by the poet. The vogue of Eliot's concept is due in part to its accord with the modern reaction against vagueness and the direct statement of feelings in poetry—an oft-cited example is Shelley's "Indian Serenade": "I die, I faint, I fail"—in favor of definiteness, impersonality, and descriptive concreteness.

See Eliseo Vivas, "The Objective Correlative of T. S. Eliot," reprinted in *Critiques and Essays in Criticism*, ed. R. W. Stallman (1949).

OCCASIONAL POEMS   are written to adorn or memorialize a specific occasion, such as a birthday, a marriage, a death, a military engagement or victory, the dedication of a public building, or the opening performance of a play. Spenser's "Epithalamion," Milton's "Lycidas," Marvell's "An Horatian Ode upon Cromwell's Return from Ireland," and Tennyson's "The Charge of the Light Brigade" are poems that have survived their occasions. Yeats's "Easter, 1916" and Auden's "September 1, 1939" are notable modern examples. The English poet laureate is often called on to meet the emergency of royal anniversaries and important public events with an appropriate literary effort.

ODE.   An ode is a long lyric poem, serious in subject, elevated in style, and elaborate in its stanzaic structure. As Norman Maclean has said, the term now calls to mind a lyric which is "massive, public in its proclamations, and Pindaric in its classical prototype" ("From Action to Image," in *Critics and Criticism*, ed. R. S. Crane, 1952). The prototype was established by the Greek poet Pindar, whose odes were modeled on the songs by the *chorus* in drama. His complex stanzas were patterned in sets of three: moving in a dance rhythm to the left, the chorus chanted the **strophe;** moving to the right, the **antistrophe;** then, standing still, the **epode.**

The **regular** or **Pindaric ode** in English is a learned imitation of Pindar's form, with all the strophes and antistrophes written in one kind of stanza, and all the epodes in another; the typical construction may be conveniently studied in Thomas Gray's "The Progress of Poesy." The **irregular ode** was introduced in 1656 by Abraham Cowley, who imitated the Pindaric style and matter but disregarded the recurrent strophic triad, allowing each stanza to find its own pattern of varying line lengths, number of lines, and rhyme scheme. This type of irregular stanzaic structure, altering freely in accordance with shifts in subject and mood, has been the most common for the English ode ever since; Wordsworth's great "Ode: Intimations of Immortality" is representative.

Pindar's odes were "encomiastic," or written to praise and glorify someone—in this instance, the winners in the Olympic games. The earlier English odes, and many later ones, were also written to eulogize something: either a person (Dryden's "Anne Killigrew"), or the arts of music or poetry (Dryden's "Alexander's Feast"), or a time of day (Collins' "Ode to Evening"), or abstract concepts (Gray's "Hymn to Adversity" and Wordsworth's "Ode to Duty"). Romantic poets perfected the personal ode of description and passionate meditation, which is stimulated by an aspect of the outer scene and turns on the attempt to solve either a private problem or a generally human one (Wordsworth's "Intimations" ode, Coleridge's "Dejection: An Ode," Shelley's "Ode to the West Wind"). Recent examples of this type are Allen Tate's "Ode to the Confederate Dead" and Wallace Stevens' "The Idea of Order at Key West."

The **Horatian ode** was originally modeled on the matter, tone, and form of the odes of the Roman Horace. In contrast to the passion and visionary boldness of Pindar's odes, Horatian odes are calm, meditative, and restrained, and they are usually **homostrophic**—that is, written in a single, repeated stanza form. Examples are Marvell's "An Horatian Ode upon Cromwell's Return from Ireland" and Keats's ode "To Autumn."

See Robert Shafer, *The English Ode to 1660* (1918); G. N. Shuster, *The English Ode from Milton to Keats* (1940); Maclean (see first paragraph); and Carol Maddison, *Apollo and the Nine: A History of the Ode* (1960)—this book includes a discussion of the odes of Pindar and Horace (Chap. 2).

OLD ENGLISH PERIOD, or the **Anglo-Saxon Period,** extended from the invasion of Celtic England by Germanic tribes (the Angles, Saxons, and Jutes) in the first half of the fifth century to the conquest of England in 1066 by the Norman French, led by William the Conqueror. Only after they had been converted to Christianity in the seventh century did the Anglo-Saxons, whose earlier literature had been oral, begin to develop a written literature. A high level of culture and learning was soon achieved in various monasteries; the eighth-century churchmen, Bede and Alcuin, were both major scholars who wrote in the standard language of international scholarship, Latin. The poetry written in the vernacular Anglo-Saxon included *Beowulf* (eighth century), the greatest of Germanic epic poems, and such lyric laments as "The Wanderer," "The Seafarer," and "Deor," all of which, though composed by Christian writers, reflect the conditions of life in the pagan past. Cynewulf was a poet who wrote on religious themes, and there survive a number of Old English saints' lives and paraphrases of books of the Bible. Alfred the Great, a West Saxon king (871–899) who for a time united all the kingdoms of southern England against a new wave of Germanic invaders, the Vikings, was no less important as a patron of literature than as a warrior. He himself translated into

Old English various books of Latin prose, supervised translations by other hands, and instituted the Anglo-Saxon Chronicle, a continuous record, year by year, of important events in England.

See H. M. Chadwick, *The Heroic Age* (1912); S. B. Greenfield, *A Critical History of Old English Literature* (1965); C. L. Wrenn, *A Study of Old English Literature* (1966).

ONOMATOPOEIA, sometimes called "echoism," is used both in a narrow and in a broad sense:

(1) In the narrow, and the more common, sense "onomatopoeia" is applied to a word, or a combination of words, whose sound seems to resemble the sound it denotes: "hiss," "buzz," "rattle," "bang." There is no exact duplication, however, of nonverbal by verbal sounds; the seeming similarity is due as much to the meaning, and to the feel of uttering the words, as to their sounds. Two lines from Tennyson's "Come Down, O Maid" are often cited as a skillful instance of onomatopoeia:

> The moan of doves in immemorial elms,
> And murmuring of innumerable bees.

John Crowe Ransom has remarked that by making only two changes in the consonants of the last line, we lose the echoic effect because we drastically change the meaning: "And murdering of innumerable beeves."

The sounds seemingly mimicked by onomatopoeic words need not be pleasant ones. Browning liked squishy and scratchy effects, as in "Meeting at Night":

> As I gain the cove with pushing prow,
> And quench its speed i'the slushy sand.

> A tap at the pane, the quick sharp scratch
> And blue spurt of a lighted match. . . .

(2) In the broad sense, "onomatopoeia" is applied to words or passages which seem to correspond to what they denote in any way whatever—in size, movement, or force, as well as sound. Alexander Pope recommends such extended verbal mimicry in his *Essay on Criticism* when he says "the sound should seem an echo of the sense," and goes on to illustrate by mimicking two different kinds of motion by the words and metrical movement of his lines:

> When Ajax strives some rock's vast weight to throw,
> The line too labors, and the words move slow;
> Not so when swift Camilla scours the plain,
> Flies o'er th'unbending corn, and skims along the main.

PANTOMIME and DUMB SHOW.   **Pantomime** is acting without speech, using only posture, gesture, bodily movement, and exaggerated facial expression to mime ("mimic") a character's actions and to express a character's feelings. Elaborate pantomimes, halfway between drama and dance, were put on in ancient Greece and Rome, and the form was revived, usually for comic purposes, in Renaissance Europe. Mimed dramas enjoyed a vogue in eighteenth-century England, and in the present century the silent movies encouraged a brief revival of the art and produced a superlative pantomimist in Charlie Chaplin. Miming survives in French masters such as Marcel Marceaux in the theater and Jacques Tati in the cinema, and England still retains the institution of the Christmas pantomime; in America, however, the sole surviving pure pantomimists are the circus clowns.

A **dumb show** is an episode of pantomime introduced into a spoken play. It was a common phenomenon in Elizabethan drama, in which it was used in imitation of Seneca, the Roman writer of tragedies. Two well-known dumb shows are the preliminary episode, summarizing the action to come, of the play-within-a-play in *Hamlet* (III. ii) and the miming of the banishment of the Duchess and her family in John Webster's *The Duchess of Malfi* (III. iv).

See R. J. Broadbent, *A History of Pantomime* (1901).

PARADOX.   A paradox is a statement which seems on its face to be self-contradictory or absurd, yet turns out to have a valid meaning. So, in the conclusion to Donne's sonnet, "Death, Be Not Proud":

> One short sleep past, we wake eternally
> And death shall be no more; *Death, thou shalt die.*

The paradox is used by almost all poets, but is a central device in *metaphysical poetry*, both in its religious and secular forms. John Donne, who wrote a collection of *Paradoxes and Problems* in prose, exploited the figure in his poetry. "The Canonization," for example, is organized as an extended proof, full of local paradoxes, of the paradoxical thesis that sexual lovers are saints.

If the paradoxical utterance combines two terms that in ordinary usage are contraries, it is called an **oxymoron;** an example is Tennyson's "O *Death in life*, the days that are no more." The oxymoron was a familiar type of *Petrarchan conceit* in Elizabethan love poetry, in phrases like "pleasing pains," "I burn and freeze," "loving hate." It is also a frequent figure in devotional prose and religious poetry, as a way of expressing the Christian mysteries, which transcend human sense and logic. As Milton describes the appearance of God, in *Paradise Lost* (III, 380):

Dark with excessive bright thy skirts appear.

Paradox is a central concern of many *New Critics*, who extend the application of the term from the rhetorical figure to encompass all surprising deviations from, or qualifications of, common perceptions or commonplace opinions. It is only in this greatly expanded sense of the term that Cleanth Brooks is able to claim, with some plausibility, that "the language of poetry is the language of paradox." (See *The Well-Wrought Urn* [1947], page 3.)

PASTORAL.   The originator of the pastoral was Theocritus, a Greek of the third century B.C. who wrote poems that represented the life of Sicilian shepherds. ("Pastor" is Latin for "shepherd.") Vergil later imitated Theocritus in his Latin *Eclogues* and established the enduring model for the traditional **pastoral:** an elaborately conventional poem expressing an urban poet's nostalgic image of the peace and simplicity of the life of shepherds and other rural folk in an idealized natural setting. The *conventions* that hundreds of later poets imitated from Vergil's imitations of Theocritus include a shepherd reclining under a spreading beech and meditating the rural muse, or piping as though he would ne'er grow old, or engaging in a friendly singing contest, or expressing his good or bad fortune with a lovely mistress, or grieving over the death of a fellow shepherd. From this last type developed the *pastoral elegy*, which persisted long after the other traditional types had ceased to be written. Other terms used synonomously with pastoral are **idyl,** from the title of Theocritus' pastorals; **eclogue** (literally, "a selection"), from the title of Vergil's pastorals; and **bucolic poetry,** from the Greek word for "herdsman."

Classical poets often described the pastoral life in terms of the lost golden age; later Christian pastoralists combined allusions to the golden age and to the Garden of Eden, and also exploited the symbolism of "shepherd" (the ecclesiastical or parish "pastor," the Good Shepherd) to give many pastoral poems a Christian range of reference. In the Renaissance the traditional pastoral was also adapted to satirical and allegorical uses. Spenser's *Shepherd's Calendar* (1579) included most of the varieties of pastoral poems current in this period.

Such was the vogue of the pastoral dream that Renaissance writers incorporated it into various other literary forms. Sidney's *Arcadia* was a long pastoral romance written in an elaborately artful prose. (**Arcadia** was a mountainous region of Greece which Vergil substituted for Theocritus' Sicily as his idealized pastoral milieu.) There was also the pastoral lyric (Marlowe's "The Passionate Shepherd to His Love"), and the pastoral drama. Fletcher's *The Faithful Shep-*

herdess is an example of this last type, and Shakespeare's *As You Like It*, based on a pastoral romance by Thomas Lodge, centers on the forest of Arden, a green refuge from the troubles and complications of ordinary life, where all enmities are reconciled, all problems resolved, and the course of true love made to run smooth.

The last important collection of traditional pastorals, and an extreme instance of the calculated and graceful display of high artifice, was Pope's *Pastorals* (1709). Five years later John Gay's *Shepherd's Week* burlesqued the type by applying its elegant formulas to the crudity of actual rustic manners and language, and inadvertently showed the way to the seriously realistic treatment of rural life. In 1783 George Crabbe published *The Village* specifically in order to

paint the cot
As Truth will paint it and as bards will not.

How far the term then lost its traditional application is indicated by Wordsworth's title for his realistic rendering of a rural tragedy in 1800: "Michael, a Pastoral Poem."

In recent decades the term "pastoral" has been expanded in various special ways. William Empson, for example, identifies as pastoral any work which contrasts simple and complicated life, to the advantage of the former: the simple life may be that of the shepherd, the child, or the working man, and it is used as an oblique way to criticize the class structure of society. Empson thus applies the term to works ranging from Marvell's poem "The Garden" to *Alice in Wonderland* and the proletarian novel. Other critics apply the term "pastoral" to any work which envisions a withdrawal from ordinary life to a place apart, close to the elemental rhythms of nature, where a man achieves a new perspective on life in the real and complex world.

See W. W. Gregg, *Pastoral Poetry and Pastoral Drama* (1906); the Introduction to *English Pastoral Poetry from the Beginnings to Marvell,* ed. Frank Kermode (1952); and for modern expansions of the concept, William Empson, *Some Versions of Pastoral* (1950), and Eleanor T. Lincoln, ed., *Pastoral and Romance: Modern Essays in Criticism* (1969).

PATHETIC FALLACY was a phrase invented by John Ruskin in 1856 to signify the attribution to natural objects of human capacities and feelings (*Modern Painters*, Vol. III, Chap. 12). As used by Ruskin—for whom "truth" was a primary artistic criterion—the term was derogatory, since it applies to descriptions, not of the "true appearances of things to us," but of "the extraordinary, or false appearances, when we are under the influence of emotion, or contemplative fancy." Two of his examples are the lines

> The spendthrift crocus, bursting through the mould
> Naked and shivering, with his cup of gold,

and Coleridge's description in "Christabel" of

> The one red leaf, the last of its clan,
> That dances as often as dance it can.

These passages, Ruskin says, however beautiful, are false and "morbid"; only in the greatest inspired poets is the use of the pathetic fallacy valid, at those rare times at which it would be inhuman to resist the pressure of powerful feelings to humanize the perceived fact.

Ruskin's contention would make not only his great romantic predecessors, but even Shakespeare, "morbid." His term is now used, for the most part, as a neutral name for a common phenomenon in descriptive poetry, in which the ascription of human traits to inanimate nature is less formally managed than in the figure called *personification*.

See Josephine Miles, *Pathetic Fallacy in the Nineteenth Century* (1942); Harold Bloom, ed., *The Literary Criticism of John Ruskin* (1965), Introduction, and pp. 62–78.

PATHOS   in Greek meant the passions, or deep feeling generally; in modern criticism, however, it is attributed to a scene or passage designed to evoke the feelings of tenderness, pity, or sympathetic sorrow from the audience. In the Victorian era a number of prominent writers exploited pathos beyond the endurance of most readers today —examples are the rendering of the death of Little Nell in Dickens' *The Old Curiosity Shop* and of the death of little Eva in Harriet Beecher Stowe's *Uncle Tom's Cabin*. (See *Sentimentalism*.) The greatest passages of literary pathos do not dwell on the pathetic circumstances but achieve the effect by understatement and omission; for example, the speech of King Lear when he is briefly reunited with Cordelia (IV. vii. 59 ff.), beginning

> Pray, do not mock me.
> I am a very foolish fond old man,

or Wordsworth's simple summation of the grief of the old man in *Michael* (11. 464–466):

> Many and many a day he thither went,
> And never lifted up a single stone.

PERIODS OF ENGLISH LITERATURE.   For convenience of discussion, historians divide the continuity of English literature into segments which are called "periods." The exact number, names, and dates of these periods vary, but the following listing conforms to widespread practice. Each period is discussed in a separate essay in this *Glossary*.

450–1066	Old English (or Anglo-Saxon) Period
1066–1500	Middle English Period
1500–1660	The Renaissance
	1558–1603 Elizabethan Age
	1603–1625 Jacobean Age
	1625–1649 Caroline Age
	1649–1660 Commonwealth Period (or, Puritan Interregnum)
1660–1798	The Neoclassical Period
	1660–1700 The Restoration
	1700–1745 The Augustan Age (or, Age of Pope)
	1745–1798 The Age of Sensibility (or, Age of Johnson)
1798–1832	The Romantic Period
1832–1901	The Victorian Period
1901–1914	The Edwardian Period
1914–	The Modern Period
	1910–1936 The Georgian Period

PERSONA, TONE, and VOICE. These terms, increasingly frequent in criticism, reflect the recent tendency to think of a work of literature, whether lyric or narrative, as a mode of speech. The concept of literature as speech implies a speaker of the total work who has determinate personal qualities, and who expresses attitudes both toward the characters and materials within his work and toward the audience to whom he addresses the work. In his *Rhetoric* Aristotle, followed by other classical rhetoricians, long ago pointed out that an orator establishes in the course of his oration an **ethos**—a personal character which itself functions as a means of persuasion; for if the personal image he projects is that of a man of rectitude, intelligence, and goodwill, the audience is instinctively inclined to give credence to him and to his arguments. The current concern with the nature and function of the author's presence in a work of imaginative literature is related to this traditional concept, and is part of the growing rhetorical emphasis in modern criticism. (See *Rhetoric and rhetorical criticism*.)

The application of the terms "persona," "tone," and "voice" varies greatly from one critic to another, and involves some of the most subtle and difficult concepts in modern philosophy and social psychology—concepts such as "the self," "personal identity," "role-playing," "sincerity." This essay will merely sketch some central uses of these terms which have proved useful in analyzing our experience with diverse works of literature.

Persona was the Latin word for the "mask" used by actors in the classical theater, from which was derived the term "dramatis personae" for the characters in a drama, and ultimately, the English word "person," a particular individual. In recent literary discussion "persona" is often applied to the first-person narrator, the "I," of a narrative poem or novel, or the lyric speaker whose voice we listen to in a lyric poem. Examples of personae are the visionary first-person narrator of Milton's *Paradise Lost* (who in the opening passages of various books discourses at some length about himself); the Gulliver who tells us about his misadventures in *Gulliver's Travels*; the "I" who carries on most of the conversation in Pope's satiric dialogue *Epistle to Dr. Arbuthnot*; the urbane and genial narrator of Fielding's *Tom Jones*, who pauses frequently for leisurely discourse with his reader; the speaker who talks first to himself, then to his sister, in Wordsworth's "Tintern Abbey"; the speaker who utters Keats's "Ode to a Nightingale," from "My heart aches" at the beginning to the ending: "Fled is that music:—Do I wake or sleep?"; and the Duke who tells the emissary about his former wife in Browning's "My Last Duchess." By calling these speakers "personae" (some critics also call them "masks") we stress the fact that they are all part of the fiction, characters invented for a particular artistic purpose. That the "I" in each of these works is not the author as he exists in his everyday life is obvious enough in the case of Swift's Gulliver and Browning's Duke, less obvious in the case of Milton, Pope, and Fielding, and does not seem obvious at all to an unsophisticated reader of the lyric poems of Wordsworth and Keats, in which we seem invited to identify the speaker with the poet himself. But even these lyric speakers exist at some remove from the men who wrote the poems, and were devised to play a role in a particular situation and to conduce to a particular effect. In each of the major lyricists the nature of the persona alters, sometimes subtly and sometimes radically, from one of his lyrics to the next. The speaker of Donne's "A Valediction: Forbidding Mourning" is very different from that of his "The Flea"; and the "I" in Wordsworth's "We Are Seven" is not identical with that of the "Intimations" ode, and neither of these with the speaker of his "Ode to Duty." (See *Lyric*.)

The modern preoccupation with **tone** dates mainly from I. A. Richards' definition of the term as expressing a literary speaker's "attitude to his listener." "The tone of his utterance reflects . . . his sense of how he stands toward those he is addressing" (*Practical Criticism*, 1929, Chaps. 1 and 3). The sense in which the word is used is indicated in the phrase "tone of voice"; the way a person speaks subtly reveals his concept of the social level, intelligence, and sensitivity of his auditor, his personal relation to him, and the stance he adopts toward him. The tone of a speech can be formal or intimate, outspoken or reticent, abstruse or simple, solemn or playful, arrogant or prayerful, angry or loving, serious or ironic, condescending or obsequious, and so on through numberless possible nuances of attitude and relationship. We can describe the tone of the speeches of characters within a narrative or dramatic work, but most current discussions deal specifically with the tone of the narrative or lyric persona himself, as he tells his story, or talks to himself, or to a nightingale, or directly to the reader. And some critical uses of "tone" are much broader, and coincide in reference with what other critics prefer to call "voice."

Voice, in a recently evolved usage, signifies the equivalent in imaginative literature to Aristotle's "ethos" in a work of persuasive rhetoric, and suggests also the traditional rhetorician's concern with the importance of the physical voice. The term in criticism points to the fact that there is a voice beyond the fictitious voices in a work, and a person behind all the *dramatis personae*, including even the first-person narrator persona. We have the sense of an all-pervasive presence, a determinate intelligence and moral sensibility, which has selected, ordered, rendered, and expressed these literary materials in just this way. The particular qualities of the author's ethos, or voice, in *Tom Jones* manifest themselves, among other things, in the fact that he has chosen to create the wise and worldly persona who ostensibly tells, and talks to the reader about, the tale. The sense of a distinctive authorial presence is no less evident in the work of writers who, unlike Fielding, pursue a strict policy of authorial noninterference, and by effacing themselves, try to give the impression that the story tells itself (see *Point of view*). There is great diversity in the quality of the authorial mind, temperament, and sensibility which pervades works, all of them "objective" in narrative technique, such as Joyce's *Ulysses*, Virginia Woolf's *Mrs. Dalloway*, Hemingway's "The Killers," and Faulkner's *The Sound and the Fury*.

Of the critics listed below who deal with this concept, Wayne C. Booth prefers the term **implied author** over "voice," in order better to indicate that the reader of a work of fiction has the sense not only of the timbre of a speaking voice, but of a total human presence. Booth's view is that this implied author is "an ideal, literary, created version of the real man"—that is, the implied author, no less than the specific narrative persona, is part of the total fiction, whom the author gradually brings into being in the course of his composition, and who plays an important role in the total effect of a work on the reader. Critics such as W. J. Ong, on the other hand, distinguish between an author's "false voice" and his "true voice," and regard the latter as the expression of the author's genuine self or identity; as they see it, for a writer to discover his true "voice" is to discover himself. All these diverse critics agree, however, that the sense of a convincing authorial presence, whose values, beliefs, and moral vision are the implicit controlling forces throughout a work, serves to persuade the reader to yield to the work that unstinting imaginative consent without which a poem or novel remains nothing more than an elaborate verbal game.

See Richard Ellmann, *Yeats: The Man and the Masks* (1948)—which discusses Yeats's theory of a poet's "masks" or "personae," both in his life and his art; Reuben Brower, "The Speaking Voice," in *Fields of Light* (1951); M. H. Abrams, ed., *Literature and Belief* (1958); James McConkey, "The Voice of the Writer," *University of Kansas City Review*, XXV (1958); W. C. Booth, *The Rhetoric of Fiction* (1961), Chap. 3; W. J. Ong, "A Dialectic of Aural and Objective Correlative" and "Voice as Summons for Belief," in *The Barbarian Within* (1962); J. O. Perry, ed., *Approaches to the Poem* (1965)—Sec. III, "Tone, Voice, Sensibility," includes selections from I. A. Richards, Reuben Brower, and W. J. Ong.

PLATONIC LOVE. In Plato's *Symposium* 210–212, Socrates recounts the doctrine of Eros (love) imparted to him by the wise woman Diotima. She bids us not to linger in the love elicited by the beauty manifested in a single human body, but to mount up as by a stair, "from one going on to two, and from two to all fair forms," and from the beauty of the body to the beauty of the mind, until we arrive at the contemplation of the Idea of "beauty absolute, separate, simple, and everlasting." From this Ideal Beauty the human soul is in exile, and of it the passing beauties of the body and of the entire world of sense are only distant and distorted reflections. Plotinus and other **Neoplatonists** (the "new Platonists," a school of Platonic philosophers of the third to the fifth century A.D.) developed the theory that all goodness, truth, and beauty in the sensible world are "emanations" (radiations) from the One or Absolute, who is the source of all being and value. From both Platonic and Neoplatonic sources Christian thinkers of the Italian Renaissance developed the theory that the true beauty of the body is only the outer manifestation of a moral and spiritual beauty of the soul, which in turn is rayed out from the absolute beauty of the one God himself. The Platonic lover reverences the physical beauty of his beloved only as a sign of the spiritual beauty that she shares with all other beautiful women, and regards her bodily beauty as the lowest rung on a ladder that leads up from sensual desire to the pure contemplation of Heavenly Beauty in God.

Some version of this idea of Platonic love is to be found in Dante and Petrarch, and in many Italian, French, and English writers of sonnets and other love poems during the Renaissance. See, for example, the exposition in Book IV of Castiglione's *The Courtier* (1528), and in Spenser's "An Hymn in Honor of Beauty." As Spenser wrote in one of the sonnets he called *Amoretti*:

> Men call you fayre, and you doe credit it. . . .
> But only that is permanent and free
> From frayle corruption, that doth flesh ensew.
> That is true beautie: that doth argue you
> To be divine and borne of heavenly seed:
> Derived from that fayre spirit, from whom al true
> And perfect beauty did at first proceed.

From this complex religious and philosophical doctrine, the modern notion that Platonic love is simply love divorced from sexual desire is a vulgarized abstraction.

The concept of Platonic love has fascinated later poets, especially Shelley; see his "Epipsychidion." But his friend Byron took a skeptical view of such lofty claims for the human Eros-impulse. "Oh Plato! Plato!" Byron sighed,

> you have paved the way,
> With your confounded fantasies, to more
> Immoral conduct by the fancied sway
> Your system feigns o'er the controlless core
> Of human hearts, than all the long array
> Of poets and romancers. . . .
> *(Don Juan, I. cxvi)*

See Plato's *Symposium* and *Phaedrus*, and the exposition of Plato's doctrine of Eros in G. M. A. Grube, *Plato's Thought* (1935), Chap. 3. Refer to J. S. Harrison, *Platonism in English Poetry of the Sixteenth and Seventeenth Centuries* (1903); Paul Shorey, *Platonism Ancient and Modern* (1938); George Santayana, "Platonic Love in Some Italian Poets," *Selected Critical Writings*, ed. Norman Henfrey (2 vols.; 1968), I, 41–59.

PLOT. The plot in a dramatic or narrative work is the structure of its actions, as these are ordered and rendered toward achieving particular emotional and artistic effects. This definition is deceptively simple, because the actions (including verbal as well as physical actions) are performed by particular characters in a work, and are the means by which they exhibit their moral and dispositional qualities. Plot and *character* are therefore interdependent critical concepts—as Henry James has said, "What is character but the determination of incident?

What is incident but the illustration of character?" Notice also that there is a difference between the plot and a mere synopsis of the course of events in a work of literature. As we usually summarize a work, we say that first this happens, then that, then that. . . . It is only when we say how this is related to that and that, and in what ways all these matters are rendered and organized so as to achieve their particular effects, that a synopsis begins to be adequate to the actual plot.

There are a great variety of plot forms. For example, some plots are designed to achieve tragic effects, and others to achieve the effects of comedy, romance, or satire (see *Genres*). Each of these types in turn exhibits an indefinite variety of plot patterns, and may be represented in the mode of drama or of narrative, and in verse or in prose. The following terms, widely current in criticism, are useful in analyzing the component elements of plots and in helping to discriminate among some traditional types of plots.

The chief character of a work, on whom our interest centers, is called the **protagonist** or **hero,** and if he is pitted against an important opponent, that character is called an **antagonist.** Hamlet is the protagonist and King Claudius the antagonist in Shakespeare's play, and the relation between them is one of **conflict.** Many, but far from all, plots deal with a conflict (Thornton Wilder's *Our Town*, for example, does not). In addition to the conflict between individuals, there may be the conflict of a protagonist against fate, or against the circumstances that stand between him and a goal he has set himself; and in some works, the conflict is between opposing desires or values in a character's own mind.

If a character sets up a scheme which depends for its success on the ignorance or gullibility of the person or persons against whom it is directed, it is called an **intrigue.** Iago intrigues against Othello and Cassio in Shakespeare's tragedy *Othello.* A number of comedies, including Ben Jonson's *Volpone* and many Restoration plays (for example, Congreve's *The Way of the World* and Wycherley's *The Country Wife*), have plots which turn largely on the success or failure of an intrigue.

As a plot progresses it arouses expectations in the audience or reader about the future course of events. An anxious uncertainty about what is going to happen, especially to those characters whose moral qualities are such that we have established a bond of sympathy with them, is known as **suspense.** If what in fact happens violates our expectations, it is known as **surprise.** The interplay of suspense and surprise is a prime source of the magnetic power and vitality of an on-going plot. The most effective surprise is one which turns out, in retrospect, to have been well grounded in what has gone before, even though we have hitherto made the wrong inference from the given facts of circumstance and character. As E. M. Forster put it, the shock of the unexpected, "followed by the feeling, 'oh, that's all right,' is a sign that all is well with the plot." A "surprise ending" in the pejorative sense is one in which the author resolves the plot without adequate earlier grounds in characterization or events, often by the use of coincidence; there are numerous examples in the short stories of O. Henry. *Dramatic irony* is a special kind of suspenseful expectation, when we foresee the oncoming disaster or triumph but the character does not.

A plot has **unity of action** (that is, it is "an artistic whole") if it is a single, complete, and ordered structure of actions, all directed toward the intended effect, in which none of the component parts, or **incidents,** is unnecessary, and as Aristotle said (*Poetics*, sec. 8), all the parts are "so closely connected that the transposal or withdrawal of any one of them will disjoint and dislocate the whole." Aristotle claimed that it does not constitute a unified plot to present a series of episodes which are strung together into a single narrative because they happen to a single character. Many *picaresque narratives*, nevertheless, such as Defoe's *Moll Flanders*, have held the interest of readers for centuries with this episodic plot structure; while even so tightly integrated a plot as that of Fielding's *Tom Jones* introduces, for variety's sake, a long, digressive story by the Man of the Hill.

A successful development which Aristotle did not foresee is the type of structural unity that can be achieved with **double plots,** familiar in Elizabethan drama. A **subplot**—a second story that is complete and interesting in its own right—is introduced into the play, and when it is skillfully managed, it serves to broaden our perspective on the main plot and to enhance rather than diffuse the overall effect. This underplot may have either the relation of analogy to the main plot (the Gloucester story in *King Lear*) or of counterpoint against it (the comic subplot involving Falstaff in *Henry IV*, Part 1). Spenser's *Faerie Queene* is an instance of a narrative romance which interweaves main plots and subplots into an intricately controlled integrity, in a way which C. S. Lewis compares to the polyphonic art of contemporary Elizabethan music.

The order of a unified plot, Aristotle pointed out, is a continuous sequence of beginning, middle, and end. The beginning initiates the action in a way which looks forward to something more; the middle presumes what has gone before and requires something to follow; and the end follows from what has gone before but requires nothing further: we are satisfied that the plot is complete. The beginning (the "initiating action," or "point of attack") need not be the actual opening stage of the specific events brought to a climax in the narrative or play. The epic, for example, plunges *in medias res* (see *Epic*), many short stories begin at the point of the climax itself, and the writer of a drama often captures our attention with a representative incident, close to an event which precipitates the central situation or conflict. Thus *Romeo and Juliet* opens with a street fight between the servants of two great houses, and *Hamlet* with the apparition of a ghost; the necessary **exposition** of antecedent matters—the feud between the Capulets and Montagues, or the posture of affairs in the Royal House of Denmark— Shakespeare weaves rapidly and skillfully into the dialogue and action of these startling opening scenes. In the novel, the modern drama, and especially the motion picture, such exposition is sometimes managed by **flashbacks:** interpolated narratives or scenes (which may be justified as a memory or a revery, or as a confession by one of the characters) which represent events that happened before the point at which the work opened. Arthur Miller's play *Death of a Salesman* and Ingmar Bergman's film *Wild Strawberries* make persistent and skillful use of this device.

The German critic Gustav Freytag, in *Technique of the Drama* (1863), characterized the typical plot of a five-act play as a pyramidal shape, consisting of a rising action, climax, and falling action. Although the total pattern that Freytag described applies to only a limited number of plays, various of his terms are frequently echoed by critics. As applied to *Hamlet*, for example, the **rising action** (the section that Aristotle called the **complication**) begins, after the opening scene and exposition, with the ghost's telling Hamlet that he has been murdered by his brother Claudius; it continues with the developing conflict between Hamlet and Claudius, in which Hamlet, despite setbacks, succeeds in controlling the course of events. The rising action reaches the **climax** of the hero's fortunes with his proof of the king's guilt by the device of the play within a play (Act III, scene ii). Then comes the **crisis,** or "turning point" of the fortunes of the protagonist, in his failure to kill the king while he is at prayer. This inaugurates the **falling action;** from now on the antagonist, Claudius, largely controls the course of events, until the **catastrophe,** in which the outcome is decided by the death of the hero, as well as of Claudius, the Queen, and Laertes. "Catastrophe" is usually applied to tragedy only; a more general term for this precipitating final scene, which is applied to both comedy and tragedy, is the **denouement** (French for "unknotting"): the action or intrigue ends in success or failure for the protagonist, the mystery is solved, or the misunderstanding cleared away.

In many plots the denouement involves a **reversal,** or **peripety,** in the hero's fortunes, whether to his failure or destruction, as in tragedy, or to his success, as in comic plots. The reversal frequently depends on a **discovery** (in Aristotle's Greek term, **anagnorisis**). This is the recognition by the protagonist of something hitherto unknown to him: Cesario reveals to the Duke at the end of *Twelfth Night* that he is really Viola; the fact of Iago's lying treachery dawns upon Othello; Fielding's Joseph Andrews discovers, on the evidence of a birthmark— "as fine a strawberry as ever grew in a garden"—that he is in reality the son of Mr. and Mrs. Wilson.

See Aristotle, *Poetics*; E. M. Forster, *Aspects of the Novel* (1927); R. S. Crane, "The Concept of Plot and the Plot of Tom Jones," in *Critics and Criticism* (1952); Humphry House, *Aristotle's Poetics* (1956); Elder Olson, *Tragedy and the Theory of Drama* (1966); Robert Scholes and Robert Kellog, *The Nature of Narrative* (1966).

POETIC DICTION.   The term **diction** signifies the selection of words in a work of literature. A writer's diction can be analyzed under such categories as the degree to which his vocabulary is abstract or concrete, Latinate or Anglo-Saxon in origin, colloquial or formal, technical or common, literal or figurative.

The poetry of almost all ages has been written in a special language, a "poetic diction," which includes words, phrases, a stylized syntax, and types of figures not current in the ordinary conversation of the time. In modern discussion, however, the term **poetic diction** is usually applied specifically to the special procedures of neoclassic writers who, like Thomas Gray, believed that "the language of the age is never the language of poetry" (letter to West, 1742). This diction was in part derived from the characteristic usage of admired earlier poets, such as Vergil, Spenser, and Milton, but was in part based on the reigning principle of *decorum*, according to which a poet must adapt the level and type of his diction to the mode and status of a particular genre. Formal satire, such as Pope's *Epistle to Arbuthnot*, because it represented a poet's direct commentary on everyday matters, permitted—indeed required—the use of language really spoken by an urbane and cultivated man of the time. But other genres, such as epic, tragedy, and ode, required a refined and special poetic diction to raise the style to the level of the form, while pastoral and descriptive poems employed a similar diction to enable them to manage lowly materials with appropriate dignity and elegance.

Prominent characteristics of much eighteenth-century poetic diction were its *archaism* and its use of recurrent *epithets*; its Latinity ("refulgent," "irriguous," "umbrageous"); the frequent invocations to, and personifications of, abstractions or inanimate objects; and the use of circumlocution, or **periphrasis**, to avoid low, technical, or common-

place terms through a roundabout, but more elegant, substitute.
Periphrases in James Thomson's *The Seasons* (1726–1730) are "the
finny tribe" for "fish," "the bleating kind" for sheep, and "from the
snowy leg . . . the inverted silk she drew" instead of "she took off
her stocking."

The following stanza from Thomas Gray's excellent period piece,
"Ode on a Distant Prospect of Eton College" (1747), demonstrates all
these devices of poetic diction. Contemporary readers took special
pleasure in the ingenious periphrases by which, to achieve the elevation
appropriate to an ode, he evaded the use of common or lowly words
such as "swim," "cage," "boys," "hoop," and "bat":

> Say, Father Thames, for thou hast seen
> Full many a sprightly race
> Disporting on thy margent green
> The paths of pleasure trace;
> Who foremost now delight to cleave
> With pliant arm thy glassy wave?
> The captive linnet which enthrall?
> What idle progeny succeed
> To chase the rolling circle's speed,
> Or urge the flying ball?

In his famed and influential attack on the doctrine of a special
language for poetry, in the Preface of 1800 to *Lyrical Ballads,* Wordsworth claimed that there is no "*essential* difference between the language of prose and metrical composition"; decried the poetic diction
of eighteenth-century writers as "artificial," "vicious," and "unnatural";
set up as the criterion for a valid poetic language that it be, not a
matter of artful contrivance, but the "spontaneous overflow of powerful feelings"; and, by a drastic reversal of the hierarchy of linguistic
decorum, claimed that the best model for such a natural expression
of feeling is not upper-class speech, but the speech of "humble and
rustic life."

See Thomas Quayle, *Poetic Diction: A Study of Eighteenth-Century
Verse* (1924); Geoffrey Tillotson, "Eighteenth-Century Poetic Diction"
(1942), reprinted in *Eighteenth-Century English Literature*, ed.
James L. Clifford (1959); M. H. Abrams, "Wordsworth and Coleridge
on Diction and Figures," in *English Institute Essays*, ed. Alan S.
Downer (1952), reprinted in part in *Coleridge*, ed. Kathleen Coburn
(1967).

POETIC JUSTICE   was a term coined by Thomas Rymer, an English
critic of the latter seventeenth century, to signify the need to distribute
earthly rewards and punishments at the close of a literary work in
proportion to the virtue or vice of the various characters. Rymer's

assumption was that a poem (in a sense which includes dramatic tragedy) is a realm of its own, and should be governed by its own high principles of decorum and morality, and not by the way things work out in the real world. Few major critics or writers since Rymer's day have acceded to this principle; it would, of course, destroy the possibility of tragic suffering, which exceeds what the protagonist has merited by his *tragic flaw*.

See Introduction to *The Critical Works of Thomas Rymer*, ed. Curt A. Zimansky (1956); M. A. Quinlan, *Poetic Justice in the Drama* (1912).

POETIC LICENSE. Dryden defined poetic license as "the liberty which poets have assumed to themselves, in all ages, of speaking things in verse which are beyond the severity of prose." In its most common sense the term is confined to language alone, to justify the poet's departure from standard prose in matters such as grammar, word order, the use of archaic or new-coined words, and the conventional use of "eye rhymes" (wind–bind, daughter–laughter). The degree and kinds of freedom allowed to poets have varied according to the conventions of each age, but in every case the justification of the freedom lies in the success of the effect. The great opening sentence of Milton's *Paradise Lost* departs from the standard colloquial prose of his time in the choice and order of words, in idiom and figurative construction, and in grammar, in order to achieve a distinctive mode of language and grandeur of announcement commensurate with his great subject and the epic form.

In a wider sense "poetic license" is applied to all the ways in which a poet is held to be free to violate the ordinary norms of speech and of literal truth, including the use of meter and rhyme and the use of fiction and myth. A special case is **anachronism**—the placing of an event or person or thing out of its actual age. Shakespeare dressed his Cleopatra in corsets and used a clock to strike the time in *Julius Caesar*. Another case is the poet's departure from geographical or historical fact, whether from ignorance or design. It does not diminish our delight in the work that Shakespeare attributed a seacoast to Bohemia in *The Winter's Tale*, or that Keats, in writing "On First Looking into Chapman's Homer," ignorantly made Cortez instead of Balboa the discoverer of the Pacific Ocean.

POINT OF VIEW   signifies the way a story gets told—the perspective or perspectives established by an author through which the reader is presented with the characters, actions, setting, and events which constitute the narrative in a work of fiction. The question of point of view has always been a practical concern of the novelist, and there have been a number of scattered observations on the matter in critical writings since the eighteenth century. Since Henry James's Prefaces to his various novels, however—collected as *The Art of the Novel* in 1934— and Percy Lubbock's *The Craft of Fiction* (1926), which codified and expanded upon James's comments, point of view has become a dominant concern of modern theorists of the novelist's art.

Authors have developed many different ways to present a story, and many extended works employ several ways within the single narrative. The simplified classification below, however, is widely recognized and will serve as a useful frame of reference. It establishes a broad division between third-person and first-person narratives, then divides third-person narratives into subclasses according to the degree and kind of freedom or limitation which the author assumes in getting the material of his story before the reader. In a **third-person narrative,** the narrator is someone outside the story who refers to all the characters in the story proper by name, or as "he," "she," "they." Thus Fielding begins *Tom Jones*: "In that part of the western division of this kingdom which is commonly called Somersetshire, there lately lived, and perhaps still lives, a gentleman whose name was Allworthy. . . ." In a **first-person narrative,** the narrator speaks as "I," and is himself a character in the story. Salinger's *The Catcher in the Rye* begins: "If you really want to hear about it, the first thing you'll really want to know is where I was born, and what my lousy childhood was like, and how my parents were occupied and all before they had me, and all that David Copperfield kind of crap. . . ."

(I) Third-person points of view:

(1) The **omniscient point of view.** This is a common term for the assumption in a work of fiction that the narrator knows everything that needs to be known about the agents and events; that he is entirely free to move as he will in time and place, and to shift from character to character, reporting (or concealing) what he chooses of their speech and actions; and also that he has "privileged" access to a character's thoughts and feelings and motives, as well as to his overt speech and actions.

Within this mode, the **intrusive narrator** is one who not only reports but freely comments on his characters, evaluating their actions and motives and expressing his views about human life in general; ordinarily, all the omniscient narrator's reports and judgments are to be taken as authoritative. This is the fashion in which many of the greatest novelists have written, including Fielding, Jane Austen, Dickens, Thackeray, Hardy, Dostoevsky, and Tolstoy. (In Fielding's *Tom Jones* and Tolstoy's *War and Peace*, the intrusive narrator goes so far as to interpolate essays suggested by the subject matter of the novels.) Alternatively, the omniscient narrator may choose to be **unintrusive,** or **impersonal:** he describes, reports, or "shows" the action in dramatic scenes, without introducing his own comments or judgments. Extreme examples of the unintrusive narrator, who gives up even the privilege of access to inner feelings and motives, are to be found in a number of Hemingway's short stories; for example, "The Killers," and "A Clean, Well-Lighted Place." (See *showing and telling,* under *Character.*)

(2) The **limited point of view.** The narrator tells the story in the third person, but confines himself to what is experienced, thought, and felt by a single character, or at most by a very limited number of characters, within the story. Henry James, who refined this narrative mode, described such a character as his "focus," or "mirror," or "center of consciousness." In a number of James's later works all the events and actions are represented as they unfold before, and filter to the reader through, the particular consciousness of one of his characters; for example, Strether in *The Ambassadors.*

Later writers developed this technique into *stream of consciousness* narration, in which we are presented with outer observations only as they impinge on the current of thought, memory, and feeling which constitute the observer's total awareness (Joyce's *A Portrait of the Artist as a Young Man*). The limitation of point of view represented both by James's "center of consciousness" narration and by the "stream-of-consciousness" narration in Joyce, Virginia Woolf, Faulkner, and others, is often said to exemplify the "self-effacing author," or "the disappearance of the author," even more effectively than the impersonal omniscient narrative. For in the latter instance, the reader remains aware that someone, or some outside voice, is telling us about what is going on; the alternative mode, however, insofar as the point of view is limited to the consciousness of a character within the story itself, aims at giving the reader the illusion that he participates in experiencing events that simply evolve before his eyes.

(II) First-person points of view:
This mode, insofar as it is consistently carried out, naturally limits the point of view to what the first-person narrator himself knows, experiences, infers, or can find out by talking to other characters. We distinguish between the narrative "I" who is a fortuitous witness of the matters he relates (Marlow in *Heart of Darkness,* and other works by Conrad); or who is a minor or peripheral participant in the story (Ishmael in Melville's *Moby-Dick,* Nick in Scott Fitzgerald's *The Great Gatsby*); or who is himself the central character in the story

(Defoe's *Moll Flanders*, Dickens' *Great Expectations*, Mark Twain's *The Adventures of Huckleberry Finn*, Salinger's *The Catcher in the Rye*).

Two other frequently discussed narrative tactics, which cut across diverse points of view, need to be mentioned:

The **self-conscious narrator** is one who is aware that he is composing a work of art and takes the reader into his confidence about the various problems involved—either seriously (Fielding's narrator in *Tom Jones* and Marcel in Proust's *Remembrance of Things Past*) or for comic purposes (Tristram in Sterne's *Tristram Shandy* and the narrator of Byron's *Don Juan*), or for purposes which are not clearly either serious or comic (Nabokov's *Pale Fire*).

The **fallible** or **unreliable narrator** is one whose interpretation and evaluation of the matters he narrates do not coincide with the implicit beliefs and norms of value held by the author, and which the author expects the reader to share with him. Henry James made repeated use of the narrator whose excessive innocence, or oversophistication, or moral obtuseness, makes him a flawed and distorting "center of consciousness" in the work; the result is an elaborate structure of ironies which, in some instances, frustrates the reader because he lacks sufficient clues to determine what the author intended as the true facts of the case, and the standards by which these facts are to be judged. (See *Irony*.) Examples of James's use of a fallible narrator are his stories "The Aspern Papers" and "The Liar." *The Sacred Fount* and *The Turn of the Screw* are works by James in which the clues for correcting the fallible narrator seem inadequate, so that the facts and evaluations intended by the author remain problematic. See, for example, the extraordinarily diverse critical interpretations collected in *A *Casebook on Henry James's "The Turn of the Screw,"* ed. Gerald Willen (1960), and in **The Turn of the Screw*, ed. Robert Kimbrough (1966).

On point of view see (in addition to the writings of James and Lubbock, mentioned above) Norman Friedman, "Point of View in Fiction," *Publications of the Modern Language Association*, LXX (1955); Leon Edel, **The Modern Psychological Novel* (rev. ed., 1964), Chaps. 3–4; W. C. Booth, **The Rhetoric of Fiction* (1961).

PRE-RAPHAELITES. In 1848 a group of English artists, including Dante Gabriel Rossetti, William Holman Hunt, and John Millais, organized the "Pre-Raphaelite Brotherhood." The aim was to replace the reigning academic style of painting by a return to the truthfulness, simplicity, and spirit of devotion which these artists found in Italian painting before the time of Raphael and the high Renaissance. The ideals of this group were taken over by a literary movement which included D. G. Rossetti himself (who was a poet as well as a painter), his sister Christina Rossetti, William Morris, and Algernon Swinburne. Rossetti's poem "The Blessed Damozel" typifies the medievalism, the pictorial realism with symbolic overtones, and the union of the flesh and the spirit, sensuousness and religiousness, associated with the earlier writings of this school. See also William Morris' *The Earthly Paradise*.

See William Gaunt, *The Pre-Raphaelite Tragedy* (1942); Graham Hough, *The Last Romantics* (1949).

PRIMITIVISM and PROGRESS.   A **primitivist** is someone who prefers what is "natural" (in the sense of what exists prior to and independently of man's reasoning and contrivance) to what is "artificial" (in the sense of what man achieves by thought, laws and conventions, and the complex arrangements of a civilized society). A useful, although not mutually exclusive, distinction is made between two manifestations of primitivism:

(1) **Cultural primitivism** is the preference of "nature" over "art" in any field of human culture and values. For example, in ethics a primitivist lauds the "natural," or innate, instincts and passions over the dictates of reason and prudential forethought; in social philosophy, the ideal is the simple and "natural" forms of social and political order in place of the anxieties and frustrations engendered by a complex and highly developed social organization; in milieu, a primitivist prefers outdoor "nature," unmodified by human intervention, to cities or artful gardens; and in literature and the other arts, he puts his reliance on spontaneity, the free expression of emotion, and the intuitive products of "natural genius," as against the reasoned adaptation of artistic means to foreseen ends and the reliance on "artificial" forms, rules, and conventions. Typically, the cultural primitivist asserts that in the modern world, the life, activities, and products of "primitive" people— who live in a way more accordant to "nature" because they are isolated from civilization—are preferable to the life, activities, and products of people living in a highly developed society, especially in cities. The eighteenth-century cult of "the Noble Savage," and the concurrent vogue of "natural" poetry written by peasants or simple working folk, were both aspects of primitivism. Cultural primitivism has played a prominent and persistent role in American thought and literature, where the "new world" was early identified both with the golden age of the past and the millennium to come, the American Indian was identified with the legendary Noble Savage, and the American pioneer was regarded as a new Adam who had cut free from the

artifice and corruptions of European civilization in order to begin a "natural" life of freedom, innocence, and simplicity. See Henry Nash Smith, *Virgin Land* (1950), and R. W. B. Lewis, *The American Adam* (1955).

(2) **Chronological primitivism** signifies the belief that the ideal stage of man's way of life lies in the very distant past, when he lived naturally, simply, and freely, and that the process of history has been a gradual "decline" from that happy stage into increasing artifice, complexity, inhibitions, and prohibitions in the psychological, social, and cultural order. Many, but not all, cultural primitivists are also chronological primitivists.

The opposite of chronological primitivism (which developed in the seventeenth century and reached its height in the nineteenth century) is the idea of **progress**: the doctrine that, by virtue of the development and exploitation of man's art, skills, and wisdom, the course of history represents an overall improvement in his lot, morality, and happiness from early barbarity to the present stage of civilization, and that this historical progress will continue indefinitely in the future— possibly to end in a final stage of social, rational, and moral perfection.

Primitivism is as old as man's recorded thought, and is reflected in the widespread myths of a vanished golden age and of a lost Garden of Eden. It achieved a special vogue, however, in the eighteenth century, in a European-wide movement in which Rousseau was a central figure. D. H. Lawrence was a recent and powerful instance of a primitivistic thinker, in his laudation of the spontaneous instinctual life, his belief in a vanished condition of man's personal and social wholeness, and his attacks on the disintegrative effects of the modern technological economy and culture. There are obvious strains of primitivism in the outlook and life-style of the current "hippie" subculture. But most men, and many writers of literature, are primitivists in some moods, longing to escape from the complications, fever, and anxieties of modern civilization into the elemental simplicities of a lost natural life, whether that is imagined as an individual's childhood, or as the classical or medieval past, or as some primitive, carefree, faraway place on earth.

See H. N. Fairchild, *The Noble Savage* (1928); J. B. Bury, *The Idea of Progress* (1932); Lois Whitney, *Primitivism and Ideas of Progress* (1934); A. O. Lovejoy and George Boas, *Primitivism and Related Ideas in Antiquity* (1948); A. O. Lovejoy, *Essays in the History of Ideas* (1948); Sigmund Freud, *Civilization and Its Discontents* (1949). A recent instance of cultural primitivism is Norman O. Brown's *Life against Death* (1959).

PROBLEM PLAY is a fairly recent dramatic type which was popularized by the great Norwegian playwright, Henrik Ibsen. In problem plays, the situation of the protagonist is so rendered as to indicate that it represents a contemporary sociological problem; often the dramatist manages—by the use of a spokesman in the play, or by the evolution of the plot, or both—to indicate that he favors a solution to the problem which is at odds with prevailing opinion. The issue may be one of the inadequate scope allowed to a woman in the middle-class nineteenth-century family (Ibsen's *A Doll's House*); or of the morality of prostitution, regarded as a typical economic phenomenon in a capitalist society (Shaw's *Mrs. Warren's Profession*); or of the crisis in the relations of black and white men and women in present-day America (in numerous current dramas and films).

One subtype of the problem play is the **discussion play,** in which the social issue is not incorporated into a plot, but expounded in the dramatic give and take of a sustained debate among the characters. See Shaw's *Getting Married* and Act III of his *Man and Superman; also his book on Ibsen's plays, **The Quintessence of Ibsenism* (1891).

PROSE, in its ordinary and most useful sense, is the sustained use of language as we ordinarily speak it, as distinguished from language patterned into recurrent units of meter, which we call *verse*. The lack of meter does not mean that the writing of distinguished prose is less an art than the writing of distinguished verse; in fact, in all literatures written prose seems to have developed later than written verse. In Old English, for example, the first prose works we possess were written by King Alfred near the end of the ninth century, more than a hundred years later than *Beowulf*.

PROSODY signifies the systematic study of versification, that is, of the principles and practice of *meter, rhyme,* and *stanza*. Sometimes the term "prosody" is extended to include also the study of sound effects such as *alliteration, assonance, euphony,* and *onomatopoeia*.

PUN. A play on words that are either identical in sound ("homonyms") or similar in sound, but are sharply diverse in meaning. Puns have had serious literary uses. The authority of the Pope goes back to the Greek pun in Matthew XVI:18, "Thou art Peter (Petros) and upon this rock (petra) I will build my church." Shakespeare used puns seriously, as well as for comic purposes; so in *Romeo and Juliet* (III. i. 101) Mercutio, bleeding to death, says, "Ask for me tomorrow and you shall find me a grave man." And John Donne's solemn "Hymn to God the Father" puns throughout on his own name and the verb "done." In the eighteenth century and thereafter, however, the literary use of the pun has been almost exclusively comic. The great exception is James Joyce's *Finnegans Wake*, which exploits puns throughout in order to help sustain its complex effect, at once serious and comic, of multiple levels of meaning.

A special type of pun, known as the **equivoque,** is the use of a single word or phrase which has two disparate meanings, in a context which makes both meanings equally relevant. An example is the epitaph suggested for a bank teller:

> He checked his cash, cashed in his checks,
> And left his window.   Who is next?

PURPLE PATCH   is a translation of Horace's phrase "purpureus . . . pannus" in his versified *Ars Poetica*. It signifies a sudden heightening of rhythm, diction, and figurative language that makes a section of verse or prose—especially a descriptive passage—stand out from its context. The term is sometimes applied without derogation to a set piece, separable and quotable, in which an author rises to an occasion. An example is the eulogy of England by the dying John of Gaunt in Shakespeare's *Richard II* (II. i, 40 ff.), beginning

> This royal throne of kings, this scept'red isle,
> This earth of majesty, this seat of Mars,
> This other Eden, demi-paradise. . . .

Other well-known examples are Byron's depiction of the Duchess of Richmond's ball on the eve of Waterloo in *Childe Harold's Pilgrimage* (Canto III, xxi–xxviii), and Pater's prose description of the *Mona Lisa* in his essay on Leonardo da Vinci in *The Renaissance*. Often, however, "purple passage" connotes disparagement of an author who has self-consciously girded himself to perform a piece of fine writing.

REALISM and NATURALISM.   Realism is used in two ways: (1) to denote a literary movement of the nineteenth century, especially in prose fiction (beginning with Balzac in France, George Eliot in England, and William Dean Howells in America); and (2) to designate a recurrent way of representing life in literature, which was typified by the writers of this historical movement.

Realistic fiction is often opposed to romantic fiction: the *romance* is said to present life as we would have it be, more picturesque, more adventurous, more heroic than the actual; realism, to present an accurate imitation of life as it is. This distinction is not invalid, but it is inadequate. Casanova, T. E. Lawrence, Winston Churchill were people in real life, but their histories, as related by themselves or others, demonstrate that truth is stranger than realism. The realist sets out to write a fiction which will give the illusion that it reflects life as it seems to the common reader. To achieve this effect he prefers as protagonist an ordinary citizen of Middletown, living on Main Street, perhaps, and engaged in the real estate business. The realist, in other words, is deliberately selective in his material and prefers the average, the commonplace, and the everyday over the rarer aspects of the contemporary scene. His characters, therefore, are usually of the middle class or (less frequently) the working class—people without highly exceptional endowments, who live through ordinary experiences of childhood, adolescence, love, marriage, parenthood, infidelity, and death; who find life rather dull and often unhappy, though it may be brightened by touches of beauty and joy; but who may, under special circumstances, display something akin to heroism.

A thoroughgoing realism involves not only a selection of subject matter but, more importantly, a special literary manner as well: the subject is represented, or "rendered," in such a way as to give the reader the illusion of actual experience. Daniel Defoe, the first novelistic realist, dealt with the extraordinary adventures of a shipwrecked mariner named Robinson Crusoe and with the extraordinary misadventures of Moll Flanders; but these novels are made to seem the very mirror held up to real life by Defoe's reportorial manner of rendering the events, whether trivial or extraordinary, in the same circumstantial, matter-of-fact, and seemingly unselective way. Writers such as Henry Fielding and Jane Austen are sometimes called realists because they often render commonplace people so well that they convince us such people really lived and talked this way. It is well, however, to reserve the term "realist" for writers who render a subject seriously, and as though it were a direct reflection of the casual order of experience, without too patently shaping it, as do Fielding and Austen, into a tightly wrought comic or ironic pattern. It makes good sense to say that Jane Austen is *more* realistic in subject and manner than the contemporary writer of romances Sir Walter Scott, or that Jane Austen's novels contain many realistic passages. The technical term, "realistic novel," however, is most usefully applied to works which are realistic both in subject and manner, and throughout the whole rather than in parts—works such as William Dean Howells' *The Rise of Silas Lapham*, Arnold Bennett's novels about the "Five Towns," and Sinclair Lewis' *Main Street*.

Naturalism is sometimes claimed to be an even more accurate picture of life than is realism. But naturalism is not only, like realism, a special selection of subject matter and a special literary manner; it is a mode of fiction that was developed by a school of writers in accordance with a special philosophical thesis. This thesis, a product of post-Darwinian biology in the mid-nineteenth century, held that man belongs entirely in the order of nature and does not have a soul or any other connection with a religious or spiritual world beyond nature; that man is therefore merely a higher-order animal whose character and fortunes are determined by two kinds of natural forces, heredity and environment. He inherits his personal traits and his compulsive instincts, especially hunger and sex, and he is subject to the social and economic forces in the family, the class, and the milieu into which he is born. The French novelist Émile Zola, beginning in the 1870s, did much to develop this theory in what he called *le roman expérimental* (that is, the novel organized in the mode of a scientific experiment). Zola and later naturalistic writers, such as the Americans Frank Norris, Stephen Crane, Theodore Dreiser, and James Farrell, try to present their subjects with an objective scientific attitude and with elaborate documentation, often including an almost medical frankness about activities and bodily functions usually unmentioned in earlier literature. They tend to choose characters who exhibit strong animal drives, such as greed and brutal sexual desire, and who are victims both of their glandular secretions within and of sociological pressures without. The end of the naturalistic novel is usually "tragic," but not, as in classical and Elizabethan tragedy, because of a heroic but losing struggle of the individual mind and will against gods, enemies, and circumstance. The protagonist of the naturalistic plot, a pawn to multiple compulsions, merely disintegrates, or is wiped out.

Aspects of the naturalistic selection and management of materials, and austere or brutal frankness of manner, are apparent in many modern novels and dramas, such as Hardy's *Jude the Obscure* (although Hardy substituted a cosmic determinism for biological and environmental determinism), various plays of Eugene O'Neill, and James Jones's novel of World War II, *The Naked and the Dead*. An enlightening exercise is to distinguish how the relation of the sexes is represented in a romance (Richard Blackmore's *Lorna Doone*), an ironic novel of manners (Jane Austen's *Pride and Prejudice*), a realistic novel (William Dean Howells' *A Modern Instance*), and a naturalistic novel (Émile Zola's *Nana*, or Theodore Dreiser's *An American Tragedy*). Movements originally opposed both to realism and naturalism (though some modern works, such as Joyce's *Ulysses*, combine aspects of all these novelistic modes) are *expressionism* and *symbolism*.

See Walter L. Myers, *The Later Realism* (1927); Erich Auerbach,

Mimesis: The Representation of Reality in Western Literature (1953);
Harry Levin, "What is Realism?" in *Contexts of Criticism* (1957),
and *The Gates of Horn: A Study of Five French Realists* (1963).

REFRAIN. A line, or part of a line, or a group of lines which is
repeated in the course of a poem, sometimes with slight changes, and
usually at the end of each stanza. It is found in many ballads and
work-poems, and is a frequent element in Elizabethan song, where it
sometimes occurs in a nonsense form as mere carrier of the melodic
line: "With a hey, and a ho, and a hey nonino." A famous refrain is
that which closes each stanza in Spenser's "Epithalamion"—"The
woods shall to me answer, and my echo ring"—in which sequential
changes indicate the altering sounds during the successive hours of
the poet's wedding day. The refrain in Spenser's "Prothalamion"—
"Sweet Thames, run softly, till I end my song"—is echoed ironically
in Part III of Eliot's *The Waste Land*, describing the Thames in our
age of polluted waters.

A refrain may consist of a single word—"Nevermore" in Poe's "The
Raven"—or of a whole stanza. If the stanza refrain occurs in a song
as a part in which all the listeners join, it is called "the chorus"; for
example, in "Auld Lang Syne" and many other songs by Robert Burns.

RENAISSANCE   ("rebirth") is the name applied to the period of European history following the Middle Ages; it is commonly said to have
begun in Italy in the late fourteenth century and to have continued
in western Europe through the fifteenth and sixteenth centuries. In this
period the arts of painting, sculpture, architecture, and literature
reached an eminence not exceeded by any civilization in any age. The
development came late to England in the sixteenth century, and did
not have its flowering until the *Elizabethan* and *Jacobean* periods;
sometimes, in fact, Milton (1608–1674) is said to be the last great
Renaissance poet.

Many attempts have been made to define "the Renaissance," as
though one essence underlay the complex features of the culture of
numerous countries over several hundred years. It has been described
as the birth of the modern world out of the ashes of the dark ages;
as the discovery of the world and the discovery of man; as the era of
untrammelled individualism in life, thought, religion, and art. Recently some historians, finding that these attributes were present in
various people and places in the Middle Ages, and also that many
elements long held to be medieval survived into the Renaissance, have
denied that the Renaissance ever existed. It is true that history is a
continuous process, and that "periods" are invented not by God but by
historians; but the concept of a period is a convenience, if not a

necessity, of historical analysis, and one is able to identify, during the span of the Renaissance, a number of events and discoveries which in the course of time altered radically the views, productions, and manner of life of the intellectual classes.

All these events may be regarded as putting a strain on the relatively closed and stable world of the great civilization of the later Middle Ages, when most of the essential truths about man, the universe, religion, and philosophy were held to be well known and permanently established. The full impact of many of these Renaissance developments did not make itself felt until the later seventeenth and the eighteenth centuries, but the very fact that they occurred in this period indicates the vitality, the audacity, and the restless curiosity of many men of the Renaissance, whether scholars, thinkers, artists, or adventurers.

(1) The new learning. Renaissance scholars of the classics, called *humanists*, revived the knowledge of the Greek language, discovered and disseminated a great number of Greek manuscripts, and added considerably to the number of Roman authors and works which had been known to the Middle Ages. The result was to enlarge immensely the stock of ideas, materials, literary forms, and styles available to Renaissance writers. In the mid-fifteenth century the invention of printing on paper from movable type made books for the first time cheap and plentiful, and floods of publications, ancient and modern, poured from the presses of Europe to satisfy the demands of the rapidly expanding literate audience. The speed of the inauguration and spread of ideas, discoveries, and types of literature in the Renaissance was made possible by this technological development.

The humanistic revival sometimes resulted in pedantic scholarship, sterile imitations of ancient works and styles, and a rigid rhetoric and literary criticism. It also bred, however, the gracious and tolerant humanity of an Erasmus, and the noble concept of the cultivated Renaissance gentleman expressed in Baldassare Castiglione's *Il Cortegiano* (*The Courtier*), published in 1528. This was the most admired and widely translated of the many Renaissance **courtesy books,** or books on the character, obligations, and training of the man of the court. It presents the ideal of the completely rounded or "universal" man, developed in all his faculties and skills, physical, intellectual, and artistic. He is trained to be a warrior and statesman, but is capable also as athlete, philosopher, artist, conversationist, and man of society. His relations to women are in accord with the quasi-religious code of *Platonic love*, and his activities are crowned by the grace of **sprezzatura**—the seeming ease and negligence with which he meets the demands of complex and exacting rules of behavior. Leonardo da Vinci in Italy and Sir Philip Sidney in England were embodiments of the courtly ideal.

(2) The new religion. The **Reformation** led by Martin Luther (1483–1546) was a successful heresy which struck at the very basis of the institutionalism of the Roman Catholic Church. This early Protestantism was grounded on the individual's inner experience of spiritual struggle and salvation. Faith (based on the word of the Bible as interpreted by the individual) was alone thought competent to save, and salvation itself was regarded as a direct transaction with God in the theater of the individual soul, without the need of intermediation by Church, priest, or sacrament. For this reason Protestantism is sometimes said to have been an extreme manifestation of "Renaissance individualism" in northern Europe; it soon, however, developed its own institutionalism in the theocracy proposed by John Calvin and his Puritan followers. England in characteristic fashion muddled its way into Protestantism under Henry VIII and Elizabeth I, empirically finding a middle way that minimized violence and hastened a stable settlement.

(3) The new world. In 1492 Columbus, acting on the persisting belief in the old Greek idea that the world is a globe, sailed west to find a new commercial route to the East, only to be frustrated by the unexpected barrier of a new continent. The succeeding explorations of this continent gave new materials and stimulus to the literary imagination; the magic world of Shakespeare's *The Tempest*, for example, is based on a contemporary account of a shipwreck on Bermuda. More important for literature, however, was the fact that economic exploitation of the new world put England at the center, rather than as heretofore at the edge, of the chief trade routes, and so helped establish the commercial prosperity that in England, as in Italy earlier, was a necessary though not sufficient condition for the development of a vigorous intellectual and artistic life.

(4) The new cosmos. The cosmos of medieval astronomy and theology was **Ptolemaic** (that is, based on the astronomy of Ptolemy, second century A.D.) and pictured a stationary earth around which rotated the successive spheres of the moon, the various planets, and the fixed stars; Heaven, or the Empyrean, was thought to be situated above the spheres, and Hell to be situated either at the center of the earth (as in Dante's *Inferno*) or else below the system of the spheres (as in Milton's *Paradise Lost*). In 1543 Copernicus published his new hypothesis concerning the system of the universe; this gave a much simpler and more coherent explanation of accumulating observations of the actual movements of the heavenly bodies, which had led to ever

greater complications of the Ptolemaic world picture. The **Copernican theory** pictured a system in which the center is not the earth, but the sun, and in which the earth is not stationary, but one planet among the many planets which revolve around the sun.

Investigations have not borne out the earlier assumption that the world picture of Copernicus and his followers delivered an immediate and profound shock to the theological and secular beliefs of thinking men. For example in 1611, when Donne wrote in "The First Anniversary" that "new Philosophy calls all in doubt," for "the Sun is lost, and th' earth," he did so only to support the ancient theme of the world's decay and to enforce a standard Christian *contemptus mundi*. Still later, Milton in *Paradise Lost* expressed a suspension of judgment between the Ptolemaic and Copernican theories; he adopted for his own poem the older Ptolemaic scheme because it was more firmly traditional and better adapted to his imaginative purposes.

Much more important, in the long run, was the effect on men's opinions of the general principles and methods of the **new science** of the great successors of Copernicus, such as the physicists Kepler and Galileo, and the English physician and physiologist, William Harvey. The cosmos of many Elizabethan writers was not only Ptolemaic, and subject throughout to God's Providence; it was also an animate universe, invested with occult powers, inhabited by demons and spirits, and often thought to control men's lives by stellar influences and to be itself subject to control by the power of witchcraft and of magic. The cosmos that emerged in the seventeenth century, as a product of the scientific procedure of constructing exact hypotheses capable of being tested by precisely measured observations, was the physical universe of René Descartes (1596–1650). "Give me extension and motion," Descartes wrote, "and I will construct the universe." This universe of Descartes and the new science consisted of extended particles of matter which moved in space according to fixed mathematical laws, entirely free from interference by angels, demons, human prayer, or occult magical powers, and subject only to the limited manipulations of scientists who, in Francis Bacon's phrase, had learned to obey nature in order to be her master. In this way the working hypotheses of the physical scientists were converted into a philosophical world view, which was made current by many popular expositions, and—together with the methodological principle that controlled observation, rather than tradition or authority, is the only test of truth in all areas of knowledge—helped constitute the climate of eighteenth-century opinion known as the *Enlightenment*.

Refer to J. Burckhardt, **Civilization of the Renaissance in Italy* (first published in 1860); H. O. Taylor, *Thought and Expression in the 16th Century* (1920); E. A. Burtt, *The Metaphysical Foundations of Modern Science* (rev. ed., 1932); W. K. Ferguson, *The Renaissance in Historical Thought* (1948); C. S. Lewis, *English Literature in the 16th Century* (1954); Marjorie Nicolson, *Science and Imagination* (1956); Thomas S. Kuhn, *The Copernican Revolution* (1957); J. H. Randall, Jr., *The Career of Philosophy* (1962), Vol. I (*From the Middle Ages to the Enlightenment*).

RESTORATION. The period takes its name from the restoration of the Stuart line (Charles II) to the English throne in 1660, at the end of the Commonwealth; it is regarded as lasting until 1700. The urbanity, wit, and licentiousness of the life centering on the court, in sharp contrast to the high seriousness and sobriety of the earlier Puritan regime, is reflected in much of the literature of this age. The theaters came back to vigorous life after the revocation of the ban placed on them by the Puritans in 1642; Etherege, Wycherley, Congreve, and Dryden developed the distinctive comedy of manners called *Restoration comedy*, and Dryden, Otway, and other playwrights developed the even more distinctive form of tragedy called *heroic drama*. Dryden was the major poet and critic, as well as one of the major dramatists. Other poets were the satirists Samuel Butler and the Earl of Rochester; other notable writers in prose were Samuel Pepys, Sir William Temple, the religious writer John Bunyan, and the philosopher John Locke.

See Basil Willey, *The Seventeenth Century Background* (1934); L. I. Bredvold, *The Intellectual Milieu of John Dryden* (1934). And see the entry *Neoclassic and Romantic*.

RHETORIC and RHETORICAL CRITICISM. In his *Poetics* Aristotle defined poetry as a mode of *imitation*—a fictional representation of human beings thinking, feeling, acting, and interacting—and focused his discussion on such elements as plot, character, thought, and diction within the work itself. In his *Rhetoric* Aristotle defined rhetorical discourse as the art of "discovering all the available means of persuasion in any given case," and focused his discussion on the various ways in which the orator deploys devices for achieving the intellectual and emotional effects on an audience that are needed to persuade them to accede to his point of view. Later classical rhetoricians concurred with this definition of rhetoric as the art of persuading an audience, and (still following Aristotle's lead) analyzed the text of a rhetorical discourse into "invention" (the finding of arguments or proofs), "disposition" (the arrangement of such matters), and "style" (the choice of words, figures, and rhythms that will most effectively express this material). They also discriminated three main categories of oratory, each of which uses characteristic devices to achieve its distinctive effects:

(1) **Deliberative**—to persuade an audience (such as a legislative assembly) to approve or disapprove of a matter of public policy, and to act accordingly.

(2) **Forensic**—to achieve (for example, in a judicial trial) condemnation or approval of a man's actions.

(3) **Epideictic**—"display rhetoric," used on ceremonial occasions to amplify the praise (or sometimes, the blameworthiness) of a person or group of persons.

Horace in his versified *Art of Poetry* declared that the aim of a poet is either to instruct or to delight a reader, or preferably to do both. Such *pragmatic criticism*, which breaks down Aristotle's distinction between poetry and rhetoric, in one or another form dominated literary theory from late classical times through the eighteenth century; discussions of poetry absorbed and expanded upon the terms of traditional rhetoric, and a poem was regarded mainly as a deployment of artistic means for achieving effects upon the reader or audience. The triumph in the early nineteenth century of *expressive* theories of literature (which conceive a work primarily as the expression of the feelings, temperament, and mental powers of the author himself), followed by the dominance, beginning in the 1920s, of *objective* theories of literature (which maintain that a work must be considered as an object in itself, independently of the mental qualities of the author and the responses of a reader) served to diminish, and sometimes to eliminate, rhetorical considerations in literary criticism. (See *Criticism*.)

Since the late 1950s, however, there has been a strong revival of interest in literature as a public act involving communication between author and reader, and this has led to the development of a **rhetorical criticism** which, without departing from a primary focus on the work as such, undertakes to analyze those elements within a poem or a prose narrative which are there primarily for the reader's sake. As Wayne Booth has said in the Preface to his influential book *°The Rhetoric of Fiction* (1961), his subject is "the rhetorical resources available to the writer of epic, novel, or short story as he tries, consciously or unconsciously, to impose his fictional world upon the reader." A number of recent critics of prose fiction and of narrative and nonnarrative poems have devoted special attention to an author's use of a variety of means—especially the authorial presence or *voice* that he projects—in order to inform, to achieve imaginative consent, and to engage the interests and guide the emotional responses of the reader to whom, whether deliberately or not, his literary work is inevitably addressed. (See *Persona, voice, and tone.*)

See C. S. Baldwin, *Ancient Rhetoric and Poetic* (1924), and George Kennedy, *The Art of Persuasion in Greece* (1963); and for recent examples of the rhetorical criticism of poetry and fiction, Wayne Booth, *The Rhetoric of Fiction* (1961); M. H. Nichols, *Rhetoric and Criticism* (1963); Donald C. Bryant, ed., *Papers in Rhetoric and Poetic* (1965); Edward P. J. Corbett, ed., *Rhetorical Analyses of Literary Works* (1969).

RHETORICAL FIGURES. It is convenient to list under this heading some common figures of speech which depart from standard, or "literal," language mainly by the arrangement of their words to achieve special effects, and not, like metaphors and other *tropes*, by a radical change of meaning in the words themselves.

An **apostrophe** is a direct address either to an absent person or to an abstract or inanimate entity. Keats begins his "Ode on a Grecian Urn" by apostrophizing the urn: "Thou still unravished bride of quietness"; and in his fine poem, "Recollections of Love," Coleridge turns suddenly from thoughts of his beloved to apostrophize the River Greta:

> But when those meek eyes first did seem
> To tell me, Love within you wrought—
> O Greta, dear domestic stream!
>
> Has not, since then, Love's prompture deep,
> Has not Love's whisper evermore
> Been ceaseless, as thy gentle roar?
> Sole voice, when other voices sleep,
> Dear under-song in clamor's hour.

If such an address is to a god or muse to assist the poet in his composition, it is called an **invocation;** so Milton invokes divine guidance at the opening of *Paradise Lost*:

> And chiefly Thou, O Spirit, that dost prefer
> Before all temples th' upright heart and pure,
> Instruct me. . . .

A **rhetorical question** is a question asked, not to evoke an actual reply, but to achieve an emphasis stronger than a direct statement. The figure is most used in persuasive discourse, and tends to impart an oratorical tone to a speech. When "fierce Thalestris" in Pope's *The Rape of the Lock* asks Belinda,

> Gods! shall the ravisher display your hair,
> While the fops envy, and the ladies stare?

she does not stay for an answer, which is obviously "No!" (By far the most common rhetorical question is one that won't take "Yes" for an answer.) Shelley's "Ode to the West Wind" closes with the most famous rhetorical question in English:

O, Wind,
If Winter comes, can Spring be far behind?

Chiasmus is a sequence of two phrases or clauses which are parallel in syntax, but with a reversal in the order of the words. So in this line from Pope the verb first precedes, then follows, the adverbial phrase:

Works without show, and without pomp *presides*.

The effect is sometimes reinforced by alliteration and other similarities in sound, as in Pope's summary of the common fate of coquettes in marriage:

A *fop* their *p*assion, but their *p*rize a *sot*.

In Yeats's "An Irish Airman Foresees His Death," the chiasmus consists in a reversal of the position of the same phrase:

The years to come seemed *waste of breath*,
A *waste of breath* the years behind.[1]

Zeugma in Greek means "yoking"; in the most common present usage, it is applied to expressions in which a single word stands in the same grammatical relation to two or more other words, but with some alteration in its meaning from one instance to the next. Here are various instances of zeugma in Pope:

Or *stain* her honour, or her new brocade.

Obliged by hunger, and request of friends.

To rest, the cushion and soft Dean *invite*.

To achieve the maximum of concentrated verbal effects within the tight limits of the *closed couplet*, Pope exploited all these language patterns with supreme virtuosity. He is the English master of the rhetorical figures, as Shakespeare is of the metaphorical figures.

For other figures of speech, of thought, and of sound see the listing under *Figurative language* in the Index.

RHYME.   In English versification the standard rhyme consists in the identity, in rhyming words, of the last stressed vowel and of all the

speech sounds following that vowel: láte–fáte; fóllow–swállow.

End rhymes, by far the most frequent type, occur at the end of a verse-line. **Internal rhymes** occur within a verse-line, as in Swinburne's

Sister, my sister, O *fleet sweet* swallow.

[1] From the *Collected Poems of W. B. Yeats.* Copyright 1919 by The Macmillan Company, renewed 1947 by Bertha Georgie Yeats. Reprinted by permission of The Macmillan Company, the Macmillan Company of Canada, Mr. M. B. Yeats, and A. P. Watt & Son.

A stanza from Coleridge's *The Ancient Mariner* illustrates the patterned use both of internal rhymes (within lines 1 and 3) and of an end rhyme (lines 2 and 4):

> In mist or *cloud*, on mast or *shroud*,
> It perched for vespers *nine*;
> Whiles all the *night*, through fog-smoke *white*,
> Glimmered the white moon-*shine*.

The numbered lines in the following stanza of Wordsworth's "The Solitary Reaper" are followed by a column which, in conventional fashion, marks the sequence of the terminal rhyme elements by a sequence of the letters of the alphabet:

1)	Whate'er her theme, the maiden sang	*a*
2)	As if her song could have no *ending*;	*b*
3)	I saw her singing at her work,	*c*
4)	And o'er the sickle *bending*—	*b*
5)	I listened, motionless and *still*;	*d*
6)	And as I mounted up the *hill*,	*d*
7)	The music in my heart I *bore*,	*e*
8)	Long after it was heard no *more*.	*e*

Lines 1 and 3 do not rhyme with any other line. Both in lines 5 and 6 and lines 7 and 8 the rhyme consists of a single stressed syllable, and is called a **masculine rhyme:** still–hill, bore–more. In lines 2 and 4, the rhyme consists of a stressed syllable followed by an unstressed syllable, and is called a **feminine rhyme:** ending–bending.

A feminine rhyme, since it involves two syllables, is also known as a **double rhyme.** A rhyme involving three syllables is called a **triple rhyme.** Such rhymes, since they coincide with surprising patness, usually have a comic quality. In *Don Juan* Byron often uses triple rhymes such as comparison–garrison, and sometimes intensifies the comic effect by permitting the pressure of the rhyme to force a distortion of the pronunciation; thus he addresses the husbands of learned wives:

> But—Oh! ye lords of ladies intellectual
>
> Inform us truly, have they not hen-pecked you all?

This maltreatment of words, in which the poet seems to surrender helplessly to the exigencies of a triple rhyme, has been thoroughly exploited by Ogden Nash:

> Farewell, farewell, you old rhinocerous,
> I'll stare at something less prepocerous.[1]

[1] Copyright, 1933, by Ogden Nash. From *Many Long Years Ago* by Ogden Nash, by permission of Little, Brown and Company, and J. M. Dent & Sons Ltd.

If the correspondence of the rhymed sounds is exact, it is called **perfect rhyme,** or else "full" or "true rhyme." Until recently almost all English writers of serious poems have limited themselves to perfect rhymes, except for an occasional *poetic license* such as **eye-rhymes,** or words whose endings are spelled alike, and in most instances were once pronounced alike, but now have a different pronunciation: prove–love, daughter–laughter. Many modern poets, however, deliberately supplement perfect rhyme with **imperfect rhyme** (also known as "partial," "near," or "slant rhyme"). This effect is fairly common in folk poetry such as children's verses, and it was employed occasionally by various writers of art lyrics such as Thomas Vaughan and William Blake. Hopkins and Yeats, however, were the first important poets fully to exploit partial rhymes, in which the rhymed vowels are either approximate or quite different, and occasionally even the rhymed consonants are similar rather than identical. Wilfred Owen constructs the following six-line stanza with two sets of partial rhymes:

> The centuries will burn rich loads
> With which we groaned,
> Whose warmth shall lull their dreamy lids,
> While songs are crooned.
> But they will not dream of us poor lads
> Lost in the ground.[1]

In his poem "The Force that through the Green Fuse Drives the Flower," Dylan Thomas uses, most effectively, such distantly approximate rhymes as (with masculine endings) trees–rose, rocks–wax, tomb–worm, and (with feminine endings) flower–destroyer–fever.

The passages quoted will illustrate some of the many effects of the device that has been called "making ends meet in verse"—the pleasure of the expected but varying chime; the reinforcement of syntax and rhetorical emphasis when a strong masculine rhyme concurs with the end of a clause, sentence, or stanza; the sudden grace of movement which may be lent by a feminine rhyme; the broadening of the comic by a pat coincidence of sound; the sometimes haunting effect of the limited consonance in partial rhymes. Cunning artificers in verse make it more than an auxiliary sound effect; they use it to enhance or contribute to the meaning of the words. When Pope satirized two contemporary pedants in the lines,

> Yet ne'er one sprig of laurel graced these ribalds,
> From slashing Bentley down to piddling Tibalds,

---

[1] From "Miners" by Wilfred Owen, *Collected Poems.* Copyright Chatto & Windus, Ltd., 1946, © 1963. Reprinted by permission of New Directions Publishing Corporation.

the rhyme, as W. K. Wimsatt has said, demonstrates "what it means to have a name like that," with its implication that the scholar is as graceless as his appellation. And in one of its important functions, rhyme ties individual lines into the pattern of a *stanza*.

See George Saintsbury, *History of English Prosody* (3 vols.; 1906–1910); H. C. K. Wyld, *Studies in English Rhymes* (1923); W. K. Wimsatt, Jr., "One Relation of Rhyme to Reason," in *The Verbal Icon* (1954).

ROMAN À CLEF (French for "novel with a key") is a novel in which the reader is expected to identify, within the apparent fiction, actual people or events. One example is Thomas Love Peacock's *Nightmare Abbey* (1818), whose characters are entertaining caricatures of such contemporary literary figures as Coleridge, Byron, and Shelley. A more recent instance is Aldous Huxley's *Point Counter Point* (1928), in which we find, under fictional names, well-known people of the twenties such as the novelist D. H. Lawrence, the critic Middleton Murry, and the right-wing political extremist, Oswald Mosely.

ROMANTIC PERIOD. The limits of the Romantic Period in English literature are usually set either at 1789 (the beginning of the French Revolution) or 1798 (the publication of Wordsworth and Coleridge's *Lyrical Ballads*) and 1832, when Scott died and the passage of the Reform Bill signaled the political preoccupations of the Victorian era. For some characteristics of the thought and writings of this great literary period, see *Neoclassic and romantic*. Major writers of the time, in addition to Wordsworth and Coleridge, were the poets Blake, Byron, Shelley, Keats, and Landor, the essayists Lamb, Hazlitt, De Quincey, and Leigh Hunt, and the novelists Jane Austen and Sir Walter Scott.

SATIRE is the literary art of diminishing a subject by making it ridiculous and evoking toward it attitudes of amusement, contempt, indignation, or scorn. It differs from the *comic* in that comedy evokes laughter as an end in itself, while satire "derides"; that is, it uses laughter as a weapon, and against a butt existing outside the work itself. That butt may be an individual (in "personal satire"), or a type of person, a class, an institution, a nation, or even (as in Rochester's "A Satyr against Mankind" and much of Swift's *Gulliver's Travels*, especially Book IV) the whole race of man. The distinction between the comic and the satiric, however, is a sharp one only at its extremes. Shakespeare's Falstaff is a comic creation, presented without derision for our unmitigated enjoyment; the puritanical Malvolio in *Twelfth Night* is for the most part comic but has aspects of satire directed

against the type of the complacent and fatuous hypocrite; Jonson's
Volpone clearly satirizes the type of man whose cleverness is put at the
service of his cupidity; and Dryden's *MacFlecknoe*, while representing
a permanent type of the pretentious *poetaster*, ridicules specifically the
living individual, Shadwell.

Satire has usually been justified by those who practice it as a cor-
rective of human vice and folly; Pope remarked that "those who are
ashamed of nothing else are so of being ridiculous." Its claim (not
always borne out in the practice) has been to ridicule the failing
rather than the individual, and to limit its ridicule to corrigible faults,
excluding those for which a man is not responsible. As Swift said,
speaking of himself in his "Verses on the Death of Dr. Swift":

> Yet malice never was his aim;
> He lashed the vice, but spared the name. . . .
> His satire points at no defect,
> But what all mortals may correct. . . .
> He spared a hump, or crooked nose,
> Whose owners set not up for beaux.

Satire occurs as an incidental element in many works whose overall
form is not satiric—in a certain character, or situation, or interpolated
passage of ironic commentary on some aspect of the human condition
or contemporary milieu. But in many literary achievements, verse or
prose, the attempt to diminish a subject by ridicule is the organizing
principle of the whole, and these works constitute the formal genre
of "satires." In discussing such writings the following distinctions will
be found useful.

(1) Critics make a broad division between formal (or "direct")
satire and indirect satire. In **formal satire** the satiric voice speaks out
in the first person; this "I" may speak either to the reader (as in
Pope's *Moral Essays*; for example, Epistle II, "Of the Characters of
Women") or else to a character within the work itself, who is called
the **adversarius** and whose major function is to elicit and guide the
satiric speaker's comments. (In Pope's "Epistle to Dr. Arbuthnot,"
Arbuthnot serves as adversarius.) Two types of formal satire are commonly distinguished, taking their names from the great Roman satirists
Horace and Juvenal. The types are defined by the character of the
persona whom the author presents as his first-person satiric speaker,
and by the attitude and *tone* that such a persona manifests toward his
subject matter and audience.

In **Horatian satire** the character of the speaker is that of an urbane,
witty, and tolerant man of the world, who is moved more often to
wry amusement than to indignation at the spectacle of human folly,
pretentiousness, and hypocrisy, and who uses a relaxed and informal

language to evoke a smile at human follies and absurdities—sometimes including his own. Pope's *Moral Essays* and other formal satires for the most part sustain a Horatian stance.

In **Juvenalian satire** the character of the speaker is that of a serious moralist who uses a dignified and public style of utterance to decry modes of vice and error which are no less dangerous because they are ridiculous, and who undertakes to evoke contempt, moral indignation, or an unillusioned sadness at the aberrations of men. Dr. Johnson's "London" and "The Vanity of Human Wishes" are types of Juvenalian satire.

(2) **Indirect satire** is cast in the form of a narrative instead of direct address, in which the objects of the satire are characters who make themselves and their opinions ridiculous by what they think, say, and do, and are sometimes made even more ridiculous by the author's comments and narrative style.

One type of indirect satire is **Menippean satire.** This is named for its Greek originator, the philosophical Cynic Menippus. It is sometimes called **Varronian satire,** after a Roman imitator, Varro; while Northrop Frye, in *Anatomy of Criticism*, pp. 308–312, suggests an alternative name, the *anatomy*, after a major English instance of the type, Burton's *Anatomy of Melancholy* (1621). It is written in prose—though with interpolated passages of verse—and is a miscellaneous form often held together by a loosely constructed narrative. Its major feature, however, is a series of extended dialogues and debates (often conducted at a banquet or party) in which a group of immensely loquacious eccentrics, pedants, literary people, and representatives of various professions or philosophical points of view serve to make ludicrous the intellectual attitudes they typify by the arguments they urge in their support. Examples are Rabelais' *Gargantua and Pantagruel*, Voltaire's *Candide*, Thomas Love Peacock's *Nightmare Abbey* and other satiric fiction, and Huxley's *Point Counter Point*, in which, as in Peacock, the central satiric scenes are discussions at a weekend in a country manor. Frye also classifies Lewis Carroll's two *Alice* books as "perfect Menippean satires."

It should be noted that any narrative or literary vehicle can be adapted to the purposes of indirect satire. Dryden's *Absalom and Achitophel* turns Old Testament history into a satiric allegory on contemporary political maneuverings. In *Gulliver's Travels* Swift converts to satiric use the current literature of voyage and discovery. Many of Addison's *Spectator* papers are satiric essays; Byron's *Don Juan* is a versified satiric form of the old episodic *picaresque* fiction; Ben Jonson's *The Alchemist*, Wycherley's *The Country Wife*, and Shaw's *Arms and the Man* are satiric plays; and Gilbert and Sullivan's *Patience* and other works, like Gay's *Beggar's Opera* and its modern adaptation by Brecht, *The Threepenny Opera*, are satiric operettas. T. S. Eliot's *The Waste Land* employs motifs from myth in a verse satire directed against the spiritual dearth in contemporary life. Most modern satire, however, is written in prose, and especially in novelistic form; for example, Evelyn Waugh's *The Loved One*, Joseph Heller's *Catch-22*, and Kurt Vonnegut, Jr.'s *Player Piano* and *Cat's Cradle*.

Good English satire has been written in every period beginning with the Middle Ages; articles in *Punch* and *The New Yorker* demonstrate that formal essayistic satire, no less than satiric novels and plays, still commands a wide audience; and W. H. Auden is a contemporary who writes excellent satiric poems. The proportioning of the examples in this article, however, indicates how large the Restoration and eighteenth century loom in satiric achievement: the greatest age of English, and probably of world, satire is the century and a half that included Dryden, the Earl of Rochester, Samuel Butler, Wycherley, Addison, Pope, Swift, Gay, Fielding, Johnson, Goldsmith, and (it should not be overlooked) the Burns of "The Holy Fair" and "Holy Willie's Prayer" and the Blake of *The Marriage of Heaven and Hell*. This was also the period of such great satirists as Boileau, LaFontaine, and Voltaire in France.

The articles on *Burlesque, Irony*, and *Wit and humor* describe some of the forms and stylistic devices available to satirists. Consult David Worcester, *The Art of Satire (1940); Ian Jack, *Augustan Satire (1952); James Sutherland, *English Satire (1958); R. C. Elliott, *The Power of Satire (1960); Gilbert Highet, *The Anatomy of Satire* (1962); Ronald Paulson, *The Fictions of Satire* (1967); Matthew Hodgart, *Satire (1969). A recent collection is John Russell and Ashley Brown, eds., *Satire: A Critical Anthology* (1967).

SENTIMENTALISM   is now a pejorative term applied, in a general sense, to an excess of emotion to an occasion, or, in a more limited sense, to an overindulgence in the "tender" emotions of *pathos* and sympathy. Since what constitutes excess or overindulgence is relative both to the judgment of the individual and to large-scale changes in culture and in literary fashion, what to the common reader of one age is a normal expression of humane feeling may seem sentimental to many later readers. The emotional responses Shelley expresses and tries to evoke from the reader in his "Epipsychidion" seemed sentimental to the *New Critics* of the 1930s, who insisted on the need for an ironic counterpoise to intense feeling in poetry. Sophisticated readers now find both the *drama* and *novel of sensibility* of the eighteenth century ludicrously sentimental, and also respond with jeers insteads of

tears to once celebrated episodes of pathos, such as many of the death
scenes, especially the death of a child, in Dickens and other Victorian
writers. And a staple of current anthologies of bad poetry are poems
which were once written, and by some people read, with deep seriousness. A useful distinction between sentimental and nonsentimental is
one which does not depend on the intensity or type of the feeling
expressed or evoked, but labels as sentimental a work or passage in
which the feeling is rendered in commonplaces and *clichés*, instead of
being freshly verbalized and sharply realized in the details of the
situation as represented.

See *Pathos*; and refer to I. A. Richards, *Practical Criticism*, Chap.
6, and Laurence Lerner, "A Note on Sentimentality," *The Truest
Poetry* (1960).

SETTING.   The setting of a narrative or dramatic work is the general
locale and the historical time in which its action occurs; the setting
of an episode or scene within a work is the particular physical location
in which it takes place. The general setting of *Macbeth*, for example,
is medieval Scotland, and the setting for the scene in which Macbeth
comes upon the witches is a blasted heath; the setting of Joyce's
Ulysses is Dublin on June 16, 1904, and its opening episode is set in
the Martello Tower, overlooking Dublin Bay. The physical setting, in
writers like Poe, Hardy, and Faulkner, is an important element in
generating the *atmosphere* of a work. The Greek term **opsis** ("scene,"
or "spectacle") is now occasionally used to denote the visible or
picturable elements in any work of literature, including a lyric poem.

When applied to a theatrical production, "setting" is synonomous
with **mise en scène,** a French term denoting the scenery and the
properties, or movable pieces of furniture, on the stage. The term
"mise en scène" sometimes includes also the positioning of the actors
in a particular scene.

SHORT STORY.   A short story is a work of prose fiction, and most of
the terms for analyzing the component parts, the types, and the various
narrative techniques of the *novel* are applicable to the short story as
well. It differs, for example, from the **anecdote**—the simple and un-
elaborated narration of a single incident—in that it organizes the
action, thought, and interactions of its characters into the artful pattern of a *plot*, which has a beginning and develops through a middle
to some sort of denouement at the end. The plot form may be comic,
or tragic, or romantic, or satiric; the story is presented to us from one
of the many available *points of view*; and it may be written in the
mode of fantasy, realism, or naturalism.

In the **tale,** or "story of incident," the focus of interest is on the course and outcome of the events, as in Poe's *The Gold Bug* or other tales of detection, in the stories of O. Henry, and in the stock but sometimes well-contrived western story in the pulp magazines. "Stories of character" focus on the revelation of a state of mind and motivation, or of moral qualities. In some of the stories of character by the Russian master of the form, Chekhov, nothing more happens than an encounter and conversation between two people. Ernest Hemingway's classic, "A Clean, Well-Lighted Place," consists only of a curt conversation between two waiters about an old man who each day gets drunk and stays on in the café until it closes, followed by a brief meditation on the part of one of the waiters. Some stories achieve a balance of interest between external action and character. Hemingway's "The Short Happy Life of Francis Macomber" is as violent in its packed events as the most lurid tale of adventure, but every detail of the action is contrived to test and reveal, with a surprising set of reversals, the moral quality of all three protagonists.

The short story, however, is a story that is short; that is, it differs from the novel in the dimension which Aristotle calls "magnitude," and this limitation imposes differences both in the effects that can be achieved and in the choice and management of the elements to achieve those effects. Edgar Allan Poe, who is sometimes called the originator of the short story as a specific genre, was at any rate its first critical theorist. He defined what he called "the prose tale" as a narrative that can be read at one sitting of from one-half hour to two hours, and that is limited to "a certain unique or single effect," to which every detail is subordinate (Review of Hawthorne's *Twice-Told Tales*, 1842). Poe's comment applies to many short stories, and it points to the economy of management which the tightness of the form always imposes in some degree. We can say that, by and large, the short story writer introduces a very limited number of characters, cannot afford the space for a leisurely analysis and sustained development of character, and cannot undertake to develop as dense and detailed a social milieu as does the novelist. He often begins his story close to, or even on the verge of, the climax, minimizes both prior exposition and the details of the setting, keeps the complications down, and clears up the denouement quickly—sometimes in a few sentences. (See *Plot.*) The central incident is selected to reveal as much as possible of the totality of the protagonist's life and character, and the details are devised to carry maximum significance. This spareness in the narrative means often gives the artistry in a good short story higher visibility than the artistry in an equally good novel.

Many distinguished short stories, however, depart from this paradigm in various ways. It must be remembered that the name covers a great diversity of prose fiction, all the way from the **short short story,** which is a slightly elaborated anecdote of perhaps 500 words, to such long and complex forms as Melville's *Billy Budd,* Henry James's *The Turn of the Screw,* and Conrad's *Heart of Darkness,* whose status between the tautness of the short story and the expansiveness of the novel is sometimes indicated by the name **novelette.**

Historically the short narrative, in both verse and prose, is one of the oldest and most widespread of literary forms. Some of the types which preceded the short story are the *fable,* the *exemplum,* the *folk-tale,* and the *fabliau.* The form of prose narrative recognizably like the contemporary short story was developed by such writers as Washington Irving, Hawthorne, and Poe in America, Sir Walter Scott in England, E. T. A. Hoffman in Germany, Balzac in France, and Gogol and Turgenev in Russia. The short story in English has flourished more in America than in England; Frank O'Connor has called it "the national art form," and its American masters include (in addition to those already mentioned) William Faulkner, Katherine Anne Porter, Eudora Welty, Flannery O'Connor, John O'Hara, J. F. Powers, John Cheever, and J. D. Salinger.

See H. S. Canby, *The Short Story in English* (1909); Sean O'Faolain, **The Short Story* (1948); Frank O'Connor, **The Lonely Voice: A Study of the Short Story* (1962).

SOLILOQUY is the act of talking to oneself. In drama it denotes the *convention* by which a character, alone on the stage, utters his thoughts aloud; the playwright uses this device as a convenient way to convey directly to the audience information about a character's motives, intentions, and state of mind, as well as for purposes of general exposition. Marlowe's *Dr. Faustus* opens with a long expository monologue, and concludes with another which expresses Faustus' frantic condition during his belated attempts to escape damnation. The best-known of all soliloquies, of course, is Hamlet's speech, "To be or not to be."

A related stage device is the **aside,** in which a character expresses his thought or intention in a short speech which, by convention, is inaudible to the other characters on the stage. Both conventions, common in Elizabethan and later drama, fell into disuse in the later nineteenth century, when increasing demands that plays convey the illusion of real life forced the dramatists to exploit indirect means for conveying information and guidance to the audience.

SONNET. A lyric poem written in a single stanza, which consists of fourteen iambic pentameter lines linked by an intricate rhyme scheme. The rhyme, in English, usually follows one of two main patterns:

(1) The **Italian** or **Petrarchan sonnet** (named after the fourteenth-

century Italian poet, Petrarch) falls into two main parts: an **octave** (8 lines) rhyming *a b b a a b b a* and a **sestet** (6 lines) rhyming *c d e c d e* or some variant, such as *c d c c d c.* Petrarch's sonnets were first imitated in England, both in form and in primary subject matter—a doting lover's hopes and pains—by Sir Thomas Wyatt in the early sixteenth century. The Petrarchan form was later used by Milton, Wordsworth, D. G. Rossetti, and other sonneteers, who sometimes made it technically easier in English (which does not have as many rhyming possibilities as Italian) by introducing a new pair of rhymes in the second half of the octave. (See *Rhyme.*)

(2) The Earl of Surrey and other English experimenters in the sixteenth century also developed a new form called the **English sonnet,** or else the **Shakespearean sonnet,** after its greatest practitioner. This stanza falls into three quatrains and a concluding couplet: *a b a b c d c d e f e f g g.* There was one especially important variant, the **Spenserian sonnet,** in which Spenser links each quatrain to the next by a continuing rhyme: *a b a b   b c b c   c d c d   e e.*

John Donne shifted from the hitherto standard subject, secular love, to a variety of religious themes in his *Holy Sonnets*, and Milton expanded the range to other matters of serious contemplation. The sonnet, except for a lapse in the English neoclassic period, has remained a popular form up to such modern poets as E. A. Robinson, W. H. Auden, and Dylan Thomas. The stanza is just long enough to permit a fairly complex lyric development, yet so short and so exigent in its rhymes as to pose a standing challenge to the artistry of the poet. The rhyme pattern of the Petrarchan sonnet has on the whole favored a statement of problem, situation, or incident in the octave, with a resolution in the sestet. The English form sometimes falls into a similar division of material and sometimes presents a repetition-with-variation of the statement in the three quatrains; the final couplet, however, usually imposes an epigrammatic turn at the end. In Drayton's fine English sonnet, "Since there's no help, come let us kiss and part," the lover brusquely declares in the first two quatrains that he is glad the affair is cleanly broken off, pauses in the third quatrain as though at the threshold, and in the last two rhymed lines suddenly drops his swagger to make one last plea. Here are the concluding quatrain and couplet:

> Now at the last gasp of love's latest breath,
> When, his pulse failing, passion speechless lies,
> When faith is kneeling by his bed of death,
> And innocence is closing up his eyes;
>> Now if thou wouldst, when all have given him over,
>> From death to life thou mightst him yet recover.

Following Petrarch's early example, a number of Elizabethan poets wrote a **sonnet sequence**, in which a series of sonnets are linked together by exploring various aspects of a relationship between lovers, or by indicating a development in that relationship which constitutes a kind of implicit plot. Shakespeare wrote his sonnets in a sequence, as did Sidney in *Astrophel and Stella* (1580) and Spenser in *Amoretti* (1595). Later examples of the sonnet sequence are D. G. Rossetti's *House of Life*, Elizabeth Barrett Browning's *Sonnets from the Portuguese*, and William Ellery Leonard's *Two Lives*. Dylan Thomas' recent *Altarwise by Owl-light* is a sequence of ten sonnets which is not about lovers, but a meditation on the poet's own life. George Meredith's *Modern Love* (1862) is a sequence of sixteen-line poems which are sometimes called "sonnets."

See T. W. H. Crosland, *The English Sonnet* (1917); L. G. Sterner, *The Sonnet in American Literature* (1930); L. C. John, *The Elizabethan Sonnet Sequences* (1938); J. B. Leishman, *Themes and Variations in Shakespeare's Sonnets* (1963).

STANZA. A stanza (Italian for "stopping place") is a grouping of the verse-lines in a poem. Usually the stanzas of a given poem are marked by a recurrent rhyme scheme, and are also uniform in the number and lengths of the component lines. Some unrhymed poems, however, are divided into stanzaic units (for example, Collins' "Ode to Evening"), and some rhymed poems are composed of variable stanzas (for example, the *irregular ode*).

Of the great variety of English stanza forms, many have no special names and must be described by specifying the number of lines, the type and number of *feet* in each line, and the pattern of the *rhyme*. Some stanzas, however, have been used so frequently that they have been given the convenience of a name, as follows:

A **couplet** is a pair of rhymed lines. The **octosyllabic couplet** has lines of eight syllables, usually consisting of four iambic feet. So in Marvell's "To His Coy Mistress":

> The grave's a fine and private place,
> But none, I think, do there embrace.

Iambic pentameter couplets are called *heroic couplets* (discussed in a separate entry).

The **tercet,** or **triplet,** is a stanza of three lines with a single rhyme. The lines may be the same length (as in Robert Herrick's "Upon Julia's Clothes," written in tercets of iambic tetrameter), or else of varying lengths. In Richard Crashaw's "Wishes to His Supposed Mistress," the lines of each tercet are successively in iambic dimeter, trimeter, and tetrameter:

> Who e'er she be
> That not impossible she
> That shall command my heart and me.

Terza rima is composed of tercets which are interlinked, in that each is joined to the one following by a common rhyme: *a b a, b c b, c d c,* and so on. Dante composed his *Divine Comedy* in terza rima; but although Sir Thomas Wyatt introduced the form early in the sixteenth century, it has not been a common meter in English, in which rhymes are much harder to find than in Italian. Shelley, however, used it brilliantly in "Ode to the West Wind," and it occurs also in the poetry of Milton, Browning, and T. S. Eliot.

The **quatrain,** or four-line stanza, is the most common in English versification, and is employed with various meters and rhyme schemes. The *ballad stanza* (in alternating four- and three-foot lines) is one common quatrain, and the **heroic quatrain,** in iambic pentameter rhyming *a b a b,* is the stanza of Gray's "Elegy Written in a Country Churchyard."

Rhyme royal was introduced by Chaucer in *Troilus and Criseyde* and other narrative poems; it is believed to take its name, however, from its later use in the verses of King James I of Scotland. It is a seven-line, iambic pentameter stanza rhyming *a b a b b c c.*

Ottava rima, as the Italian name indicates, has eight lines; it rhymes *a b a b a b c c.* Like terza rima and the *sonnet,* it was brought from Italian into English by Sir Thomas Wyatt. Although employed by a number of earlier poets, it is peculiarly the stanza which helped Byron discover what he was born to write, the satiric poem *Don Juan*:

> Juan was taught from out the best edition,
> Expurgated by learned men, who place,
> Judiciously, from out the schoolboy's vision,
> The grosser parts; but, fearful to deface
> Too much their modest bard by this omission,
> And pitying sore his mutilated case,
> They only add them all in an appendix,
> Which saves, in fact, the trouble of an index.

Spenserian stanza is a still longer form devised by Edmund Spenser for *The Faerie Queene*—nine lines, the first eight iambic pentameter and the last iambic hexameter (an *Alexandrine*), rhyming *a b a b b c b c c.* Enchanted by Spenser's gracious movement and music, many poets have attempted the form in spite of its difficulties. Its greatest successes have been in poems which, like *The Faerie Queene,* move in a leisurely way, with ample time for unrolling the richly textured stanzas: James Thomson's "The Castle of Indolence," Keats's "The Eve of St. Agnes," Shelley's "Adonais," and the narrative section of Tennyson's "The Lotus Eaters."

There are also various elaborate stanza forms imported from France, such as the rondeau, the villanelle, and the triolet, containing intricate repetitions of rhymes and lines, which have been used mainly, but not exclusively, for *light verse*. Their revival by W. H. Auden, William Empson, and other poets is a sign of renewed interest in high metrical artifice. Dylan Thomas' "Do not go gentle into that good night" is a **villanelle;** that is, it consists of five tercets and a quatrain, all on two rhymes, and with systematic later repetitions of lines 1 and 3 of the first tercet.

The nature and history of the various stanzas are discussed and exemplified in R. M. Alden, *English Verse* (1903).

STOCK CHARACTERS   are character types that recur repeatedly in a particular literary genre, and so are recognizable as part of the *conventions* of the form. The old Greek comedy had three stock characters who fulfilled the functions of the standard plot: the **alazon,** or imposter and self-deceiving braggart; the **eiron,** or self-deprecatory and understating character, whose contest with the alazon is central to the comic plot; and the **bomolochos,** buffoon, whose antics add an extra comic element. (See Lane Cooper, *An Aristotelian Theory of Comedy,* 1922.) In his *Anatomy of Criticism* (1957), pp. 171 ff., Northrop Frye has revived these old terms, added a fourth, the **agroikos,** the rustic or easily deceived character, and identified the recurrence of these types (very broadly defined) in comic plots through our own time.

Elizabethan romantic comedy, such as Shakespeare's *As You Like It* and *Twelfth Night,* often turned on a heroine disguised as a handsome young man; and a stock figure in the Elizabethan comedy of intrigue was the clever servant who, like Mosca in Jonson's *Volpone,* connives with his master to fleece another stock character, the stupid "gull." Nineteenth-century comedy, on stage and in fiction, exploited the stock Englishman with a monocle, an exaggerated Oxford accent, and a defective sense of humor. Western stories and films generated the tight-lipped sheriff who lets his gun do the talking, while a familiar figure in the fiction of the recent past was the stoical Hemingway hero, unillusioned but faithful to his primal code of honor and loyalty in a civilization grown effete and corrupt. The beat or hipster who, with or without the help of drugs, has opted out of the Establishment, is an even more recent stock character.

The evaluation of a character in literature does not depend on whether or not an author incorporates an established type, but on how well he recreates it into a convincing individual. Two of Shakespeare's greatest characters are patently conventional. Falstaff is a re-rendering in part of the *Vice,* the comic tempter of the medieval morality play, and in part of the familiar braggart soldier, the "miles gloriosus" of

Renaissance and Roman comedy, whose ancestry goes back to the Greek alazon. And Hamlet combines the stock attributes of the hero of Elizabethan *revenge tragedies* with those of the Elizabethan melancholic man.

STOCK RESPONSE.   An habitual and stereotyped reaction, in place of one which is genuinely and aptly responsive to a given stimulus. The term may be applied either to the response to a situation or topic that an author expresses in his work, or to the response of a reader to a passage within the work; in either case, the connotation is derogatory. I. A. Richards, in his *Practical Criticism* (1930), Chap. 5, gave currency to this term by citing and analyzing stock responses by students who wrote critiques on unidentified poems presented for their inspection.

STOCK SITUATIONS   are the counterparts in plot of stock characters; that is, they are often-used incidents or sequences of actions in a drama or narrative. Instances range from single situations—the eavesdropper who is hidden behind a bush or under a table, or the suddenly discovered will or birthmark—to the overall pattern of a plot. The Horatio Alger books are all variations on the rags-to-riches-by-pluck-and-luck plot, and we often recognize the stock boy-meets-girl story in the opening episode of popular fiction or motion pictures.

A number of modern critics distinguish certain recurrent character-types and elements of plot, such as the sexually irresistible but fatal enchantress, the sacrificial scapegoat, and the underground journey, as "archetypal" components which are held to recur, not because they are functional literary conventions, but because, like dreams and myths, they express elemental and universal human impulses, anxieties, and needs. See *Archetype.*

STREAM OF CONSCIOUSNESS   was a phrase used by William James in his *Principles of Psychology* (1890) to characterize the unbroken flow of thought and awareness in the waking mind; it has now been adopted to describe a narrative method in modern fiction. Long passages of introspection are found in novelists such as George Meredith and Henry James, and as early as 1888 a minor French writer, Edouard Dujardin, wrote a short novel, *Les Lauriers Sont Coupés* (*The Laurels Have Been Cut*), which is a rather crude but sustained attempt to represent all the scenes and events as they impinge upon the consciousness of the central character. The stream of consciousness, as it was refined after World War I, is a mode of narration that undertakes to capture the full spectrum and flow of a character's mental process, in which sense perceptions mingle with conscious and half-conscious thoughts, memories, feelings, and random associations.

Some critics use "stream of consciousness" interchangeably with the term **interior monologue**. It is useful, however, to employ the former as the inclusive term, denoting all the diverse techniques employed by authors to describe or to represent the overall state and process of consciousness in a character. "Interior monologue" can then be reserved to denote specifically the technique that undertakes to reproduce the course and rhythm of consciousness just as it occurs in a character's mind, with no (or at any rate, with minimal) intervention by the author as guide or commentator, and without tidying the vagaries of the mental process into grammatical sentences or into a logical and narrative order. The interior monologue, in its radical form, is sometimes described as the exact reproduction of consciousness; but since sense perceptions, feelings, and some aspects of thought itself are nonverbal, it is clear that the author must convert these elements into some kind of verbal equivalent, and much of this conversion is a matter of narrative convention rather than of unedited, point-for-point reproduction.

James Joyce perfected various techniques of stream-of-consciousness narration in *Ulysses* (1922). Here is a passage of interior monologue from the "Lestrygonian" episode, in which Leopold Bloom saunters through Dublin, observing and musing:

> Pineapple rock, lemon platt, butter scotch.   A sugarsticky girl shoveling scoopfuls of creams for a christian brother.   Some school treat.   Bad for their tummies.   Lozenge and comfit manufacturer to His Majesty the King.   God.   Save.   Our. Sitting on his throne, sucking red jujubes white.

Dorothy Richardson sustains a stream-of-consciousness narrative, focused exclusively on the mind of her heroine, throughout the twelve volumes of her novel *Pilgrimage* (1915–1938); Virginia Woolf employs the procedure as the chief narrative mode in several novels, including *Mrs. Dalloway* (1925) and *To the Lighthouse* (1927); and William Faulkner exploits it brilliantly in the first three of the four parts of *The Sound and the Fury* (1929).

See Leon Edel, *The Modern Psychological Novel* (1955); Robert Humphrey, *Stream of Consciousness in the Modern Novel* (1954); Melvin Friedman, *Stream of Consciousness: A Study in Literary Method* (1955).

STYLE   is the manner of linguistic expression in prose or verse—it is *how* a speaker or writer says whatever he says. The characteristic style of a work or a writer may be analyzed in terms of its *diction*, or characteristic choice of words; its sentence structure and syntax; the density and types of its figurative language; the patterns of its rhythm and of its component sounds; and its rhetorical aims and devices.

In traditional theories of *rhetoric*, styles were classified into three main levels: the **high** (or grand), the **middle** (or mean), and the **low** (or base, or plain) **style.** The doctrine of *decorum* required that the level of style in a work be appropriate to the speaker, the occasion, and the dignity of its literary genre. Recently Northrop Frye has introduced a variant of this ancient and long-persisting theory of stylistic levels in literature. He makes a basic differentiation between the **demotic style** (which is modeled on the language, rhythms, and associations of ordinary speech) and the **hieratic style** (which employs a variety of formal elaborations that separate the literary language from ordinary speech). Frye then proceeds to distinguish a high, middle, and low level in each of these classes. See *The Well-Tempered Critic* (1963), Chap. 2.

In analyzing style two types of sentence structure are often distinguished:

The **periodic sentence** is one in which the parts, or "members," are so composed that the completion of the sense—that is, the closure of the syntax—remains suspended until the end of the sentence; the effect tends to be formal or oratorical. An example is the fine opening sentence of Boswell's *Life of Samuel Johnson*:

> To write the Life of him who excelled all mankind in writing the lives of others, and who, whether we consider his extraordinary endowments, or his various works, has been equalled by few in any age, is an arduous, and may be reckoned in me a presumptuous task.

In the **nonperiodic,** or **loose, sentence**—which is more relaxed and conversational in effect—the component members are continuous, but so loosely joined that the sentence would have been syntactically complete if a period had been inserted at one or more places before the actual close. So in Addison's sentences in *Spectator 105*, describing the limited topics in the conversation of a mere man-about-town:

> He will tell you the names of the principal favourites, repeat the shrewd sayings of a man of quality, whisper an intrigue that is not yet blown upon by common fame; or, if the sphere of his observations is a little larger than ordinary, will perhaps enter into all the incidents, turns, and revolutions in a game of ombre. When he has gone thus far he has shown you the whole circle of his accomplishments, his parts are drained, and he is disabled from any farther conversation.

Another distinction made with increasing frequency in discussing prose style is that between parataxis and hypotaxis:

A **paratactic style** is one in which the members within a sentence, or else a sequence of complete sentences, are put one after the other without any expression of their connection or relations except (at most) the noncommittal connective, "and." Hemingway's style is characteristically paratactic. The members in this sentence from *The Sun Also Rises* are joined merely by "ands": "It was dim and dark and the pillars went high up, and there were people praying, and it smelt of incense, and there were some wonderful big buildings." And the curt sentences in "Indian Camp" omit all connectives: "The sun was coming over the hills. A bass jumped, making a circle in the water. Nick trailed his hand in the water. It felt warm in the sharp chill of the morning."

A **hypotactic style** is one in which the temporal, logical, and syntactic relations between members and sentences are expressed by words (such as "when," "then," "because," "therefore") or by phrases (such as "in order to," "as a result") or by the use of subordinate phrases and clauses. The typical sentences in this article are hypotactic.

A very large set of terms are used to classify types of style, such as "pure," "ornate," "florid," "gay," "sober," "simple," "elaborate," and so on. Styles are also classified according to a literary period or tradition ("the *metaphysical* style," "Restoration prose style"); according to an influential work ("Biblical style," *euphuism*); according to a type of use ("a scientific style," "journalese"); or according to the distinctive practice of an individual author (the "Shakespearean" or "Miltonic style"; "Johnsonese"). Historians of English prose style, especially in the seventeenth and eighteenth centuries, have distinguished between the vogue of the "Ciceronian style," which is elaborately constructed, highly periodic, and typically builds to a climax, and the opposing vogue of the clipped, concise, pointed, and uniformly stressed sentences in the "Attic" and "Senecan styles." See *Style, Rhetoric, and Rhythm: Essays by Morris W. Croll*, ed. J. M. Patrick and others (1966), and George Williamson, *The Senecan Amble: A Study in Prose Form from Bacon to Collier* (1951).

General treatments of style: J. M. Murry, *The Problem of Style* (1925); Herbert Read, *English Prose Style* (1928); Bonamy Dobrée, *Modern Prose Style* (1934); P. F. Baum, *The Other Harmony of Prose* (1952); Erich Auerbach, *Mimesis: The Representation of Reality in Western Literature* (1953). For attempts to distinguish and analyze "mannerist," "baroque," and "rococo" styles in seventeenth-century and later poetry and prose, see Wylie Sypher, *Four Stages of Renaissance Style* (1955), and *Rococo to Cubism in Art and Literature* (1960).

SURREALISM, "superrealism," was launched as a concerted movement in France by André Breton's *Manifesto on Surrealism*, 1924. The ex-

pressed aim was a revolution against all restraints on the free functioning of the human mind. These restraints included the logical
reason, standard morality, social and artistic conventions, and the control of artistic creation by forethought and intention. To ensure the
unhampered operation of the deep mind, which they regarded as the
only source of valid knowledge and art, surrealists turned to "auto-
matic writing" (writing delivered over entirely to the promptings of
the unconscious mind), and to exploiting the material of dreams, of
states of mind between sleep and waking, and of natural or artificially
induced hallucinations.

Surrealism was a revolutionary movement in painting, sculpture,
and the other arts, as well as literature; it often united briefly with one
or another revolutionary political and social movement; and it spread
rapidly over both Europe and America. It is more important, however,
in its general influence than in the work of the relatively small group
of its professed adherents such as André Breton, Louis Aragon, and
the painter Salvador Dali. The influence, direct or indirect, of sur-
realist innovations can be found in many modern writers in prose and
verse who have broken with conventional modes of artistic organization to experiment with free associations, violated syntax, nonlogical
and nonchronological order, dreamlike and nightmarish sequences,
and the juxtaposition of bizarre, shocking, or seemingly unrelated
images. In England and America such effects can be found in a wide
range of writings, from the poetry of Dylan Thomas to the flights of
fantasy, hallucinative writing, startling inconsequences, and *black
humor* in the novels of Henry Miller, Thomas Pynchon (*V*), and
William Burroughs (*Naked Lunch*).

See *Literature of the absurd*; and refer to David Gascoyne, *A Short
Survey of Surrealism* (1935); A. E. Balakian, *Literary Origins of
Surrealism* (1947); Herbert Read, *The Philosophy of Modern Art*
(1955); H. M. Block, "Surrealism and Modern Poetry," *Journal of
Aesthetics and Art Criticism*, XVIII (1959).

SYMBOL. A symbol, in the broadest sense of the term, is anything
which signifies something else; in this sense all words are symbols.
As commonly used in discussing literature, however, symbol is applied
only to a word or set of words that signifies an object or event which
itself signifies something else; that is, the words refer to something
which suggests a range of reference beyond itself. Some symbols are
"conventional" or "public"; thus "the Cross," "the Red, White, and
Blue," "the Good Shepherd" are terms that signify symbolic objects of
which the further significance is fixed and traditional in a particular
culture. Poets, like all of us, use such conventional symbols; many

poets, however, also use "private" or "personal symbols," which they develop themselves. Often they do so by exploiting preexisting and widely shared associations with an object or action—for example, the general tendency to associate a peacock with pride and an eagle with heroic endeavor, or to associate the rising sun with birth and the setting sun with death, or to associate climbing with effort or progress and descent with surrender or failure. Some poets, however, often use symbols whose significance they mainly generate for themselves, and these set the reader a more difficult problem in interpretation.

Take as an example the word "rose," which in its literal meaning is a kind of flower. In Burns's line, "O my love's like a red, red rose," the word "rose" is a *simile*; and in the lines by Winthrop Mackworth Praed

> She was our queen, our rose, our star;
> And then she danced—O Heaven, her dancing!

the word "rose" is a *metaphor*. In the long medieval dream vision *The Romance of the Rose* we read about a half-opened rose to which the dreamer's access is aided by a character called "Fair Welcome," but impeded or forbidden by other characters called "Reason," "Shame," and "Jealousy": we readily recognize that the whole narrative is an *allegory* about an elaborate courtship, in which most of the agents are personified abstractions and the rose itself represents the lady's love. Then we read William Blake's poem "The Sick Rose":

> O Rose, thou art sick.
> The invisible worm
> That flies in the night
> In the howling storm:
>
> Has found out thy bed
> Of crimson joy:
> And his dark secret love
> Does thy life destroy.

This rose is not the vehicle for a simile or metaphor, because it lacks the paired subject—"my love," or the girl referred to as "she," in the examples just cited—which is characteristic of these figures. And it is not an allegorical rose since, unlike the flower in *The Romance of the Rose*, it is not part of an obvious double order of correlated references, one literal and the second allegorical, in which the allegorical reference of the rose is precisely fixed by its function within the literal narrative. Blake's rose *is* a rose—yet it is also something more than a rose: words such as "bed," "joy," "love," which do not comport literally with an actual flower, together with the sinister tone and the intensity of the feeling, press the reader to infer that the described object has a further range of unspecified reference which makes it a symbol. But Blake's rose is a personal symbol and not—like the symbolic rose in the closing cantos of Dante's *Paradiso* and other Christian poems—an element in a set of traditional and widely known religious symbols, in which concrete objects of this passing world are regarded as signifying the truths of a higher and eternal realm. Only from the implicit suggestions in Blake's poem itself—the sexual connotations of "bed" and "love," especially in conjunction with "joy" and "worm"—supplemented by our knowledge of related elements in Blake's other poems, as well as by our normal associations with the objects described in this poem, do we gradually infer that Blake's lament for a crimson rose which has been entered and sickened unto death by a dark and secret worm symbolizes the destruction wrought by furtiveness, deceit, and hypocrisy in what ought to be a frank and joyous relationship of physical love. Various critics of the poem, however, have proposed differing interpretations of its symbolic significance. It is an attribute of many private symbols, and one reason why they are an irreplaceable literary device, that they suggest a direction, or a broad area of reference rather than, like an item in an allegorical narrative, a single and specific reference.

See W. B. Yeats, "The Symbolism of Poetry" (1900) in *Essays and Introductions* (1961); W. Y. Tindall, *The Literary Symbol* (1955); Harry Levin, "Symbolism and Fiction," in *Contexts of Criticism* (1957); Isabel C. Hungerland, *Poetic Discourse* (1958), Chap. 5; Maurice Beebe, ed., *Literary Symbolism* (1960).

SYMBOLIST MOVEMENT.   Various English Romantic poets employed private symbols in their poetry; Shelley, for example, repeatedly made symbolic use of objects such as the morning and evening star, a boat moving upstream, winding caves, and the conflict between a serpent and an eagle. William Blake, however, exceeded all his contemporaries in the use of a persistent and sustained symbolism, both in his lyric poems and prophetic epics. His procedure had no close parallel until the **Symbolist Movement** in France, which began with Baudelaire's *Fleurs du Mal* (1857) and was continued by such major poets as Rimbaud, Verlaine, Mallarmé, and Valérie. The techniques of the French **Symbolists,** who exploited private symbols in a poetry of rich suggestiveness rather than explicit statement, had an immense influence throughout Europe, and (especially in the 1890s and later) in England and America as well, on poets such as Arthur Symons, Ernest Dowson, Yeats, Eliot, Pound, Dylan Thomas, Hart Crane, E. E. Cummings, and Wallace Stevens.

English and European literature since World War I has been a notable era of symbolism in literature. Many major writers of the period—poets, novelists, and dramatists—exploit symbols which are in part drawn from religious and esoteric traditions and in part developed by themselves. Some of the notable works of the age are symbolist throughout: in their settings, their agents, and their actions, as well as in their diction. Instances of a persistently symbolic procedure occur in lyrics (Yeats's "Byzantium" poems, Dylan Thomas' series of sonnets *Altarwise by Owl-light*), in longer poems (Hart Crane's *The Bridge*, Eliot's *The Waste Land*, Stevens' "Comedian as the Letter C"), and in novels (Joyce's *Ulysses* and *Finnegans Wake*, Faulkner's *The Sound and the Fury*).

See Arthur Symons, *The Symbolist Movement in Literature* (rev. ed., 1919); Edmund Wilson, *Axel's Castle* (1936); C. M. Bowra, *The Heritage of Symbolism* (1943); Kenneth Cornell, *The Symbolist Movement* (1951); Edward Engelberg, ed., *The Symbolist Poem* (1967). For William Blake's complex symbolism, refer to S. Foster Damon, *A Blake Dictionary: The Ideas and Symbols of William Blake* (1965).

SYNESTHESIA   is the experience of two or more modes of sensation when only one sense is being stimulated. In literature the term is applied to descriptions of one kind of sensation in terms of another; color is attributed to sounds, odor to colors, sound to odors, and so on. A complex example of this phenomenon, sometimes also called "sense transference" or "sense analogy," is this passage from Shelley's "The Sensitive Plant":

> And the hyacinth purple, and white, and blue,
> Which flung from its bells a sweet peal anew
> Of music so delicate, soft, and intense,
> It was felt like an odor within the sense.

The varicolored, bell-shaped flowers send out a peal of music which affects the sense as though it were (what in fact it is) the scent of the hyacinths. Keats, in the "Ode to a Nightingale," calls for a draught of cool wine

> Tasting of Flora and the country green,
> Dance, and Provençal song, and sunburnt mirth;

tasting, that is, of sight, color, motion, sound, and heat. This type of imagery can be found, in scattered examples, in literature since Homer. It was especially exploited, however, by the French *Symbolists* of the middle and later nineteenth century; see Baudelaire's sonnet "Correspondances," and Rimbaud's sonnet on the color of vowel sounds: "A black, E white, I red, U green, O blue."

Refer to June Downey, *Creative Imagination* (1929); R. H. Fogle, *The Imagery of Keats and Shelley* (1949), Chap. 3.

TENSION has been a common descriptive and evaluative word in literary criticism since Allen Tate proposed it as a term to be made by "lopping the prefixes off the logical terms *ex*tension and *in*tension." In technical logic the "intension" of a word is the abstract set of attributes which must be possessed by any object to which the word can be literally applied, and the "extension" of a word is the specific object or class of objects to which it literally applies. The meaning of good poetry, according to Tate, "is its 'tension,' the full organized body of all the extension and intension that we can find in it." ("Tension in Poetry," 1938, in *On the Limits of Poetry*, 1948.) It would seem that by this statement Tate means that a good poem incorporates both the abstract and the concrete, the general idea and the particular image, in an integral whole.

Other critics use "tension" to characterize poetry that manifests an equilibrium of the serious and the ironic, or "a pattern of resolved stresses," or a harmony of opponent tendencies, or any other mode of that stability-in-conflict which is the favorite way in the *new criticism* for conceiving the organization of a good poem. And some critics, dubious perhaps about the validity of Tate's logical derivation of the term, simply apply "tension" to any poem in which the elements seem tightly rather than loosely interrelated.

THREE UNITIES. In the sixteenth and seventeenth centuries, critics of the drama in Italy and France added to Aristotle's recommendation of *unity of action* two other unities, to constitute the rules of drama known as "the three unities." On the assumption that "verisimilitude"— the achievement of an illusion of reality in the audience—requires that the action represented in a play approximate the actual conditions of the staging of the play, they imposed the "unity of place" (that the action be limited to a single location) and the "unity of time" (that the time represented be limited to the two or three hours it takes to act the play, or at most to a single day of either twelve or twenty-four hours). Mainly because of the strong influence of Shakespeare, whose plays represent frequent changes of place and the passage of many years, the rules of the unities were never so dominant in English *neoclassicism* as in Italy and France; a final blow was the famous attack against them in Dr. Johnson's "Preface to Shakespeare" (1765). Since the mid-eighteenth century in England, the unities of time and place have been regarded as optional devices, available to the playwright for special effects of dramatic concentration.

See J. W. H. Atkins, *English Literary Criticism: Seventeenth and Eighteenth Centuries* (1957).

TRAGEDY. The term is broadly applied to literary, and especially to dramatic, representations of serious and important actions which turn out disastrously for the chief character. Detailed discussions of the tragic form properly begin—although they should not end—with Aristotle's classic analysis in the *Poetics*. Aristotle based his theory on induction from the only examples available to him, the tragedies of Greek dramatists such as Aeschylus, Sophocles, and Euripides. In the subsequent two thousand years and more, many new and artistically effective types of serious plots ending in a catastrophe have been developed—types that Aristotle had no way of foreseeing. The innumerable attempts to stretch Aristotle's analysis to apply to all later tragic forms serve merely to blur his critical categories and to obscure important differences among diverse types of tragic plays. When flexibly managed, however, Aristotle's concepts apply in some part to many tragic plots, and they serve at least as a suggestive starting point for establishing the differentiae of the various non-Aristotelian modes of tragic construction.

Aristotle defined tragedy as "the imitation of an action that is serious and also, as having magnitude, complete in itself," in the medium of poetic language, and in the manner of dramatic rather than narrative presentation, incorporating "incidents arousing pity and fear, wherewith to accomplish the catharsis of such emotions." Precisely how to interpret Aristotle's **catharsis**—which in Greek signifies "purgation," or "purification," or both—is much disputed. On two matters, however, a number of modern commentators agree. Aristotle in the first place sets out to account for the undeniable, if extraordinary, fact that many tragic representations of suffering and defeat leave an audience feeling not depressed, but relieved, or even exalted. (One recent commentator, however, interprets Aristotle's "catharsis" as applying not to an effect on the audience, but to an element within the play itself: it signifies, he claims, the purgation of the guilt attached to the hero's tragic act, through the demonstration by the course of the drama that the hero performed this act without knowledge of its nature. See Gerald Else, *Aristotle's Poetics*, 1957, pp. 224–232, 423–447.) In the second place, Aristotle uses this distinctive effect, "the pleasure of pity and fear," as the basic way to distinguish the tragic from comic or other forms, and he regards the dramatist's aim to produce and maximize this effect as the principle which determines both the choice of the tragic protagonist and the organization of the tragic plot.

Accordingly, Aristotle says that the tragic hero will most effectively evoke both our pity and our terror if he is neither thoroughly good nor thoroughly evil but a mixture of both; and also that the tragic effect will be stronger if the hero is "better than we are," in the sense that he is of higher moral worth. Such a man is exhibited as suffering a change in fortune from happiness to misery because of a mistaken act, to which he is led by his **hamartia**—his "error of judgment" or, as it is often though less literally translated, his **tragic flaw**. (One common form of hamartia in the Greek tragedies was **hubris**, that "pride," or overweening self-confidence, which leads a man to disregard a divine warning or to violate a moral law.) The tragic hero accordingly moves us to pity because, since he is not an evil man, his misfortune is greater than he deserves; but he moves us also to fear, because we recognize similar possibilities of error in our own lesser and fallible selves. Aristotle also grounds his analysis of "the very structure and incidents of the play" on the same principle; the plot, he says, which will most effectively evoke "tragic pity and fear" is one in which the events develop through complication to a *catastrophe* in which there occurs a sudden *reversal* in the hero's fortune from happiness to disaster.

The Middle Ages, lacking direct knowledge either of classical tragedies or of Aristotle's theory, conceived tragedy to be simply the story of an eminent person who, whether deservedly or not, is brought from prosperity to wretchedness by an unpredictable turn of the wheel of fortune. The short narratives in "The Monk's Tale" of *The Canterbury Tales* are all, in Chaucer's own term, "tragedies" of this kind. With the Elizabethan era came both the beginning and the acme of dramatic tragedy in England. The tragedies of this period owed much to the native religious drama, the *miracle* and *morality plays*, which had developed independently of classical influence; but a most important contribution came from the Roman writer, Seneca, whose plays became widely known earlier than those of the Greek tragedians.

Senecan tragedy was written to be recited, rather than acted; but to English playwrights, who thought that these tragedies had been intended for the stage, they provided the model for a fully developed five-act play with a complex plot and a formal and elaborate style of dialogue. Senecan drama, in the Elizabethan age, had two main lines of development. One of these consisted of academic tragedies, written in close imitation of the Senecan models, including the use of a *chorus*, and usually constructed according to the rules of the *three unities*, which had been elaborated by Italian critics of the age; the earliest English example was Sackville and Norton's *Gorboduc* (1562). The other and much more important development was written for the popular stage, and is called the **revenge tragedy,** or (in its most sensational form) the **tragedy of blood**. This type of play derived from Seneca's favorite materials of revenge, murder, ghosts, mutilation, and carnage, but while Seneca had relegated such matters to long reports of offstage actions by messengers, the Elizabethan writers had them acted out on stage to satisfy the audience's appetite for violence and horror. Thomas Kyd's *The Spanish Tragedy* (1586) established this popular form, based on a murder and the quest for vengeance and including a ghost, insanity, suicide, a play-within-a-play, sensational incidents, and a gruesomely bloody ending. Marlowe's *The Jew of Malta* and Shakespeare's *Titus Andronicus* belong in this convention; and from this lively but unlikely source came one of the greatest of tragedies, *Hamlet*, as well as Webster's fine horror plays, *The Duchess of Malfi* and *The White Devil*.

Many of the best tragedies in the brief flowering time between 1585 and 1625, by Marlowe, Shakespeare, Chapman, Webster, Beaumont and Fletcher, and Massinger, deviate radically from the Aristotelian norms. Shakespeare's *Othello* is one of the few plays which accords entirely with Aristotle's basic criteria for the tragic hero and plot. The hero of *Macbeth*, however, is not a good man who commits a tragic error, but an ambitious man who knowingly turns great gifts to evil purposes and therefore, although he retains our sympathy by his courage and self-insight, entirely deserves his destruction at the hands of his morally superior antagonists. Shakespeare's *Richard III* presents first the success, then the ruin, of an utterly malign protagonist who nonetheless arouses in us a kind of reluctant admiration by his intelligence and by the shameless candor of his ambition and malice. Most Shakespearean tragedies, like Elizabethan tragedies generally, depart from Aristotle's paradigm by introducing humorous incidents or scenes, called *comic relief*. There developed also in this age the *tragicomedy*, a popular non-Aristotelian form which produced a number of artistic successes. And in the later seventeenth century the Restoration period produced the curious form, a cross between epic and tragedy, called *heroic tragedy*.

Until the close of the seventeenth century almost all tragedies were written in verse and had as protagonists men of high rank, whose fate affected the fortunes of a state. A few minor Elizabethan tragedies, such as *A Yorkshire Tragedy* (of uncertain authorship), had as the chief character a man of the lower class, but it remained for eighteenth-century writers to popularize the **bourgeois,** or **domestic tragedy,** which was written in prose and presented a protagonist from the common ranks who suffers a commonplace or domestic disaster. George Lillo's *The London Merchant: or, The History of George Barnwell* (1731), which represents a merchant's apprentice who falls into the toils of a heartless courtesan and comes to a bad end by robbing his employer and murdering his uncle, is still read, at least in college courses.

Since that time most successful tragedies have been in prose, and represent middle-class, or occasionally even working-class, heroes and heroines. One of the more notable recent tragedies, Arthur Miller's *The Death of a Salesman* (1949), relies for its tragic seriousness on the degree to which Willy Loman, in his bewildered defeat by life, is representative of the ordinary man whose aspirations reflect the false values of a commercial society; the effect on the audience is one of compassionate understanding rather than of tragic pity and terror. A term sometimes applied to the typical protagonist in modern serious plays, to signify his discrepancy from the heroes of traditional tragedies, is the **anti-hero**: a man who, instead of manifesting largeness, dignity, power, and heroism in the face of fate, is petty, ignominious, ineffectual, or passive. Extreme instances are the characters who people the meaningless world of Samuel Beckett's dramas—the tramps, Vladimir and Estragon, in *Waiting for Godot,* or the blind and paralyzed old man, Hamm, who is the protagonist in *Endgame.*

Tragedy since World War I has been innovative in many other ways, including the experimentation with various ancient types. Eugene O'Neill's *Mourning Becomes Electra,* for example, is an adaptation of Aeschylus' *Oresteia,* with the locale shifted from Greece to New England, the poetry altered to rather flat prose, and the tragedy of fate converted into a tragedy of the psychological compulsions of a family trapped in a tangle of Freudian complexes. T. S. Eliot's *Murder in the Cathedral* is a poetic drama which incorporates elements from two early forms, the medieval *miracle play* (dealing with the martyrdom of a saint) and the medieval *morality play.*

See *Plot,* and refer to A. C. Bradley, **Shakespearean Tragedy* (1904); F. L. Lucas, **Tragedy: Serious Drama in Relation to Aristotle's Poetics* (1927); H. D. F. Kitto, **Greek Tragedy* (3d ed., 1954); John Gassner, *Masters of the Drama* (1940); H. J. Muller, **The Spirit of Tragedy* (1956); Elder Olson, **Tragedy and the Theory of Drama* (1961); R. B. Sewall, ed., **Tragedy: Modern Essays in Criticism* (1963).

TRAGICOMEDY   was a type of Elizabethan and Jacobean drama which mingled both the subject matter and the forms of traditional tragedy and comedy: (1) Its important characters included both people of high degree and people of low degree. According to the reigning critical theory, only upper-class characters were appropriate to tragedy, while members of the lower classes were the proper subject of comedy. (2) It consisted in a serious action which threatened a tragic disaster to the protagonist, yet, by an abrupt change of circumstance, ended happily. As John Fletcher wrote in his Preface to *The Faithful Shep-*

herdess, tragicomedy "wants deaths, which is enough to make it no tragedy, yet brings some near it, which is enough to make it no comedy, which must be a representation of familiar people. . . . A god is as lawful in [tragicomedy] as in a tragedy, and mean people as in a comedy."

Shakespeare's *Merchant of Venice* is a tragicomedy, both because it mingles people of high degree with lowly characters (such as Shylock and the clown, Launcelot Gobbo) and also because the developing threat of death to Antonio is suddenly reversed at the end by Portia's ingenious casuistry in the trial scene. Francis Beaumont and John Fletcher developed, in *Philaster* and numerous other plays, a mode of tragicomedy which employs a romantic and fast-moving plot of love, jealousy, treachery, intrigue, and disguises, and ends in a melodramatic reversal of fortune for the protagonists, who had hitherto seemed headed for disaster. Shakespeare wrote his late plays, *Cymbeline* and *The Winter's Tale,* in this very popular mode of the tragicomic romance. "Tragicomedy" is sometimes applied also to plays with *double plots,* one serious and the other comic.

See E. M. Waith, *The Pattern of Tragicomedy in Beaumont and Fletcher* (1952); M. T. Herrick, *Tragicomedy (1955).

UTOPIAS and DYSTOPIAS. *Utopia* was the title of a book about an imaginary commonwealth written in Latin (1515–1516) by the Renaissance humanist, Sir Thomas More. The title plays on two Greek words, "outopia" (no place) and "eutopia" (good place); and the term **Utopia** has come to signify the class of fiction which represents an ideal political state and way of life. The first and greatest instance of the type was Plato's *Republic,* which sets forth, in dialogue form, the eternal Idea of a commonwealth that can only be distantly approximated by political organizations in the actual world. Most Utopias since Plato's, beginning with that of Sir Thomas More, represent their ideal place under the fiction of a distant country reached by some venturesome traveler. There have been many Utopias written since More gave impetus to the genre, some as mere Arcadian dreams, others as blueprints for social and technological progress. They include Francis Bacon's *New Atlantis* (1627), Edward Bellamy's *Looking Backward* (1888), William Morris' *News from Nowhere* (1891), and James Hilton's *Lost Horizon* (1934).

The Utopia can be distinguished from representations of imaginary places which, either because they are superior to the real world or manifest exaggerated versions of some of its unsavory aspects, are used primarily as vehicles for *satire* on human life and society: Swift's *Gulliver's Travels* (1726), Samuel Butler's *Erewhon* (1872). Another related but distinctive form is that of **science fiction,** represented by the works of H. G. Wells, Jules Verne, and many current writers, which explores the marvels of discovery and achievement that may result from scientific development. There are also diverse cross-forms; for example, an aspect or tendency of present scientific research is attacked, by imagining its disastrous or apocalyptic conclusion, as in Kurt Vonnegut, Jr.'s, *Cat's Cradle* and Michael Crichton's *The Andromeda Strain.*

The term **Dystopia** ("bad place") has recently come to be applied to works of fiction which represent a very unpleasant imaginary world, in which certain ominous tendencies of our present social, political, and technological order are projected in some future culmination. Examples are Aldous Huxley's *Brave New World* and George Orwell's *1984.*

See J. A. Hertzler, *The History of Utopian Thought* (1923); Lewis Mumford, *The Story of Utopias* (1922); Karl Mannheim, *Idealogy and Utopia* (1934); and the anthology, J. W. Johnson, ed., *Utopian Literature: A Selection* (1960).

VICTORIAN PERIOD.   The beginning of the Victorian Period is dated sometimes as 1832 (the passage of the first Reform Bill) and sometimes as 1837 (the accession of Queen Victoria); it extends to the death of Victoria in 1901. The year 1870 is often used to divide "early Victorian" from "late Victorian." Much writing of the period, whether imaginative or didactic, in verse or in prose, reflected current social, economic, and intellectual problems—for example, the industrial revolution and its effects on the economic and social structure; rapid urbanization and the deterioration of rural England; massive poverty, growing class tensions, and pressures toward political and social reform; and the impact on philosophy and religious fundamentalism of the theory of evolution, and of the rapid extension of "positivism" (the method of investigation and proof developed in the physical sciences) into all areas of speculation and inquiry. It was an age of immense and variegated and often self-critical literary activity. The derogatory connotations of the term "Victorian" in our time— sexual priggishness, narrow-mindedness, respectability, complacency —are based on the actual attitudes and values of many members of the rapidly expanding Victorian middle class; but current attacks on these attitudes merely echo the attacks by numerous men of letters within the age itself. The most eminent poets were Tennyson, Browning, and Arnold; the most prominent essayists were Carlyle, Ruskin, Arnold, and Pater; the most distinguished of many excellent novelists (this was the greatest age of English fiction) were Dickens, Thackeray, George Eliot, Meredith, Trollope, Hardy, and Samuel Butler.

See *Pre-Raphaelites* and *Aestheticism and Decadence*; and refer to G. M. Young, *Victorian England: Portrait of an Age* (2d ed., 1953); Jerome Buckley, *The Victorian Temper* (1951); W. E. Houghton, *The Victorian Frame of Mind* (1957).

WIT, HUMOR, and the COMIC. Both "wit" and "humor" now denote species of the **comic:** any element in literature that is designed to amuse or to excite mirth in the reader or audience. Wit and humor, however, had a variety of other meanings in earlier literary criticism, and a brief comment on their history will help clarify the difference between them in present usage.

Wit once meant the mental faculty of "intelligence" or "inventiveness," a sense it still retains in the term "half-wit." In the sixteenth and seventeenth century it came to be used for ingenuity in literary invention, and especially for the ability to discover brilliant, surprising, and paradoxical figures; hence "wit" was often applied to the style of poetry we now call *metaphysical*. And in the eighteenth century there were frequent attempts to distinguish the "false wit" of Cowley and other metaphysical stylists, who were said to aim at a merely superficial dazzlement, and "true wit," regarded as the apt phrasing of truths whose enduring validity is attested by their very commonplaceness. So Pope defined "true wit" in his *Essay on Criticism* as "What oft was thought, but ne'er so well expressed."

The present use of the term derives from its seventeenth-century application to a brilliant and paradoxical style. "Wit," that is, denotes a kind of verbal expression which is brief, deft, and intentionally contrived to produce a shock of comic surprise. The surprise is usually the result of an unforeseen connection or distinction between words or concepts, which frustrates the listener's expectation only to satisfy it in a different way. Philip Guedalla wittily said: "History repeats itself. Historians repeat each other." The trite comment about history turns out to be unexpectedly appropriate, with an unlooked for turn of meaning, to the writers of history as well. "The only sure way to double your money," remarked the American comedian Abe Martin, "is to fold it and put it in your hip pocket." The resulting laughter, in a famous phrase of Immanuel Kant, arises "from the sudden transformation of a strained expectation into nothing"; it would be more accurate to say, however, "from the sudden satisfaction of an expectation, but in a way we did not in the least expect."

Abe Martin's remark is what Sigmund Freud calls "harmless wit," which evokes a laugh or smile without malice. What Freud calls "tendency wit" is aggressive wit; it is a derisive turn of phrase, directing the laugh at a particular object or butt. "Mr. James Payn," in Oscar

Wilde's barbed comment on a contemporary novelist, "hunts down the obvious with the enthusiasm of a short-sighted detective. As one turns over the pages, the suspense of the author becomes almost unbearable." As Wilde's comment demonstrates, wit characteristically is couched in the form of an *epigram*.

Repartee is a term aptly taken from fencing to signify a contest of wit, in which each person tries to cap the remark of the other, or to turn it to his own purpose. Attacking Disraeli in Parliament, Gladstone remarked that "the honorable gentleman will either end on the gallows or die of some loathsome disease." To which Disraeli rejoined: "That depends on whether I embrace the honorable gentleman's principles or his mistresses." *Restoration comedies* usually included episodes of sustained repartee. The classic example is the discussion of their marriage contract by Mirabel and Millamant in Act IV of Congreve's *The Way of the World*.

Humor derives from the theory of the "four humours" and from the application of the term "humorous" to one of the comically eccentric characters in the Elizabethan *comedy of humours*. As we now use the word, humor may be ascribed both to a comic speech and to a comic appearance or mode of behavior. A humorous speech differs from a witty speech in one or both of two ways: (1) wit, as we saw, is always intended by the speaker to be comic, but some speeches that we find humorous are intended by the speaker to be serious; and (2) a humorous saying is not cast in the neat, epigrammatic form of a witty saying. For example, the chatter of the old Nurse in *Romeo and Juliet* is humorous only to the audience, not to the speaker; similarly, the discussion of the mode of life of the goldfish in Central Park by the inarticulate and irascible taxi driver in Salinger's *The Catcher in the Rye* is unintentionally but superbly humorous, and is not cast in the form of a witty turn of phrase.

More important is the difference that wit is always verbal, while humor has a much broader range of reference. We find humor, for example, in the way Charlie Chaplin looks, dresses, and acts, and also in the sometimes wordless cartoons in *The New Yorker*. In a thoroughly humorous situation, the sources of the fun are complex. In Act III, scene iv, of *Twelfth Night*, Malvolio's appearance and actions, and his speech as well, are humorous, but all despite his own very solemn intentions; and our comic enjoyment is increased by our knowledge of the hilarity of the hidden auditors onstage. One source of the greatness of a comic creation like Falstaff is that he exploits the full gamut of comic possibilities. Falstaff is humorous in the way he looks and in what he does; what he says is sometimes witty, and at all other times humorous; while his actions and speech are sometimes uninten-

tionally humorous, sometimes intentionally humorous, and not infre-
quently—as in his whimsical account to his skeptical auditors of how
he bore himself in the highway robbery, in the second act of *Henry IV*,
1—they are humorous even beyond his intention.

One other point needs to be made about humor. In the normal use,
the term refers to what is purely **comic**: it evokes, as it is sometimes
said, sympathetic laughter, or else laughter which is an end in itself.
If we extend Freud's distinction between harmless and tendency wit,
we can say that humor is the "harmless" form of the comic. There is,
however, another mode of the comic, "tendency comedy," in which
we are made to laugh at a person not merely because he is ridiculous,
but because he is being ridiculed—the laughter is derisive, with some
element of contempt or malice, and serves as a weapon against its
ridiculous subject. Tendency comedy and tendency wit, but not
humor, are among the major devices that a writer employs in *satire*,
the literary art of derogating by deriding a subject.

See Sigmund Freud, *Wit and Its Relation to the Unconscious*
(1916); Max Eastman, *Enjoyment of Laughter* (1936); D. H. Monro,
The Argument of Laughter (1951); Louis Cazamian, *The Development of English Humor* (1952); Louis Kronenberger, *The Thread of
Laughter* (1952); George Williamson, *The Proper Wit of Poetry*
(1961).

Index of Terms

The first number, in **boldface**, identifies the page containing the main discussion of a term; on the text page, the term is printed in boldface. Succeeding numbers, in *italics*, identify other pages on which the term occurs, in a context that illustrates its use or amplifies its meaning; on these text pages, the term is printed in italics.

Some entries in the Index are followed by a list of related terms. These lists identify the diverse entries that deal with the types and features of such comprehensive topics as *Style, Figurative language,* or *Novel.*

Terms likely to be mispronounced—most of these are borrowings from foreign languages—are followed (in parentheses) by a very simplified guide to pronunciation. This guide marks the stress—in some instances, both the primary and secondary stress—and indicates the pronunciation of those parts of a word about which a student is apt to be in doubt. The following vowel marks are used:

ā (fate)	ĭ (pin)
ă (pat)	ō (rope)
ä (father)	ŏ (pot)
ē (meet)	oo (food)
ĕ (get)	ŭ (cut)
ī (pine)	

Additional Terms

Additional Terms

Additional Terms

Additional Terms

Additional Terms

Additional Terms

Additional Terms

Additional Terms

Additional Terms

Additional Terms

Additional Terms

Additional Terms

Additional Terms

Additional Terms